THE CHANGING FACE OF EUROPEAN BANKS AND SECURITIES MARKETS

Also by Jack Revell

BANKING AND ELECTRONIC FUND TRANSFERS

CHANGES IN WEST EUROPEAN PUBLIC BANKS AND THEIR IMPLICATIONS FOR SPAIN

COMPETITION AND REGULATION OF BANKS
(*with Edward P. M. Gardener and Christopher Barclay*)

COSTS AND MARGINS IN BANKING: AN INTERNATIONAL SURVEY

SECURITISATION: HISTORY, FORMS AND RISKS
(*with Edward P. M. Gardener*)

SOLVENCY AND REGULATION OF BANKS

THE BRITISH FINANCIAL SYSTEM

THE FUTURE OF SAVINGS BANKS: A Study of Spain and the Rest of Europe

THE WEALTH OF THE NATION: The National Balance Sheet of the United Kingdom, 1957–61

The Changing Face of European Banks and Securities Market

Edited by

Jack Revell
Professor Emeritus, University of Wales
Consultant Director, Institute of European Finance, Bangor

St. Martin's Press

First published in Great Britain 1994 by
THE MACMILLAN PRESS LTD
Houndmills, Basingstoke, Hampshire RG21 2XS
and London
Companies and representatives
throughout the world

A catalogue record for this book is available
from the British Library.

ISBN 0–333–60478–4

Printed in Great Britain by
Antony Rowe Ltd
Chippenham, Wiltshire

First published in the United States of America 1994 by
Scholarly and Reference Division,
ST. MARTIN'S PRESS, INC.,
175 Fifth Avenue,
New York, N.Y. 10010

ISBN 0–312–10645–9

Library of Congress Cataloging-in-Publication Data
The Changing face of European banks and securities markets / edited by
Jack Revell.
p.   cm.
Includes bibliographical references and index.
ISBN 0–312–10645–9
1. Banks and banking—Europe.   2. Securities industry—Europe.
I. Revell, Jack.
HG2974. C43   1994
332.1'094—dc20   93–29483
                                                                  CIP

CONTENTS

PART I COMPETITION IN BANKING MARKETS

Chapter 1 European Banking: An Analysis of Competitive
Conditions   **3**
*Philip Molyneux, D.M. Lloyd-Williams and
John Thornton*

Chapter 2 Competition in Banking Markets: Lessons from
the Italian Case   **30**
Riccardo Cesari, Vittorio Conti and Marco Onado

List of Tables

List of Figures

Preface

The twelve chapters of this volume deal with issues that are the main topics of discussion about the banking systems and the wider financial systems of European countries at the present time, and the few chapters that appear to be about the systems of particular countries are concerned with issues that have their counterparts in most of the other countries. The chapters fall naturally into four groups, each of which forms a part of the volume with three chapters:

Part I   Competition in Banking Markets
Part II   Bank Organisation and Strategy
Part III Bank Regulation and Crises
Part IV Securities Markets and Financial Centres

The line of argument is from the ever-increasing competition, further magnified by the single European market, and its effects on the organisation, strategy, regulation and crises of banks and the parallel effects of competition and internationalisation on securities markets and international financial centres. The topics are representative of turbulent times in the financial systems of Western Europe.

The chapters are all papers read at meetings of the European Association of University Teachers in Banking and Finance; ten from the September 1992 meeting in Bangor and two from the September 1991 meeting in Siena. The idea of bringing these papers together in one volume arose because the 1992 meeting marked the tenth anniversary of the Association. In other years the papers are published in a variety of journals, and most of them appear as Research Papers in the series published by the Institute of European Finance.

The first meeting of the Association was held in Würzburg in 1982, and it was there that members first came into contact with the Wolpertinger, an (allegedly) mythical beast from Bavaria. The full name of the Association is a bit of a mouthful, so we all refer to it as the 'Wolpertinger Club'. The word club is also a better description of the nature of the Association because membership is by invitation, and we avoid all the recent alarming increase in university bureaucracy by having no subscription and no officers; we just meet together at a different European university each year, and the host university has a burst of administrative activity each ten or twelve years. The universities from which our members come co-operate closely in research, staff exchange visits and student exchange through the EC Erasmus scheme. For the rest we are a group of close friends, united by a common interest in the industrial economics of banking and financial systems.

My task as editor of this collection of papers has been made immeasurably easier by the ready co-operation of the contributors: they all replied on time to my requests, which were fewer because the papers had already been prepared. I thank them all. I should also like to thank the other members for their forbearance in accepting my choice of papers without demur even though, because of restraints on space, I have had to leave out many high-quality papers that did not fit easily into the chosen themes.

I must also thank Ted Gardener for giving me full access to the facilities of the Institute of European Finance, without which I could hardly have coped. In the Institute Linda Jeavons produced several drafts of the various chapters with great speed and accuracy, and Christine Owen was, as usual, a tower of strength in organising the production of the volume, right down to camera-ready copy and the final proof-reading. Maureen Simmons prepared the index at incredible speed. Finally the thanks of all of us are due to the publishers for accepting the proposal for the volume so readily and for their co-operation throughout. It goes without saying that any errors and omissions that remain after the lengthy process are mine alone.

JACK REVELL

Notes on the Contributors

Jean-Paul Abraham is Executive Director in charge of General Services at Banque Paribas Belgique; he teaches Financial Economics at the Facultés Notre-Dame de la Paix, Namur, and at the Katholieke Universiteit Leuven.

Nadia Bervaes took her degree of Commercial Engineer at the Katholieke Universiteit Leuven in July 1991 and is at present a graduate student in the MBA Program at the University of Chicago.

Riccardo Cesari obtained a degree in Statistics and Economics in Bologna in 1983 and went on to take a D.Phil. in Oxford in 1988 with a thesis on 'Risks and equilibrium prices of contingent claims, with application to Italian securities'. In 1983 he was research assistant to Prometeia, the association for econometric research in Bologna, and since 1984 he has been a member of the research staff of the Bank of Italy in Rome. He has published papers on risk and return in financial and credit markets, regional economic problems and econometric methods for financial models.

Francesco Cesarini is full Professor of Banking in the Faculty of Banking, Finance and Insurance at the Catholic University of Milan. He is the author of several publications on monetary and banking issues, and on problems relating to stock exchange and corporate financial instruments; he was co-author of the green book commissioned by the Italian Treasury on *Il Sistema Creditizio e Finanziario Italiano*. Alongside academic and research activity he serves as chairman of Banca Agricola Milanese and as deputy chairman of the Stock Exchange Council.

Vittorio Conti obtained a degree in economics at the Catholic University of Milan and went on to become a D.Phil. student in Oxford. From 1971 to 1976 he served as an economist in the economic research department of the Bank of Italy in Rome. Since 1976 he has been a lecturer in economic theory at the Catholic University and since 1984 the head of the economic research and planning department at Banca Commercale Italiana in Milan. He has published articles on inventory investment decisions, productivity in manaufacturing industry, input-output models,

international trade and the banking industry. He is at present involved in
research into banking and bank strategic planning. A book entitled
Financial Markets Liberalisation and the Role of Banks, of which he is
joint editor, has just been published.

Edward P.M. Gardener is Professor and Chairman of the School of
Accounting, Banking and Economics and Director of the Institute of
European Finance in the University of Wales, Bangor. He has directed
research projects for a wide range of bodies, including HM Treasury,
the British Bankers' Association and the European Free Trade Association. Current research interests are in bank financial management, bank
strategy, capital adequacy and regulation. Recent books include (co-
author) *Changes in Western European Banking* and (editor) *The Future
of Financial Systems and Services*.

Elisabetta Gualandri studied at the University of Modena and at the
University College of North Wales, Bangor, where she took the MA in
Financial Economics. She is now Associate Professor of Banking and
Economics at the University of Modena, Dipartimento di Economia
Aziendale. Her main fields of research interest include supervision of
financial institutions, comparative financial systems, and asset and liabi-
lity management. She is the author of *Normative di Vigilanza e Sistemi
Finanziari: Gran Bretagna, Francia e Italia* and of many other publica-
tions.

Anne Guinotte took her degree of Licenciée et Maître en Sciences
Economiques at the Facultés Notre-Dame de la Paix, Namur, in
September 1991.

Richard Harrington is Senior Lecturer in Economics at the University
of Manchester. He has written and published widely on financial institutions and financial markets and has acted as consultant to a number of
national and international organisations, including the Building Societies
Association and the OECD, for which he prepared a monograph on asset
and liability management by banks. He previously worked in insurance
in the City of London.

Andrea Landi is Associate Professor of Banking and Economics at the
University of Venice, Dipartimento di Economia c Direzione Aziendale.
His main fields of interest include competition in banking markets, effi-
ciency and productivity of credit institutions and the theory of financial

intermediation. He is the author of *Dimensioni, Costi e Profitti delle Banche Italiane* as well as many other publications.

Ted Lindblom is Senior Lecturer at Gothenburg School of Economics and Commercial Law, where he is director of postgraduate studies in business administration and programme co-ordinator of an MBA course in international business administration. His main research interests concern pricing strategies and management control, and he has co-authored a paper on a risk-neutral strategy for industrial conversion to natural gas. In the banking field he has recently published two books (in Swedish): one, of which he was co-author, concerns increasing competition within the financial and insurance industries, and the other analyses banks' cost structures and pricing of payment services.

Michael Lloyd-Williams is the present NatWest Lecturer in Banking and Finance in the School of Accounting, Banking and Economics at the University of Wales, Bangor. His research interests include industrial economics as applied to the European banking industry, with particular reference to the prevailing competitive conditions.

Philip Molyneux is Senior Lecturer in Banking and Finance in the School of Accounting, Banking and Economics at the University of Wales, Bangor, and is Deputy Director of the Institute of European Finance. His current research interests include structure and performance issues in European banking. He has published many articles and was the co-author of *Changes in Western European Banking*.

Ian Morison has been Midland Bank Professor of Banking and Finance at Loughborough University since 1988. His first career was as a financial journalist, serving as banking correspondent and deputy financial editor on *The Times* between 1966 and 1974. He then moved to the Inter-Bank Research Organisation, heading its public policy group until 1980, when he was apointed head of public affairs at the Committee of London Clearing Bankers. Between 1983 and 1988 he was assistant general manager and corporate affairs director at Midland Bank, with responsibility for strategic planning and external relations. He was director of the Loughborough Banking Centre from 1989 to 1992. In addition to organisation theory, his current research interests include banking strategy and financial ethics. Authored and co-authored works include *Banking Act 1979* and *Economics of the City*.

Marco Onado is Professor of Banking in the University of Bologna. In the academic year 1983-84 he was a visiting professorial fellow at the University College of North Wales, Bangor. His main research interests are the economics of banking (competition, costs and margins) and the regulation and supervision of banks and financial institutions. His most recent books are *Il Mercato Monetario e Finanziario in Italia* (with E. Monti) and *Economia dei Sistemi Finanziari*.

Javier Quesada took his degree at the University of Valencia and received his PhD from the University of Cincinatti. He is Associate Professor of Economics in the University of Valencia and director of the financial area of the Instituto de Investigaciones Económicas (IVIE). His main research interests, on which he regularly organises workshops and meetings in IVIE, are monetary economics and banking and finance, including regulatory aspects. He is co-author of *Dinero y el Sistema Bancario: Teoría y Análisis del Caso Español*.

Jack Revell is Professor Emeritus of the University of Wales, having been Professor of Economics at the University College of North Wales from 1969 to 1983. He was Director of the Institute of European Finance there from 1973 to 1985 and is now Consultant Director. He has undertaken consultancies for various organisations, including the United Nations, the Statistical Office of the European Communities, the OECD, HM Treasury and the Spanish savings bank research foundation. Among his publications are *Solvency and Regulation of Banks*, *Costs and Margins in Banking* and *Mergers and the Role of Large Banks*.

Tad Rybczynski is honorary Visiting Professor at the City University, London, a position which he has held since 1987, having been Visiting Professor there between 1974 and 1987; previously he was Visiting Professor at the University of Surrey between 1968 and 1974. He is a Fellow of the Chartered Institute of Bankers. He was the economic adviser to Lazard Bros. between 1973 and 1986 and a director of Lazard Securities from 1963 to 1986. City University has given him the honorary degree of DSc. Among the many positions that he has held is membership of the Monopolies and Mergers Commission in 1978 and 1982. He has been the recipient of various awards, both at home and overseas. He is editor and contributor to a number of books and has also written a large number of articles for learned and professional journals.

John Thornton has been a senior economist at the International Monetary Fund since 1983 and spent a year (1990/91) researching in the Institute of European Finance at Bangor. Formerly Vice President International Capital Market Research at Merrill Lynch and Senior Economist in the Bank of America International Financial Centre. He has also worked in the treasury and corporate strategy departments of Fisons. His current research interests include international banking and monetary economics. He has published widely on issues in money and banking.

Synopses of Contributions

PART I COMPETITION IN BANKING MARKETS

Chapter 1   Competitive Conditions in Banking Markets
Philip Molyneux, D.M. Lloyd-Williams and John Thornton

The only empirical study of competitive conditions within banking in the European Community as a whole has been that by Price Waterhouse (the Cecchini Report), and the few studies of competitive conditions in individual countries have used market structure variables such as concentration ratios and branch numbers. The present investigation departs from this traditional approach by using a non-structural measure of competition, the Rosse-Panzar statistic. The results indicate that monopolistic competition is present in Germany, the United Kingdom, France and Spain; by contrast the results for Italy suggest monopoly or short-run oligopoly.

Chapter 2   Competition in Banking Markets: Lessons from the Italian Case
Riccardo Cesari, Vittorio Conti and Marco Onado

Whereas the underlying hypothesis of the Cecchini Report was traditional international trade theory, with its assumption of perfectly competitive market conditions, the present study takes advantage of Italian statistics on local banking markets to emphasise the information asymmetries of imperfect markets that are stressed in recent developments of finance theory. Traditional market share statistics do not show significant changes in Italy, but the use of the shift-and-share technique brings out a number of differences in the more competitive conditions of recent years.

Chapter 3   New Forms of Competition Facing the Spanish Banking System
Javier Quesada

This contributions serves to emphasise the change in many recently deregulated banking systems, particularly in smaller countries, as they begin to adopt features that are commonplace in the more developed countries. Spain is like many other countries in developing independent pension funds, which may well become of great importance in supporting the growth of the stock exchange. Investment funds of various sorts (money market funds, fixed-income funds and variable-income funds) have become far more important after a recent change in their tax treatment. Finally, the government intends to introduce personal pension funds, but the delay in their introduction may be due to their effect on the public sector deficit. Some of the investment funds will contain mainly government paper, and the author sees these as a partial replacement for the resources made available to the government by investment coefficients on the banks, now being reduced.

PART II BANK ORGANISATION AND STRATEGY

Chapter 4 Bank Marketing, Organisation and Performance
Edward P.M. Gardener

This is a discussion of research being carried out by the author in the Institute of European Finance to follow up earlier work on the dominance of marketing considerations on bank strategy. Recent developments have tended towards the reinstatement of the supply side as a major factor. The organisational structure of banks depends to a great extent on bank strategy, and the author is conducting a case study of retail banking to see how far organisational structure can be linked to performance.

Chapter 5 Organisational Changes in UK Clearing Banks: the Causes and Consequences
Ian Morison

This paper follows the organisational change of the clearing banks from the position that obtained up to the 1960s, with each bank branch a microcosm of the whole bank, to their present structures as financial conglomerates. The organisational hierarchy of a modern clearing bank is now primarily split according to products, commercial banking products on the one hand and capital markets products on the other. Within commercial banking the second-order grouping is typically by customers, whereas within the capital markets area the second-order grouping typically remains products. Geography is now only of third-order importance. By moving away from traditional organisational forms, banks have upset both staff and customers, and there are many instances of the reversal or modification of organisational changes made only a few years previously.

Chapter 6   Strategies of Major British Banks since Big Bang
Jack Revell

This contribution starts with the premise that in the past six years the categorical imperative of the major banks has been the achievement and maintenance of the required capital ratios. Bank capital has traditionally been fed mainly from retained earnings, but these have been non-existent in three of the six years. The first part of the paper analyses the failure to improve the factors that determine profits, principally cost reduction, and the impact of provisions for bad debts, both Third World and domestic. The banks were thus driven to maintain the capital ratios by recourse to the capital market and by asset sales and securitisation. Emphasis is placed on the effects of excessive lending secured on property and the determination of the banks to maintain their dividend levels even under the most adverse conditions.

PART III BANK REGULATION AND CRISES

Chapter 7   Liquidity Management and Lender-of-Last-Resort Functions: Recent Developments in the Italian Banking System
Francesco Cesarini

This contribution examines lending by the Bank of Italy to banks in recent years. A change has been made in the regulation of required reserves so that average compliance during a month suffices and banks are allowed access to their reserves for limited periods in case of need. This and other changes have tended to replace bilateral relations between the Bank of Italy and individual banks by impersonal relations through the market. There has thus been liberalisation in reserve requirements as a weapon of monetary policy, but central bank lending to banks that are illiquid but not insolvent is still restrained by an out-of-date list of assets that they can pledge as security. The author urges that this aspect of central bank lending should also be liberalised.

Chapter 8   Diversification and Conflicts of Interest: the Effects of the New Regulation in Italy
Elisabetta Gualandri and Andrea Landi

The initial assumption of the analysis is that the economies of scope that banks achieve in the management of information may be even more important than economies of operating costs for those banks that combine credit activity and securities operations. These economies of scope give rise to conflicts of interest. The paper analyses the various kinds of conflicts of interest and shows that the authorities must choose a balance between the economies and the protection of customers from abuse of bank control of information. This theme is analysed in different countries, with particular reference to UK legislation and its Chinese walls. The effects of the new Italian legislation on the operational and organisational strategies of diversified financial intermediaries are then described and contrasted with those in the United Kingdom and other European countries.

Chapter 9   Credit Losses in Nordic Banks
Ted Lindblom

Although the profits of banks in all European countries have fallen through the joint effects of rising operating costs and loan loss provisions, particularly on loans secured on property, the effects have been most drastic in Scandinavian countries. In Norway the government has been obliged to take more than half the banking system into its ownership, and banks in Sweden and Finland have needed considerable government help. What these countries have in common is recent deregulation, leaving inexperienced banks to seek market share without regard for credit risks. The analysis of the situation in Norway and Sweden given in this paper differs from other comparisons that have been made by conducting individual examinations of five Norwegian and five Swedish banks that have been in difficulties. The comparisons, presented largely in graphical form, are conducted for each country separately.

PART IV SECURITIES MARKETS AND FINANCIAL CENTRES

Chapter 10 The Internationalisation of Bond Markets
Richard Harrington

Although internationalisation is apparent in all security trading, it is in the bond markets, comprising government and public sector bonds, domestic private sector bonds, foreign bonds and eurobonds, that this trend has been proceeding most rapidly. The removal of exchange controls has been one of the most important factors. This paper shows a convergence of domestic and international bond markets, particularly in the United Kingdom, where the market was reopened to foreign issues and there was a revival of issues by domestic companies after many years in which high interest rates had reduced such issues to a trickle. Another manifestation of the trend to internationalisation has been the growth of the Ecu bond market. The general conclusion is of rapid change, in which it is becoming realistic to talk of different currency segments of a world bond market.

Chapter 11 The Development of European Capital Markets: the Main Trends and their Implications
Tad Rybczynski

This paper charts the expansion and changing character of the capital markets in Western Europe. These changes have been impelled by a growing variety of financial instruments, including derivatives and synthetic products, the strong trend towards securitisation (as opposed to the use of bank finance), privatisation and a rising recourse to capital markets by public bodies. Their character is changed by internationalisation, represented by a growing volume of cross-border transactions, and a strong trend towards segmentation into wholesale and retail markets. Two other important influences on change in capital market are the growing weight of institutional investors and fund managers in most countries, and the impact of technology and telecommunications.

Chapter 12 The Competitiveness of European International Financial Centres

Jean-Paul Abraham, Nadia Bervaes and Anne Guinotte

After a discussion of the theory and history of international financial centres, this paper concentrates on ranking the existing centres in several ways. The main emphasis is on reporting the results of a survey in which a group of banking experts was asked to rank the six centres of London, Paris, Frankfurt, Luxembourg, Zurich and Brussels. They were given a list of forty-seven criteria, grouped into four main blocks, and they were first asked to weight the importance of each criterion before scoring the centre on each of the forty-seven criteria. At the end of the survey London emerged in first place by a large margin on practically all counts, followed in order by Luxembourg, Frankfurt, Paris, Zurich and Brussels. Except for the unexpected prominence of Luxembourg, these results are borne out by the other surveys quoted. (A further survey on the same lines comparing Amsterdam, Brussels Copenhagen, Madrid and Milan has since been carried out; the results of the two surveys have been published in one volume by the Institute of European Finance as Research Monograph no. 93/1 with the same title as this chapter.)

General Notes

Symbols in Tables

-   nil or negligible
...   not available or not applicable

Billion

One thousand million (10^9)

PART I

COMPETITION IN BANKING MARKETS

CHAPTER 1
EUROPEAN BANKING -
AN ANALYSIS OF COMPETITIVE CONDITIONS

Phil Molyneux
D.M. Lloyd-Williams
and
John Thornton

INTRODUCTION

Banking in the European Community is expected to experience marked
changes during the coming years as a result of the completing of a single
market in financial services. Price Waterhouse (1988), Neven (1990)
and Vives (1991) have investigated the impact of European integration
on the competitive conditions in banking and financial markets and all
have shown that there are significantly different competitive conditions
existing in the different country banking systems. However, only the
Price Waterhouse study for the European Commission on the 'costs of
non-Europe' can lay claim to be an empirical investigation of competitive conditions across European banking systems. The study estimated
likely price falls from completing the internal market on a standard set
of financial products. The possible gains from European integration
were reflected in the corresponding differentials between the prices in
individual countries compared with the level at which overall prices
were estimated to settle when the internal market is completed. For
every single product large differences were observed in prices across
countries, thus implying different competitive environments[1].

Because the Price Waterhouse study suggests that integration will
result in an increase in competition and significant welfare gains, '... the
crucial issue seems to be the impact of the process under way on the
degree of competition in banking ...' (Vives 1991, p. 9). However, few
studies have directly addressed the problem of estimating competitive
conditions in individual banking markets. Instead, competitive conditions are almost exclusively inferred from market structure variables
such as concentration ratios, branch numbers, numbers of banks, or
from anecdotal evidence (see Bröker 1989; Baltensperger and Dermine
1990; Neven 1990; Bruni 1990; Caminal, Gual and Vives 1990 and
Gardener and Molyneux 1990 amongst many). In this paper we

3

depart from this traditional approach and investigate competitive conditions in European banking markets using a non-structural measure of competition, namely, the Rosse-Panzar statistic.

The rest of this paper is organised as follows. Firstly, we give a brief review of the re-regulation of European Community banking aimed at fostering greater competition, and outline the important structural characteristics of the national markets. Secondly, we review some previous studies evaluating non-structural measures of competition in banking markets, while the following section presents our analysis of competitive conditions in EC banking markets. Some conclusions are offered in the final section.

STRUCTURE OF EUROPEAN COMMUNITY BANKING

The regulatory environment

Over the last thirty years the European Community has introduced banking legislation aimed at harmonising regulations and fostering competition. In this regard, Baltensperger and Dermine (1990) identify three distinct regulatory time periods: deregulation of entry to domestic markets from 1957 to 1973; attempts towards harmonisation of banking regulations from 1973 to 1983; and the recent European integration and 'internal market' proposal of freedom of cross-border services, single banking licence, home country control and mutual recognition.

Under the 1957 Treaty of Rome, the internal market was viewed as one which allowed 'free movement of goods, persons and services', and the objective was to transform segmented national markets into a common single market. In July 1965 the Commission proposed a Directive on the Abolition of Restrictions on Freedom of Establishment and Freedom to Provide Services in Respect of Self-employed Activities of Banks and other Financial Institutions. This was adopted by the EC Council of Ministers in 1973 and aimed to ensure the equal treatment of national and other firms of member states relating to entry into domestic markets and the conditions under which banks are allowed to operate. Subsidiaries of non-member country banks were to be regarded as EC undertakings in every way. From 1973 onwards very little discrimination remained as to entry into member states although cross-border competition was still severely hampered by capital restrictions.   In addition, there was no co-ordination of banking supervision, so banks operating in different countries were subject to different prudential requirements. This led to the second period of attempts to harmonise regulations.

Advances in harmonisation came in 1977 with the adoption of the First Directive on the Co-ordination of Laws, Regulations and Administrative Provisions Relating to the Taking up and Pursuit of the Business of Credit Institutions (hereafter known as the First Banking Co-ordination Directive). This directive established a definition of credit institutions and the principle of home country control, whereby supervision of credit institutions operating in various member countries would be now the responsibility of the home country of the parent bank. A directive on the Supervision of Credit Institutions on a Consolidated basis was adopted in 1983, along with two other directives relating to bank accounting formats and consumer protection in 1986. Baltensperger and Dermine (1990) state that, despite the above legislation, European banking markets were still far from full integration. A bank wishing to operate in another country still had to be authorised by the supervisors of the other country. It remained subject to supervision by the host country and its range of activities could be constrained by host country laws. In addition, most countries' bank branches had to be provided with earmarked endowment capital as if they were new banks. Finally, the supply of cross-border services was severely impaired by the restrictions on capital flows.

The difficulty encountered by full harmonisation of national regulations prompted a new approach towards European integration. In 1983 a White Policy Paper on financial integration enunciated clearly a renewed commitment to the Treaty of Rome and in 1985 the EC Commission proposed its White Paper on the completion of the internal market by 1992. In relation to banking the White Paper set guidelines for a single banking licence, home country control and mutual recognition. These principles were incorporated in the 1988 Second Banking Co-ordination Directive, which was passed by the EC Council of Ministers on 15 December 1989. It set out to eliminate the remaining intra-EC barriers to freedom of establishment in the banking sector and provides for full freedom of banking services across intra-EC boundaries. The main aim of this legislation is to harmonise laws and rules for credit institutions so that they can set up and operate freely across the Community, subject to adequate supervision. To this end the directive provides for minimum capital requirements, the monitoring and vetting of bodies that have substantial bank shareholding, controls over banks' long-term participation in non-financial companies, and the establishment of a single banking 'passport' to permit activity anywhere within the Community.

The principle of the single banking 'passport' is of particular importance. Once a credit institution is authorised to do banking business by its home supervisor (home country control) it will have a 'passport' to sell its products and services throughout the Community as long as there is prior harmonisation of essential supervisory rules (mutual recognition). A vital reinforcing feature of the Second Banking Directive is the associated supervisory arrangements. The Own Funds Directive (1988) was formally passed by the EC Council of Ministers in April 1989, along with the Solvency Ratio Directive in December 1989. The former aims to harmonise the definition of the capital, whereas the latter harmonises the solvency ratios for EC credit institutions. Other directives harmonising regulations on accounting for foreign branches, reorganisation and winding-up procedures, and deposit insurance have also been adopted. Accompanying all the above legislation is the proposal for full liberalisation of capital flows and all restrictions will be removed by the end of 1992, apart from those in Greece and Portugal where restrictions will disappear by 1995.

Structural characteristics of European banking

Despite differences relating to establishment and branching, every banking system in the European Community has a group of dominant or 'core banks' which are recognised by both the authorities and general public[2]. In many European countries there has been a trend for local and regional banks to form groups that could effectively compete against the national 'core' banks. Those countries with a large number of mutual and co-operative banks, such as Germany, Spain, Italy and France, tend to have a stronger regional focus than countries which have a small number of relatively large private banks, such as the United Kingdom.

Table 1.1 illustrates the various structural characteristics of EC banking markets at the end of 1989. It shows that the German, UK and French banking systems are by far the largest. The usual concentration measures show that, of the four largest banking sectors, Italy and France have the most concentrated markets. The market power of the major banks in Belgium, the Netherlands, Spain and most of the smaller countries also appears to be significant. It is interesting to note that, of the four largest banking markets, it is those in which regulations have historically been the most restrictive - France through nationalisation and Italy through branching restrictions and government ownership - which are the most concentrated. In fact, state-owned banks account for around 42 per cent of total banking sector assets in France and 67 per cent in Italy

Table 1.1 Market concentration and size of banking sectors in Europe, 1989

Number of banks in market[1]	Country	Size of banking sector Assets ($bn)	Concentration % of total market[3] Assets 10-firm	5-firm	Deposits 10-firm	5-firm
4,390	Germany	2,519.4	42.1	26.3	30.2	21.8
784	UK	2,280.2	38.6	28.7	36.9	27.5
1,999	France	1,850.2	58.3	42.4	57.8	42.2
1,100	Italy	1,105.0	58.4	35.8	53.9	33.3
491	Spain	600.4	60.3	37.3	60.9	37.9
169	Netherlands	463.7	72.9	67.5	83.0	77.3
120	Belgium	321.2	81.8	70.9	96.0	87.8
143	Luxembourg	317.1	43.2	26.7	43.0	26.5
169	Denmark	169.8	64.2	47.6	65.6	50.1
41	Greece	85.6	64.3	46.8	75.3	69.9
27	Portugal	70.9	77.5	53.7	83.9	58.4
47	Ireland	44.5	87.6	66.2	88.9	67.5

Notes: 1. Figures for 1988
2. Sources of information for banking sector size obtained from individual countries' banking associations and central banks
3. 10-firm and 5-firm concentration ratios calculated using data taken from the IBCA Credit Rating Agency (London) database

(see Gardener and Molyneux 1990, pp. 240 and 252), proportionally much higher than in the other large banking sectors.

It is a peculiar feature of banking markets that in almost every developed country, a handful of large banks tend to emerge over time, either through government encouragement or the workings of the market mechanism.   From a general perspective, however, it is difficult to appraise the competitive implications of increased concentration, especially in the light of contestable markets theory.   The traditional viewpoint would suggest that increased concentration fosters collusion and anti-competitive practice whereas contestability suggests otherwise.   It is, nevertheless, clear that there appears to be a current preference for larger size in many banks within different European countries.   The desire to obtain economies of scale and scope is presumably the main driving force behind this trend.

The Price Waterhouse/Cecchini findings

The economic analysis of completing the internal market in financial services after 1992 (published in detail in Price Waterhouse 1988 and summarised in Cecchini 1988) provides an indication of the kind of competitive forces that may be released when the internal market is completed.   Table 1.2 summarises the estimated price falls, hypothesised from completing the internal market, on a standard set of financial products as reported by the EC 'Cecchini' study.   The estimated gains from 1992 are reflected in the corresponding differences between the prices in individual countries compared with the level at which overall prices are estimated to fall when the internal market is completed. Although the data are not forecasts and have been estimated subject to strong assumptions, they represent a heroic attempt to suggest possible post-1992 developments.   The theoretical, potential price reductions shown in Table 1.2 indicate the different competitive conditions that exist in the three main financial services sectors for eight EC countries. It can be seen that price falls for banking products are expected to be the largest in Germany, Spain, France, Italy and the United Kingdom.   The indicative price reductions shown in Table 1.2 reflect more accurately expected price falls and shows that price falls for financial services as a whole are expected to be the largest in Spain, Italy, France and Belgium. Despite some reservations (see, for example, Neven 1990), these figures do appear to illustrate limited competition in banking services between and within EC countries.

Table 1.2 **Estimate of potential falls in financial product prices as a result of completing the EC internal market (per cent)**

	Belgium	West Germany	Spain	France	Italy	Luxem- bourg	Nether- lands	UK
Theoretical, potential price reductions[1]								
Banking	15	33	34	25	18	16	10	18
Insurance	31	10	32	24	51	37	1	4
Securities	52	11	44	23	33	9	18	12
Total	23	25	34	24	29	17	9	13
Indicative price reductions[2]								
All financial services								
Range	6-16	5-15	16-26	7-17	9-19	3-13	0-9	2-12
Centre of range	11	10	21	12	14	8	4	7

Source: Commission of the European Communities (1988)
Notes: 1. These data show the weighted averages of the theoretical potential falls of selected financial product prices
2. Indicative price falls are based upon a scaling down of the theoretical potential price reductions, taking into account roughly the extent to which perfectly competitive and integrated conditions will not be attained, plus other information for each financial services sub-sector, such as gross margins and administrative costs as a proportion of total costs

PREVIOUS STUDIES

As noted previously, there have been few empirical studies testing for competitive conditions using non-structural measures in the banking industry. In this section we focus on the work of Shaffer (1981a, 1981b, 1982); Nathan and Neave (1989 and 1991); and Lloyd-Williams, Molyneux and Thornton (1991). Shaffer uses the so-called Rosse-Panzar 'H' statistic (see Rosse and Panzar 1977 and Panzar and Rosse 1982 and 1987) to assess quantitatively the competitive nature of the banking market. The H statistic measures the sum of elasticities of total revenue with respect to input prices, and Rosse and Panzar show that this sum, called H, cannot be positive if a firm is a profit-maximising monopoly. Bresnahan (1989, p. 1036) has pointed out that a negative H need not necessarily imply a situation of monopoly and Perrakis (1991) and Nathan and Neave (1991) have formally shown that a negative H value is consistent with a conjectural variations short-run oligopoly. The logic for this is as follows: under monopoly or conjectural variations short-run oligopoly conditions an increase in input prices will increase marginal costs, reduce equilibrium output and subsequently reduce total revenue. In the case of perfect competition the H statistic is unity because any increase in input prices increases both marginal and average costs without altering the optimal output of any individual firm[3]. In the long run, demand adjusts so that the selling price and total revenue rise by the same amount as cost, and $H = 1$. Shaffer notes that H is also unity for a natural monopoly operating in a perfectly contestable market and also for a sales-maximising firm subject to breakeven constraints. A critical feature of the H statistic is that the test must be undertaken '... on observations which are exclusively in long-run equilibrium' (Shaffer 1982, p. 228)[4].

Shaffer's (1982) study (which is a refined version of Shaffer 1981a and 1981b) examines the competitive position for a sample of unit banks in New York by estimating a revenue equation of the form:

$$\ln TR = a + b(\ln PL) + c(\ln PK) + d(\ln PF) + e(\ln AST)$$
$$+ f(\ln MKt) + g[(C+D)/Dep] + h[(C+I)/Loan] + iD6$$

where: $\ln$ = natural logarithm

TR = total interest revenue

PL = annual wage, salary and benefits per full-time equivalent employee (unit price of labour)

PK = ratio of annual expenses of premises, furniture, fixtures and equipment to the balance sheet total of these items (unit price of capital)

PF = ratio of annual interest expenses to total funds (unit price of funds)

AST = bank assets

MKT = total market deposits in commercial banks
C+D/Dep = ratio of cash and due from depository institutions to total deposits
C+I/Loan = ratio of commercial and industrial loans to total loans
D6 = 1 (for six largest banks)
= 0 (for other banks)

In the above equation it is postulated that total revenue can be explained by independent variables such as interest and other costs. The first three independent variables, PL, PK and PF are input prices, while AST, MKT, (C+D)/Dep and (C+I)/Loan are proxies for other variables affecting equilibrium revenues. Total assets (AST) are entered as an independent variable to control for economies or diseconomies of scale, and total market deposits (MKT) are included as a proxy for aggregate local demand for banking services. The variables (C+D)/Dep and (C+I)/Loan are used to account for the effects of different levels of correspondent banking activity and different business mix. The six largest banks were distinguished from others using a dummy variable D6. If assets (AST) are sufficient to explain size effects, D6 should not be significant. If large size and oligopoly power are associated, D6 should be significant.

To test that the observations are in long-run equilibrium Shaffer uses a regression-relating Return on Assets (ROA) to input prices on the grounds that, in equilibrium, rates of return should not be statistically correlated with input prices. If, however, the market is in disequilibrium, an increase (decrease) in factor prices would be reflected in a temporary decline (increase) in the rate of return producing a negative correlation between factor prices and the rate of return. The same, Shaffer argues, is true if Return on Equity (ROE) is used as the dependent variable. Shaffer estimates the following equation, where the independent variables are as defined above:

$$\ln \text{ROA} = a + b(\ln\text{PL}) + c(\ln\text{PK}) + d(\ln\text{PF}) + e(\ln\text{AST})$$
$$\text{or } \ln \text{ROE} \quad + f(\ln\text{MKT}) + g[(C+D)/\text{DEP}] + h[(C+I)/\text{Loans}]$$
$$+ i\text{D6}$$

A finding of $H < 0$ implies disequilibrium whereas $H = 0$ would tend to confirm equilibrium. Table 1.3 summarises how the H statistic can be interpreted for both the competitive environment and equilibrium tests.

Shaffer estimated values of H ranging from 0.32 to 0.36 for the competitive stance test and -0.30 and -0.59 (not significantly different

Table 1.3   Interpreting the Rosse-Panzar H statistic

Competitive environment test	Equilibrium test
$H<0$ Monopoly or conjectural variations short-run oligopoly	$H<0$ disequilibrium
$0>H<1$ Monopolistic competition	$H=0$ equilibrium
$H=1$ Perfect competition	
or $H=1$ Natural monopoly in a perfectly contestable market	
or $H=1$ Sales maximising firm subject to a breakeven constraint	

from zero) for the equilibrium test, indicating that banks were behaving neither as monopolists nor as perfectly competitive firms in long-run equilibrium. The results suggest that the competitive forces preventing monopolistic conduct were primarily potential rather than actual.

Nathan and Neave (1989) use Shaffer's methodology to study data for Canadian banks, trust companies and mortgage companies between 1982 and 1984. They estimate the following model:

$$\ln \text{TRLL} = a + b(\ln \text{PF}) + c(\ln \text{PKB}) + d(\ln \text{PL}) + e(\ln \text{AST}) + f(\ln \text{BR}) + g\text{D6}$$

where TRLL = total revenue less provision for loan losses

PF = interest expenses/total deposits (unit price of funds)

PKB = premises expenditure/number of branches (unit price of capital)

PL = wages and salary expenses/number of employees (unit price of labour)

AST = total assets

BR = number of branches/total number of branches in the system

D = 1 (for the six largest banks)

= 0 (for the other banks)

For commercial banks, the 1982 value of $H = 1.058$ and does not differ significantly from unity, but for 1983 and 1984 $H = 0.680$ and 0.729, both significantly different from zero and unity. The Nathan and Neave results reject the monopoly, conjectural variations short-run oligopoly hypotheses and (except in 1982) the perfect competition hypotheses. They conclude that commercial bank revenues behave as if earned under monopolistic competition, which suggests 'that contestability theory has at least as much descriptive validity regarding the current behaviour of the Canadian banking industry as do theories of monopoly or oligopoly' (p. 586). The regression results for trust and mortgage companies yield similar results to those of the commercial banks.

Lloyd-Williams, Molyneux and Thornton (1991) test for evidence of contestability on a sample of 72 Japanese commercial banks for 1986 and 1988. They find that the 1986 values of H range between -0.004 and -0.006, which are both significantly different from zero and unity. They are, therefore, unable to reject the monopoly or conjectural variations short-run oligopoly hypotheses for Japanese commercial banks in 1986. However, for 1988 the values of H range between 0.245 and 0.423, suggesting that Japanese commercial banking revenues behaved as if earned under monopolistic competition.

In a recent critique of the above methodology Perrakis (1991) presents a conjectural variations oligopoly model which results in a reduced form revenue equation identical to that used by Shaffer (1982) and Nathan and Neave (1989), 'which is totally independent of the degree of competition prevailing in the industry' (p. 729). Perrakis argues that the H statistic is only relevant for assessing the degree of competitiveness in the extreme cases of monopoly and perfectly competitive long-run equilibrium and that the H value can obtain many values (even negative) if the sector operates as a conjectural variations oligopoly. Nathan and Neave (1991), in their reply to Perrakis, show that his oligopoly model is not empirically plausible because it does not allow for H values greater than zero. With positive values of H it is possible to reject the hypothesis of conjectural variations short-run oligopoly. It also does not show the independence he claims since Shaffer (1983) has already noted that H is a function of conjectural variation. Nathan and Neave (1991) suggest that 'Perrakis's point is not really about independence but rather about econometric identifiability (of H)' (p. 734, fn. 3), and they address this problem by estimating translog equations, consistent with an underlying optimisation model. The translog estimates for Canadian banks and trust companies between 1983 and 1987 yield similar results to the earlier findings with H values for banks and trust companies ranging between zero and one. They state that revenues behaved as if earned under monopolistic competition, and this, they argue, is consistent with a contestable market given empirical observations of the competitiveness of the Canadian banking system.

THE EUROPEAN BANKING MARKET: METHOD, DATA AND RESULTS

In this section we report results from estimating a model similar to those of Shaffer (1982) and Nathan and Neave (1989) on a sample of German, UK, French, Italian and Spanish banks for the period 1986 to 1989[5]. Accounting data were obtained from International Bank Credit Analysis Ltd (IBCA), a London-based bank credit rating agency. Table 1.4 shows the number of banks from each country in the sample.

Table 1.4   Number of European banks

	1986	1987	1988	1989
Germany	115	149	162	149
United Kingdom	109	157	178	171
France	96	142	179	138
Italy	n.a.	170	318	169
Spain	37	105	165	156

Source: International Bank Credit Analysis Ltd

Rosse-Panzar tests were performed cross-sectionally on the data for individual countries for the years 1986 through to 1989. The form of the revenue equation used was as follows:

$$\ln\text{TRASS} = a + b(\ln\text{PL}) + c(\ln\text{PK}) + d(\ln\text{PF}) + e(\ln\text{ASS}) + f(\ln\text{LNASS}) + g(\ln\text{CAPASS}) + h(\ln\text{IBTDEP})$$

where: ln =   natural logarithm
    TRASS =   total interest revenue per dollar of assets
    PL =   personnel expenses per dollar of assets
         (proxy for unit price of labour)
    PK =   capital expenses per dollar of fixed assets
         (proxy for unit price of capital)
    PF =   ratio of annual interest expenses to total funds
         (unit price of funds)
    ASS =   bank assets
    LNASS =   loans to assets ratio
    CAPASS =   total risk capital to assets ratio
    IBTDEP =   interbank deposits to total deposits

The independent variables include firm-specific variables and are similar to those used in previous studies. A number of control variables are included to take account of other risk, cost and size characteristics. Since the dependent variable, TRASS, is not risk-adjusted, we employ two variables to account for firm-specific risk, the total risk capital to assets ratio (CAPASS) and the loans to assets ratio (LNASS). We expect CAPASS to be negatively related to the total revenue dependent variable since lower capital ratios should lead to higher bank revenue. The coefficient on the loans to assets ratio (LNASS) is expected to be positively related as higher proportions of loans on the bank's books are expected to generate greater revenue. The asset size of banks (ASS) is included to take account of scale economies. Finally, the coefficient on the interbank deposits to total deposits (IBTDEP) ratio is included to account for differences in deposit mix.

The competitive position and equilibrium tests are shown for the years from 1986 to 1989 in Table 1.5. The sign on the coefficients for the price of capital proxy (PK) varies across country and over years and is rarely statistically significant at the 5 per cent level, whereas the coefficients for the price of labour proxy (PL) and the unit price of funds (PF) are almost always positive and often statistically significant. In the case of the other independent variables, looking at the results for 1986 through to 1989, the sign on the asset size (ASS) coefficient is mainly negative, indicating that size-induced differences between banks may lead to lower total revenues per dollar of assets. Bearing in mind the significance tests, the majority of equations also report positive coefficients for the loans to asset ratio (LNASS), suggesting that banks with a higher proportion of loans on their balance sheets generate higher total revenue per dollar of assets, and negative coefficients on the interbank

Table 1.5 Competitive position and equilibrium tests for European banks, 1986-89

LH variable	Constant	ln PK	ln PL	ln PF	ln ASS	ln (LN/ASS)	ln (CAP/ASS)	lnIBTDEP	$\bar{R}^2$	H
1986 TR/ASS										
Germany	-2.2422*	-0.0030	-0.1465	0.1132*	0.0500*	0.0189	-0.0067	-0.0245*	.44	- 0.0363
	(-10.12)	(-0.12)	(3.61)	(4.95)	(3.38)	(0.47)	(-0.10)	(-2.69)		882.1[a]
										789.3[b]
UK	-0.4881	0.0183	0.0268	0.5831*	-0.0006	0.0881	0.0719	-0.0139	.87	0.6282
	(-1.03)	(1.09)	(0.92)	(4.31)	(-0.11)	(0.56)	(0.95)	(-0.81)		141.1[a]
										20.5[b]
France	0.0103	0.0190	0.1518*	0.3819*	0.0267	0.0361	0.1156*	-0.0150	.68	0.5526
	(0.10)	(0.57)	(5.36)	(9.25)	(1.81)	(1.17)	(3.05)	(-1.10)		176.4[a]
										15.0[b]
Italy	Insufficient data - Missing observations for PF and IBTDEP									
Spain	-1.3617*	0.0612	0.0689*	0.2425*	0.0017	0.0627	-0.0064	-0.0224	.22	0.3726
	(-4.36)	(1.22)	(2.15)	(3.48)	(0.11)	(0.59)	(-0.13)	(-1.36)		42.1[a]
										126.8[b]

continued

Table 1.5 (continued)

LH variable	Constant	ln PK	ln PL	ln PF	ln ASS	ln (LN/ASS)	ln (CAP/ASS)	lnIBTDEP	R^2	H
1986 ROA										
Germany	-1.5231 (-1.57)	-0.0433 (-0.40)	0.2943 (1.66)	0.1930 (1.93)	0.0465 (0.72)	-0.1550 (-0.87)	0.7864* (2.70)	-0.1259* (-2.62)	.26	0.4440 2.4[a]
UK	-7.317 (-1.28)	0.2123 (1.04)	-0.3801 (-1.09)	-1.014 (-0.62)	-0.0235 (-0.34)	-0.0830 (-0.04)	0.5596 (0.61)	-0.2433 (-1.17)	.01	-1.1818 0.50[a]
France	-1.3804* (-3.12)	0.1386 (1.03)	0.2403* (2.06)	0.3291 (1.95)	0.1264* (2.04)	-0.3812* (-3.04)	1.0596* (6.86)	0.0389 (0.07)	.44	0.7080 2.3[a]
Italy	Insufficient data - Missing observations for PF and IBTDEP									
Spain	-5.561 (-1.74)	0.0025 (0.01)	-0.4413 (-1.37)	0.2400 (0.29)	0.1383 (0.88)	-1.3651 (-0.87)	0.9615 (1.87)	-0.0962 (-0.59)	.18	-0.1988 3.1[a]

continued

Table 1.5 (continued)

LH variable	Constant	ln PK	ln PL	ln PF	ln ASS	ln (LN/ASS)	ln (CAP/ASS)	lnIBTDEP	$\bar{R}^2$	H
1987 TR/ASS										
Germany	-2.7814* (-13.95)	0.0015 (0.08)	-0.0018 (-0.05)	0.0511* (2.48)	0.0432* (3.30)	0.0936* (2.90)	0.0802 (1.46)	-0.0359* (-3.38)	.38	0.0508 260.9[a] 0.8[b]
UK	-1.4445* (-3.46)	0.0011 (0.05)	0.0114 (0.26)	0.0747* (5.05)	0.0014 (0.16)	0.5785* (2.16)	0.1488 (1.73)	0.0014 (0.11)	.90	0.0872 2114.5[a] 117.5[b]
France	0.2503* (2.14)	0.0430 (1.59)	0.2053* (7.20)	0.5769* (16.04)	-0.0006 (-0.05)	0.0023 (0.09)	0.0248* (0.78)	-0.0317* (-2.47)	.72	0.8252 143.6[a] 170.8[b]
Italy	-0.8466* (-2.22)	-0.1323 (-1.48)	-0.2576* (-2.95)	0.1321* (2.32)	-0.0583* (-11.11)	0.1670 (1.52)	-0.0674 (-0.92)	-0.0353 (-1.00)	.36	-0.2578 18.5[a] 8.1[b]
Spain	-1.5784* (-8.04)	0.0174 (0.94)	0.0373 (1.87)	0.1373* (2.74)	-0.0121* (-2.23)	0.0810* (2.60)	0.0217 (1.42)	-0.0145* (-2.78)	.23	0.1920 1369.9[a] 8.8[b]

continued

Table 1.5 (continued)

LH variable	Constant	ln PK	ln PL	ln PF	ln ASS	ln (LN/ASS)	ln (CAP/ASS)	lnIBTDEP	$\bar{R}^2$	H
1987 ROA										
Germany	-2.0565* (-2.24)	-0.1502 (-1.66)	0.1727 (1.03)	0.1721 (1.82)	0.1087 (1.80)	-0.1242 (-0.83)	1.0304* (4.09)	-0.1426* (-2.91)	.25	0.1946 0.5ᵃ
UK	-2.826 (-1.64)	0.0338 (0.33)	-0.3132 (-1.76)	0.16862* (2.76)	-0.0434 (0.16)	0.1692 (0.15)	0.8639* (2.43)	-0.1071* (-2.13)	.81	-0.1108 11.1ᵃ
France	-1.2480* (-2.64)	0.1275 (1.17)	0.3241* (2.80)	0.1649 (1.16)	0.1719* (3.35)	-0.2606* (-2.39)	1.3365* (10.28)	0.0868 (1.66)	.54	0.6165 7.0ᵃ
Italy	-3.331* (-2.95)	0.1173 (0.40)	-0.2657 (-0.94)	0.3163 (1.84)	-0.4311* (-2.77)	-0.4481 (-1.38)	-0.0176 (-0.07)	-0.0649 (-0.61)	.16	0.1679 0.2ᵃ
Spain	-3.140 (-1.12)	-0.0369 (-0.16)	0.0721 (0.23)	-0.4726 (-0.73)	-0.9463 (-1.38)	-0.3774 (-0.89)	0.8446* (3.86)	-0.1122 (-1.69)	.23	-0.4374 0.3ᵃ

continued

Table 1.5 (continued)

LH variable	Constant	ln PK	ln PL	ln PF	ln ASS	ln (LN/ASS)	ln (CAP/ASS)	lnIBTDEP	$\bar{R}^2$	H
1988 TR/ASS										
Germany	-2.7829* (-13.77)	0.0070 (0.36)	-0.00151 (-0.04)	0.0433* (2.16)	0.0305* (2.28)	0.0873* (2.63)	0.0517 (0.89)	-0.0291* (-2.30)	.24	0.0488 165.1[a] 265.4[b]
UK	-0.0353 (-0.19)	-0.0294 (-1.66)	0.0565 (1.94)	0.8579* (15.75)	-0.0054 (-1.00)	-0.0332 (-0.29)	-0.0430 (-0.79)	-0.0082 (1.35)	.97	0.8850 152.5[a] 129.4[b]
France	0.2127* (2.09)	-0.0011 (-0.05)	0.1775* (6.61)	0.6029* (15.68)	-0.0087 (-0.68)	0.0303 (1.48)	-0.0104 (-0.32)	-0.0197 (-1.55)	.40	0.7793 207.0[a] 60.8[b]
Italy	-1.2905* (-3.96)	-0.8887* (-2.02)	0.1257* (2.49)	0.0884* (2.59)	-0.0331 (-1.59)	0.1019 (1.79)	0.6622 (1.63)	-0.0341* (-2.86)	.29	-0.6736 59.2[a] 399.3[b]
Spain	-2.2152 (-1.70)	0.0356 (1.83)	0.1815* (9.13)	0.5384* (15.43)	-0.0081 (-0.98)	0.0177 (0.79)	-0.0701* (-3.56)	-0.0086 (-1.11)	.71	0.7556 265.8[a] 147.5[b]

continued

Table 1.5 (continued)

LH variable	Constant	ln PK	ln PL	ln PF	ln ASS	ln (LN/ASS)	ln (CAP/ASS)	lnIBTDEP	$\bar{R}^2$	H
1988 ROA										
Germany	-4.3833* (-5.57)	-0.1449 (-1.92)	-0.1782 (-1.24)	-0.0514 (-0.66)	0.1628* (3.11)	0.1752 (1.34)	1.0711* (4.73)	-0.1259* (-2.55)	.21	-0.3745 1.86[a]
UK	-3.452* (-3.34)	-0.1342 (-1.40)	-0.1320 (-0.83)	0.8191* (2.77)	-0.0079 (-0.27)	-1.1041 (-1.77)	-0.0204 (-0.07)	-0.0427 (-1.29)	.28	0.6792 1.49[a]
France	-1.3333* (-2.96)	-0.0737 (-0.74)	0.39220* (3.24)	-0.0399 (-0.23)	0.1652* (2.89)	-0.3465* (-3.83)	1.1894* (8.27)	0.1209* (2.08)	.40	0.2786 2.8[a]
Italy	-6.653* (-5.31)	-0.0176 (-0.14)	-0.7089 (-3.42)	-0.1742 (-1.56)	-0.0127 (-0.14)	-0.4816* (-2.47)	0.4865* (3.26)	-0.0137 (-0.26)	.43	-0.9007 30.7[a]
Spain	-0.2318 (-0.27)	-0.0688 (-0.59)	0.2681 (1.82)	-0.0269 (-0.12)	0.0186 (0.37)	-0.1149 (-0.81)	1.3181* (8.61)	0.0145 (0.32)	.40	0.1724 6.2[a]

continued

Table 1.5 (continued)

LH variable	Constant	ln PK	ln PL	ln PF	ln ASS	ln (LN/ASS)	ln (CAP/ASS)	lnIBTDEP	$\bar{R}^2$	H
1989 TR/ASS										
Germany	-2.0152* (-6.54)	0.0721* (2.32)	0.2365* (5.18)	0.1610* (5.23)	0.0327 (1.62)	-0.0667 (-1.53)	-0.1374 (-1.72)	-0.0394 (1.27)	.25	0.4697 96.1[a] 67.8[b]
UK	-0.0869 (-0.40)	-0.0063 (-0.42)	0.0557* (2.37)	0.8031* (9.91)	-0.0129* (-2.23)	0.1871* (2.07)	-0.0385 (-0.75)	-0.0374* (-2.37)	.86	0.8525 68.6[a] 193.8[b]
France	0.2027 (2.18)	0.2470 (0.95)	0.1548* (6.60)	0.5919* (15.51)	-0.0060 (-0.50)	0.0297 (1.64)	0.0319 (1.08)	-0.0140 (-0.96)	.68	0.7714 342.6[a] 286.2[b]
Italy	5.1860* (4.57)	-0.2036 (-1.86)	-1.4302* (-4.97)	0.7393* (7.33)	-0.3260* (-3.79)	0.1328 (0.43)	0.3340* (2.48)	-0.0489 (-0.75)	.83	-0.8945 17.8[a] 15.2[b]
Spain	-0.7502* (-3.52)	0.0562 (2.07)	0.1493* (4.60)	0.3660* (8.09)	-0.0088 (-0.85)	0.0187 (0.81)	-0.0630* (-2.27)	-0.0020 (-0.17)	.36	0.5715 286.4[a] 172.9[b]

continued

Table 1.5 (continued)

LH variable	Constant	ln PK	ln PL	ln PF	ln ASS	ln (LN/ASS)	ln (CAP/ASS)	lnIBTDEP	$\bar{R}^2$	H
1989 ROA										
Germany	-3.4981*	0.0289	0.1352	0.2198*	0.1171*	0.2278	0.6912*	-0.2820*	.28	0.3839
	(-4.47)	(0.37)	(1.03)	(2.58)	(2.34)	(1.91)	(3.47)	(-3.70)		2.73[a]
UK	-7.3981*	0.1618	-0.8794*	0.1538	-0.0495	-1.8635*	0.3643	0.0055	.63	-0.5638
	(-5.40)	(1.71)	(-5.90)	(0.30)	(-1.35)	(-3.25)	(1.12)	(0.05)		6.6[a]
France	-1.6954*	0.1037	0.2860*	0.0324	0.1514*	-0.0669	1.2401*	0.0944	.34	0.4221
	(-3.44)	(0.71)	(2.27)	(0.15)	(2.31)	(-1.53)	(7.09)	(1.16)		2.53[a]
Italy	-5.296*	-0.0417	-0.3725	0.0483	-0.0038	-0.3914	0.3326	-0.0703	.30	-0.3660
	(-3.69)	(-0.30)	(-1.58)	(0.35)	(-0.03)	(-1.81)	(1.79)	(-0.79)		2.38[a]
Spain	-1.1226	-0.0922	0.2656*	-0.3812*	0.0627	-0.0647	1.3418*	0.0464	.53	-0.2078
	(-1.41)	(-0.90)	(2.04)	(-2.26)	(1.54)	(-0.70)	(11.11)	(1.10)		97.7[a]

continued

Table 1.5   (continued)

Notes: t-statistics in parentheses
  a)   F statistic for testing the hypothesis H=0 at 5% level
        of significance
  b)   F statistic for testing the hypothesis H=1 at 5% level
        of significance
  *   values significant at the 5% level

deposits total deposits ratio (IBTDEP), which implies that banks that engage in a large proportion of wholesale funding earn lower revenue per dollar of assets. The signs on the capital to assets ratio (CAPASS) appear to be indeterminate. Finally, long-run equilibrium tests, which use the return on assets (ROA) as the dependent variable, illustrate that for the majority of the regressions the data are in long-run equilibrium and, therefore, the H statistics can be meaningfully interpreted. The White (1980) heteroscedasticity test confirmed the absence of heteroscedasticity in the data, apart from the United Kingdom equation for 1989. There also appears to be no strong evidence of multicollinearity as indicated by the Belsley statistic (Belsley, Kuhn and Welsch 1980) with all the total revenue equations having values less than 25.

Table 1.6 summarises the H statistic and equilibrium results and shows that for Germany (except for 1987), the United Kingdom, France and Spain the H values are positive and significantly different from zero and unity when in equilibrium. This leads us to reject the monopoly, conjectural variations short-run oligopoly and the perfect competition hypotheses for these banking markets. As for long-run equilibrium, the evidence provided by the test indicates that for the Spanish market only the results for 1986 and 1987 may be used. This is consistent with casual observation, since between September 1987 and 1989 this market underwent dramatic changes, which included a price war among major banks, and this can hardly be considered a situation of long-run equilibrium. The statistics computed for Italy (1988), France (1987) and the United Kingdom (1987 and 1989) also have to be ignored because of a similar problem.

Thus, in equilibrium, commercial bank revenues in these markets behave as if earned under monopolistic competition. This situation is certainly better than joint monopoly, but is nonetheless different, as others suppose, from what strict contestable markets theory would

Table 1.6   The Rosse-Panzar 'H' statistic and equilibrium results

	1986	1987	1988	1989
Germany	0.2566 E	0.0508[a]E	0.0488 E	0.4697 E
United Kingdom	0.6282 E	0.0872 D	0.8850 E	0.8525 D
France	0.5526 E	0.8252 D	0.7793 E	0.7714 E
Italy	n.a.	-0.2578 E	-0.6786 D	-0.8945 E
Spain	0.3726 E	0.1920 E	0.7556 D	0.5715 D

Notes: All data significantly different from 1 and 0 unless stated
a   = not significantly different from 0
E   = denotes data in long-run equilibrium
D   = denotes data in disequilibrium

imply. The theory of contestability (see Baumol, Panzar and Willig 1982) establishes conditions under which potential competitors will guarantee perfectly competitive pricing by incumbents, that is if long-run average cost curves are flat-bottomed or if incumbents can all produce at the minimum point on a U-shaped average cost curve in equilibrium, given the market demand function. A monopolistically competitive outcome would reflect the threat of hit-and-run entry only if these cost and demand conditions were not satisfied, a question that deserves further empirical investigation. The results for Italy, however, tell a different story. The H values for 1987 at -0.2578 and -0.8945 for 1989, where the data are in long-run equilibrium, are both significantly different from zero and unity. The methodology is, therefore, unable to reject the monopoly or conjectural variations short-run oligopoly hypotheses for Italian commercial banks in those two years. (Italian results for 1988 also suggest this but, because the data do not represent long-run equilibrium values, they cannot be interpreted as such.)

CONCLUSION

EC banking legislation has established relatively free access to member countries' banking systems over the last three decades. This would suggest that, other things being equal, competitive conditions in European banking have increased. However, the degree of concentration in each member country's banking system would seem to indicate that a restricted competitive environment continues to prevail. In this paper we follow recent research into competitive conditions in banking markets and utilise the Rosse-Panzar statistic to test the competitive conditions in major European banking markets between 1986 and 1989. Our results indicate that monopolistic competition is prevalent in Germany, the United Kingdom, France and Spain. The results for Italy suggest that banks are earning revenue as if under monopoly or conjectural variations short-run oligopoly conditions. We suggest that further empirical study could be undertaken to evaluate whether a monopolistically competitive outcome is consistent with contestable markets theory.

NOTES

1. See Neven (1990) on the problems associated with interpreting price differences as varying degrees of price competition.
2. For example, in the United Kingdom: Barclays, National Westminster, Midland, Lloyds; in France: Crédit Agricole, BNP, Crédit Lyonnais, Société Générale, Paribas; in Italy: Banca Nazionale del Lavoro, Istituto Bancaria Sao Paolo, Monte dei Paschi di Siena; and in Germany: Deutsche Bank, Dresdner Bank and Commerzbank.
3. This statement is true only under one or more of three conditions: (a) the firm produces a single output; (b) the production function is homethetic; or (c) factor prices change by equal proportions across observations in the sample. Condition (a) is certainly false for large banks and we can find no evidence from the empirical banking literature that (b) holds. Our input price data, however, do show that (c) holds in the majority of cases and thus we maintain the assumption that $H = 1$ under long-run perfect competition.
4. Bresnahan (1989, p. 1037) in two critical observations notes that for the methodology to give convincing results all cost shifters must be correctly specified and entered into the equation. Although it was impossible to account for all cost shifts in our empirical investigation, our model, we believe, is sufficient to account for this theoretical point. In addition, he also argues that shifts in the cost function are unlikely to identify fully the degree of market power in

any industry, simply because the market power coefficient is part of the supply relationship and its identification requires more information, coming from the demand side of the market.

5. Since Perrakis (1991) has questioned the consistency of these reduced form revenue equations, we also estimated translog revenue functions for each country using the approach as suggested by Nathan and Neave (1990 and 1991). The parameter estimates using the translog model were nearly all insignificant and the explanatory variables were subject to severe multicollinearity. Because of their unreliability we do not report these results.

LIST OF REFERENCES

Baltensperger, E. and J. Dermine (1990), 'European banking: prudential and regulatory issues' in J. Dermine (ed.), *European Banking in the 1990s* (Oxford: Blackwell)

Baumol, William J.; John C. Panzar and Robert D. Willig (1982), *Contestable Markets and the Theory of Industry Structure* (San Diego: Harcourt Brace Jovanovich)

Belsley, D.A.; E. Kuhn and R.E. Welsch (1980), *Regression Diagnostics: Identifying Influential Data and Sources of Collinearity* (New York)

Bresnahan, T. (1989), 'Empirical studies of industries with market power' in R. Schmalensee and R.D. Willig (eds), *Handbook of Industrial Organisation*, 2, chap. 17, 1011-57

Bröker, G. (1989), *Competition in Banking* (Paris: OECD)

Bruni, F. (1990), 'Banking and financial regulation towards 1992: the Italian case' in J. Dermine (ed.), *European Banking in the 1990s* (Oxford: Blackwell)

Caminal, R.; J. Gual and X. Vives (1990), 'Competition in Spanish banking' in J. Dermine (ed.), *European Banking in the 1990s* (Oxford: Blackwell)

Cecchini, P. (1988), *The European Challenge in 1992: the Benefits of a Single Market* (Aldershot: Gower Press)

Commission of the European Communities (1988), *European Economy: the Economics of 1992* (Brussels: European Commission)

Dermine, J. (1991), 'Discussant on banking competition and European integration' by X. Vives in A. Giovanni and C. Mayer (eds), *European Financial Integration* (London: CUP)

Gardener, E.P.M. and P. Molyneux (1990), *Changes in Western European Banking* (London: Unwin Hyman)

Lloyd-Williams, D.M.; P. Molyneux and J. Thornton (1991), 'Competition and contestability in the Japanese commercial banking market', Institute of European Finance, Research Papers in Banking and Finance, no. 16 (Bangor: Institute of European Finance)

Molyneux, P. (1989), '1992 and its impact on local and regional banking markets', *Regional Studies*, **23**, 6, 523-33

Nathan, Alli and Edwin H. Neave (1989), 'Competition and contestability in Canada's financial system: empirical results', *Canadian Journal of Economics*, **22**, 3 (August), 576-94

Nathan, Alli and Edwin H. Neave (1990), 'Competitiveness and contestability in Canadian banks and trust companies: further results', *Queen's University School of Business Working Paper* (September)

Nathan, Alli and Edwin H. Neave (1991), 'Reply to Perrakis', *Canadian Journal of Economics*, **22**, 3 (August), 727-35

Neven, D.J. (1990), 'Structural adjustment in European retail banking: some views from industrial organisation' in J. Dermine (ed.), *European Banking in the 1990s* (Oxford: Blackwell)

Panzar, J.C. and J.N. Rosse (1982), 'Structure, conduct and comparative statistics', *Bell Laboratories Economic Discussion Paper*, no. 248 (March)

Panzar, J.C. and J.N. Rosse (1987), 'Testing for monopoly equilibrium', *Journal of Industrial Economics*, **35**, 443-56, Marquandt

Perrakis, Stylianas (1991), 'Assessing competition in Canada's financial system: a note', *Canadian Journal of Economics*, **22**, 3 (August), 727-32

Price Waterhouse (1988), 'The cost of non-Europe in financial services' in *Research of the Cost of Non-Europe*, **9** (Brussels: Commission of the European Communities)

Rosse, J.N. and J.C. Panzar (1977), 'Chamberlin vs. Robinson: an empirical test for monopoly rents', *Bell Laboratories Economic Discussion Paper*, no. 90

Shaffer, Sherrill (1981a), 'Banking: competition or monopoly power?', Banking Studies Department, Federal Reserve Bank of New York (March)

Shaffer, Sherrill (1981b), 'Empirical test for competitive conduct', Banking Studies Department, Federal Reserve Bank of New York (August)

Shaffer, Sherrill (1982), 'A non-structural test for competition in financial markets', in *Bank Structure and Competition*, Conference Proceedings, Federal Reserve Bank of Chicago, pp. 225-43

Shaffer, Sherrill (1983), 'Non-structural measures of competition', *Economics Letters*, **12**

Vives, X. (1991), 'Banking competition and European integration' in A. Giovanni and C. Mayer (eds), *European Financial Integration* (London: CUP)

White, H. (1980), 'A heteroskedasticity-consistent covariance matrix estimator and a direct test for heteroskedasticity', *Econometrica*, **48**, 817-38

CHAPTER 2
COMPETITION IN BANKING MARKETS:
LESSONS FROM THE ITALIAN CASE

Riccardo Cesari
Vittorio Conti
and
Marco Onado

FOREWORD

The 1980s have witnessed an increasing interest in the banking industry. Many studies, mainly theoretical, have analysed the peculiarity of competition in banking markets. This interest stems, on the one hand, from the increase in competition fostered by recent deregulation in domestic markets and, on the other hand, from the expectations about the competition between national systems that will be determined by the implementation of the Second Banking Co-ordination Directive.

With specific reference to the European side of the problem, there is a widespread belief that competitive forces will increase and will put significant pressure on national banking systems. This will eventually force the convergence of individual structures, which are still very different as far as cost structures, market conditions and operating efficiency are concerned (Conti 1990). The sign and speed of changes are by no means clear. On the one hand, some apply to the banking markets the traditional theory of international trade. This is, for example, the underlying hypothesis of the Cecchini Report. On the other hand, many argue that banking markets are different, on the ground of the information asymmetries which have been particularly stressed in recent developments of financial theory.

This approach looks very attractive, because of its theoretical consistency: if intermediaries exist precisely because of the imperfections which are embodied in financial markets (and particularly in retail banking markets), it is impossible to use the traditional international theory whose main hypothesis is the perfection of market conditions. The difficulty arises when one tries to predict the final outcome of integration between imperfect markets and particularly when one tries to test these hypotheses empirically. Some have examined experience in regional markets. Others have tried to infer from changes in national markets what will happen to the European markets. All suffer from insufficient data on local markets and from not taking into account the

30

level of risk, a fundamental dimension of financial activity. This failure is partly due to a very heroic assumption that risks are equal between banks, which is once again inconsistent with the hypothesis of market imperfections.

The Italian case from this point of view is particularly interesting for at least two reasons:

- data are available for local markets, and classified by size of bank loan, location and size of the bank. Moreover, these data refer to the quantity of loans, interest rates and bad debts
- in the 1980s competition has been dramatically increased by deregulation (phasing out of credit ceilings; liberalisation of branching etc.).

This paper briefly reviews the theory on competition in banking markets in the next section; as a typical model is based on the different behaviour of incumbent banks and new entrants, the shift-and-share technique seems particularly suited to capture the difference in these two classes of banks as far as risks and prices are concerned. Data on the Italian banking system are then used to analyse how competition has worked in recent years. Handling these conclusions with care, a few implications for future European competition are drawn in the last section.

COMPETITION IN BANKING MARKETS

The typical efficient financial contract cannot be used because of the risk involved or, in other words, because of the informative asymmetries between the lender and the borrower. This very fact makes competition less direct and straightforward than in markets where both parties share the same amount of information. This is particularly true in retail banking markets, especially loan markets, where asymmetries are stronger and the assessment of risk is the main task of the lender. Risk is therefore a fundamental component of the market price and of the profit for the intermediary.

This approach tends to identify lending as the main product of financial intermediaries. While intrinsically multi-product firms, financial units and especially banks exist precisely because of their capacity to produce information during their lending activity (Conti and Noera 1988). One can therefore argue that it is not possible to adopt for banking markets the contestable market hypothesis recently developed by Baumol *et al.* (1982). While - even with reference to the Italian situation - some give a positive answer (Di Battista and Grillo 1988) others are more sceptical (Galli and Onado 1990) and point to the peculiarity of banking markets - particularly retail markets - as an element which loosens the effects of potential competition.

Only a segment of financial markets meets the strict theoretical requirements of potential competition. This is the case of wholesale services, which can be offered across borders and are not dependent on physical presence (Montgomery 1991). Only for these perfectly tradable services do conditions of success depend on cost advantages. In retail markets the existence of informational asymmetries strengthens customer relationships and gives to the incumbent a competitive advantage over the potential new entrant. This advantage does not necessarily lead to a higher price: the convenience of maintaining the customer relations suggests not making complete use of the monopolistic position (Sharpe 1991). On the other hand, the new entrant can successfully enter the market only after acquiring the same degree of information (which is costly and time consuming) or, alternatively, by acquisition or merger with the incumbent, which can be a mixed blessing for the degree of competition and economic welfare.

The consequences of this approach are twofold. On the one hand, and in opposition to the more radical version of the structure-conduct-performance model, one can argue that new entries in the market can have asymmetric effects. In financial contracts the risk is not immediately evident, while costs connected with the acquisition of information are borne as soon as the new branch starts its operation. It is therefore reasonable that a new entrant tends to concentrate its supply on the market where information is more available. In so doing, not only does the new entrant lower its costs, but it can also make a better assessment of risks. The segment where information costs are minimal is typically the market for major corporate clients. New entrants tend therefore to concentrate on the already competitive segment of the market. The effects of structural conditions and particularly of the elimination of barriers to entry tend to be gradual. The increase in the number of participants does not immediately affect price conditions and other traditional indicators of performance. The result, at least in the short run, can be an overheating of competition in the already competitive segment of the market.

From another point of view, it has been argued that the new entrant is in a disadvantageous position as far as risk assessment is concerned and is therefore more likely to accept *lemons* among its customers. The price to be paid for entering new markets is therefore to accept greater risks for a given level of interest rate. Even in this case, the more radical version stresses the potential instability which is intrinsically embodied in competition when applied to banking markets. This leads to a structural trade-off between competition and stability. In a less radical version this leads to the conclusion that deregulation must be followed by changes in structural conditions (and not the other way round) to absorb suboptimal conditions determined by competition.

The interest of scholars and regulators is now focused on how European competition will work. Which forces will lead the restructuring of domestic financial systems as soon as institutional and regulatory barriers have been cut down? The faith in the rationality of the invisible hand is often entangled with fears about the prices that are likely to be paid to competition.

Two recent studies deserve to be mentioned here. Montgomery (1991) moves from the hypothesis that a process of integration between different areas (within a single country or among different countries) should progressively lead from a structure based on local banks to a structure based on multi-regional banks. These banks can provide a more efficient way of transferring funds but will not necessarily determine an improvement in the competitive conditions and/or in the efficiency of the financial system. That happens when the entry of new banks pushes local banks out of the market, thus destroying customer relationships that have been built over time. The relationship between lenders and borrowers is part of the productive capital of the economy as the result of long-term processes. An empirical test on Italian data is used to demonstrate this two-sided result; a further step is to consider this as an example of the effects of financial integration between different regions in the United States, between different countries in Europe, or whatever.

In a more general paper Vives (1991) builds the hypothesis that the integration will phase out the collusive behaviour which is typical of retail markets. Given the intrinsic imperfection of financial markets, the ideal conditions of competition will never be attained. This will lead banks to soften competition through mergers, acquisitions and accords. These structural changes will be the main forces to lead market integration, not the hit-and-run strategies made possible by deregulation in contestable markets.

An empirical test is presented only by Montgomery but the reliability of the test is, to say to the least, very poor; the main weakness is not to take into account an indicator of risk. This is tantamount to supposing that risk is equal for all the areas examined and, within each area, for all lenders. Cesari and Villani (1989) provided an interesting attempt to take into account both risk and price, distinguishing new entrants from incumbents. Their shift-and-share technique allows for managing the enormous amount of data and, particularly, for distinguishing a *subjective - discretionary risk*, as defined by the concentration of loans in more risky industries or in more risky customers in each industry, and an *objective* (or *environmental*) *risk*, as defined by the difference between the average degree of riskiness in each area and the average riskiness of the country. According to their analysis, it will be local banks that in a situation of greater competition will be bound to stick to the customer of lower quality and are therefore exposed to greater risks.

THE SHIFT-AND-SHARE TECHNIQUE

If we define risk as the ratio of bad debts (S) on loans (I), according to the approach used by Cesari and Villani (1989), using the *shift-and-share* technique, it is possible to define for each area (A), the risk differential DR between local banks (BL) and external banks (BE) as the difference of riskiness for each class *vis-à-vis* the riskiness of the area.

$$DR = \left[\frac{S}{I}\right]^{BE} - \left[\frac{S}{I}\right]^{BL} = [\ \left[\frac{S}{I}\right]^{BE} - \left[\frac{S}{I}\right]^{A}\ ] - [\ \left[\frac{S}{I}\right]^{BL} - \left[\frac{S}{I}\right]^{A}\ ] \tag{1}$$

The first term in square brackets (DR1) can be divided for the i categories of customers in two components. The first refers to the differential in riskiness (weighted by portfolio composition I_i/I). The latter to the differential in composition (weighted by the riskiness S_i/I_i).

$$DR1 = \Sigma_i [\ \left[\frac{S_i}{I_i}\right]^{BE} - \left[\frac{S_i}{I_i}\right]^{A}\ ]\ \left[\frac{I_i}{I}\right]^{BE} + \Sigma_i [\ \left[\frac{I_i}{I}\right]^{BE} - \left[\frac{I_i}{I}\right]^{A}\ ]\ \left[\frac{S_i}{I_i}\right]^{A} \tag{2}$$

By the same token, the second term of equation (1) can be written as:

$$DR2 = \Sigma_i [\ \left[\frac{S_i}{I_i}\right]^{BL} - \left[\frac{S_i}{I_i}\right]^{A}\ ]\ \left[\frac{I_i}{I}\right]^{BL} + \Sigma_i [\ \left[\frac{I_i}{I}\right]^{BL} - \left[\frac{I_i}{I}\right]^{A}\ ]\ \left[\frac{S_i}{I_i}\right]^{A} \tag{3}$$

To give emphasis to informational factors, we can split the risk differential DR into two parts: R_1, equal to the difference between the first terms of (2) and (3) and R_2, equal to the difference between the second terms. We get:

$$DR = DR1 - DR2 = R_1 + R_2 \tag{4}$$

In particular:

$$R_1 = \Sigma_i \left[\left(\frac{S_i}{I_i} \right)^{BE} - \left(\frac{S_i}{I_i} \right)^A \right] \left(\frac{I_i}{I} \right)^{BE} - \Sigma_i \left[\left(\frac{S_i}{I_i} \right)^{BL} - \left(\frac{S_i}{I} \right)^A \right] \left(\frac{I_i}{I} \right)^{BL} \qquad (5)$$

This expression can be interpreted as the greater risk that the external bank has to bear (given its portfolio composition) for entering a new market, having less information than local banks. Alternatively stated, it can be interpreted as the advantage that comes to a local bank from consolidated customer relationships.

The second term R_2 can be written as:

$$R_2 = \Sigma_i \left[\left(\frac{I_i}{I} \right)^{BE} - \left(\frac{I_i}{I} \right)^{BL} \right] \left(\frac{S_i}{I_i} \right)^A \qquad (6)$$

which can be interpreted as a preference factor for particular classes of borrowers, which in turn can derive from risk aversion (if there are structural differences in riskiness) or from factors connected to the costs necessary to produce the loan (including the cost of information).

The same procedure can be applied to interest rates (r) applied by local and external banks.

$$DT = r^{BE} - r^{BL} = [r^{BE} - r^A] - [r^{BL} - r^A] \qquad (7)$$

which can be written as:

$$DT = T_1 + T_2 \qquad (8)$$

where:

$$T_1 = \Sigma_i [(r_i)^{BE} - (r_i)^A] \left(\frac{I_i}{I} \right)^{BE} - \Sigma_i [(r_i)^{BL} - (r_i)^A] \left(\frac{I_i}{I} \right)^{BL} \qquad (9)$$

$$T_2 = \Sigma_i \left[\left(\frac{I_i}{I} \right)^{BE} - \left(\frac{I_i}{I} \right)^{BL} \right] (r_i)^A \qquad (10)$$

T_1 can be viewed as the rate differential the external bank has to accept (conditions of composition being given) to operate in new markets, having less information than local banks or as the price advantage deriving from consolidated customer relationships.

R_1 and T_1 can therefore be interpreted as measures (respectively on the risk and rate side) of information asymmetries.

The following criteria have been adopted:
- local markets identified by the province

- banks defined as local (incumbent) or external (new entrants) according to the location of their headquarters
- loans, bad debts and rates classified by:
  - local/external banks
  - size of the loan
  - institutional and size class of banks
- risk measured by the ratio of bad debts to loans

Beside differentials previously defined, we have run regressions of the type:

$$y_{ij} = \alpha + \Sigma_i \beta_i Dp_i + \Sigma_j \gamma_j Dt_j \qquad (11)$$

where:

$Dp_i = $ *dummy* variable for i-th province
$Dt_i = $ *dummy* variable for j-th year
Dependent variables are DR, R_1 R_2, DT, T_1 and T_2 as defined by equations (1), (5), (6), (7), (9) and (10)

THE RESULTS: MARKET SHARES

Three characteristics of the market at the beginning of the period must be stressed:

- the external banks had quite a large market share (63.1 per cent), as shown by 1986 data in Figure 2.1
- the segmentation was quite evident, taking into account the size of banks. The share of local banks was particularly strong in the lower classes of loans. As external banks, the share of small banks (especially small saving banks) in the upper classes was practically zero (Figure 2.2)
- while interest rates were practically equal for all classes of loans (but on average lower for external banks: Figure 2.3) the level of risk was higher in many classes and lower on the average (Figure 2.4). A suboptimal condition (lower rates - higher risks) seemed to characterise the condition of external banks in the small loan market

After four years of strong competition (a really new component of the Italian scene) the situation has changed due to:

- a demand factor: the relative increase of lower classes of loans
- a supply factor: the dramatic increase of minor banks (particularly saving banks) and the stronger presence of external banks in lower classes of loans. The traditional segmentation does not hold any

longer. Competition has led to a reshuffle of market share in individual segments, rather than to a change in aggregate market shares for individual banks

Figure 2.1 Market share of external banks by size of loans

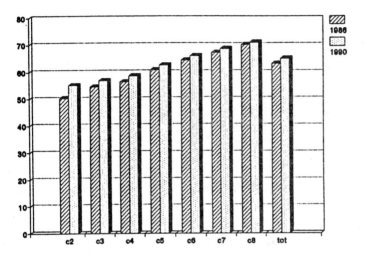

Figure 2.2 Market share of external banks by bank size and category

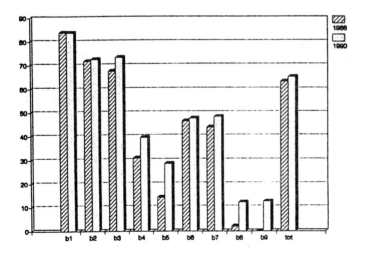

Figure 2.3   Interest rates 1986: external banks versus local banks

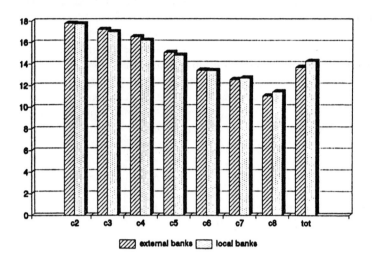

Figure 2.4   Risk 1986: external banks versus local banks

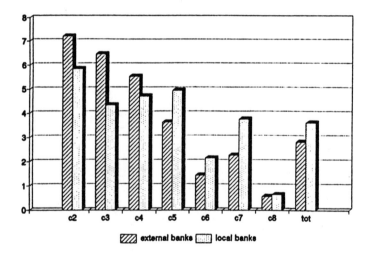

From the aggregate data it is, however, quite difficult to sum up the effects of competition over the period examined. Rate and risk differentials show only minor changes over the period (see Figures 2.5 and 2.6). From this point of view, data interpreted at face value seem to lead to the conclusion that even in an integrated country, even in a period of deregulation and greater competition, differences tend to remain.

Shift-and-share technique changes the picture. Holding portfolio composition equal, it appears that over the period conditions have changed dramatically. In almost every area, the information disadvantage has dropped, both in the risk dimension and in the rate dimension. Competition seems to have made risk and rates almost equal across banks. On the other hand, the relationship of rate differential to *risk* differential has almost disappeared. Banks which accept higher risks in new markets cannot charge higher prices any longer.

The regression (practically a pooling of data over the period) for the overall risk-return differential shows a significant positive relationship between risk and rate (see Figure 2.7): higher risk differentials are associated with higher rate differentials. This situation is however different from one area to another. In some areas, due to lower competitive conditions, external banks are better off and can more than compensate the higher costs of information as measured by loan riskiness.

Figure 2.5   Interest rates 1990: external banks versus local banks

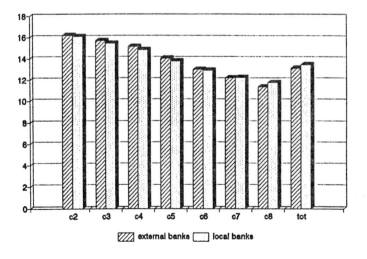

Figure 2.6   Risk 1990: external banks versus local banks

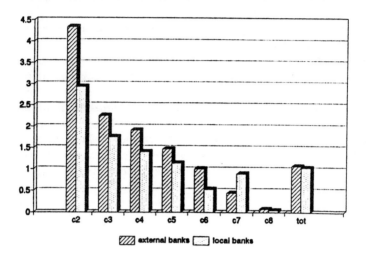

Figure 2.7   Rate and risk differentials: external banks versus local banks

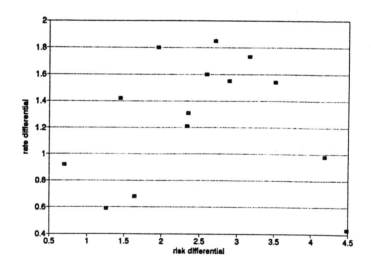

Looking at what we have defined as the information disadvantage (Figure 2.8) these findings are reinforced with two important qualifications:

- in many areas the risk differential is equal to or less than zero: the information disadvantage has disappeared
- all areas of Figure 2.7 where the rate-risk relationship was suboptimal lie on the horizontal axis thus proving the importance of this factor

Moreover, Figures 2.9 and 2.10 show that in most areas the disadvantage has disappeared in the risk component (Figure 2.9) while rate differentials tend to converge, although the rates charged by local banks are still higher (Figure 2.10). It is finally important to stress that the risk differential is higher mainly for minor banks, and particularly saving banks. In other words, the banks that built significant market shares in new segments (the large corporate clients) had to pay a high price in terms of risk.

Figure 2.8   Information disadvantage: external banks versus local banks

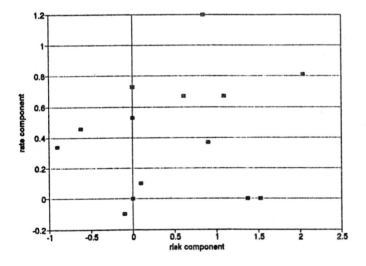

Figures 2.9 Information disadvantage: risk component

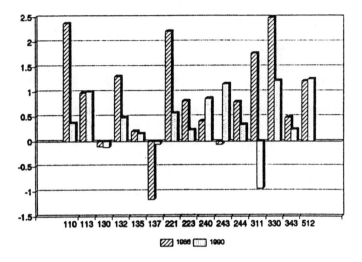

Figure 2.10 Information disadvantage: rate component

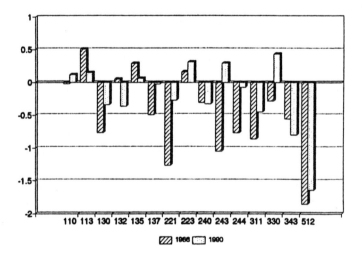

Figure 2.11 Risk differential: external versus local by bank size

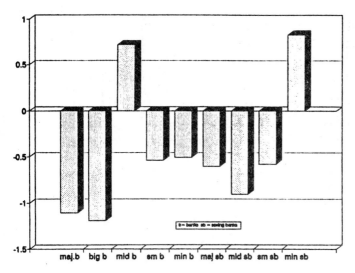

SUMMARY AND CONCLUSIONS

The theory of banking competition has been dominated by two different (and opposite) forms of pessimism. On the one hand, many argue that the new entrant bank can overcome the information barriers only at a high price (or it cannot overcome them at all) and so it can exert only a limited competitive pressure. On the other hand, particular emphasis has been given to the potential instability that competition can determine. The consequence is a permanent trade-off between competition and stability. As the latter is the supreme good of financial markets, competition must be carefully if not avoided, at least controlled. This state of mind has been largely responsible for various forms of market segmentation that prevailed in all financial systems at least until the 1970s and that determined a situation of low competition in all retail markets.

Italy was by no means an exception from this point of view.

■ an increase in banking competition led to a significant reshuffle of market shares in different market segments. The entrance into new markets has been much more significant than changes in total market shares. In other words, when competition increases, a preferred habitat strategy does not seem feasible. Major banks have gained market shares in the small loan sector. This change was favoured by the very lax Italian discipline on individual loan size

- traditional data (total market shares, aggregate interest rates) do not show significant changes over the period
- the shift-and-share technique shows that this change has been dominated by a 'virtuous' risk-rate relationship. New entrants did not seem to be handicapped by information asymmetries, even when they did not adopt a preferred habitat strategy
- This situation is not, however, common to all banks. Minor banks seem particularly worse off when they enter new markets (in the Italian case the big loans segment). Minor banks seem particularly ill-suited to act as external banks (Cesari and Villani 1989; Faini, Galli and Giannini 1991). These banks have a lower cost of information when they operate in local markets. When entering new markets, they do not seem ready or able (or both) to sustain the higher marginal cost of information. From this point of view, the marginal cost of information seems much more important in shaping the effects of bank competition than the average cost of production.

The Italian experience confirms the importance of information asymmetries in loan markets, and suggests the existence of at least three stages in bank competition:

- *segmentation*: when competition (for structural or cyclical reasons) is not particularly strong, different classes of banks tend to operate in different segments of the market. A sort of preferred habitat behaviour (or quiet-life attitude) tends to prevail. The capacity of banks to assess risks is obviously important, but once risks emerge, differences between banks are more than compensated for by rate differentials
- *convergence* (once market share of external banks is reasonably large): when competition becomes stronger, rates (all conditions being equal) tend to converge. The information disadvantage becomes particularly important, especially in the risk component. As the marginal cost of information is different for each bank or class of bank, many lenders (in Italy, minor banks that entered the large corporate loans segment) are worse off
- *restructuring*: this stage (which seems the inevitable outcome of the Italian experience) can lead to structural changes aiming at reducing the information costs for lenders

It is in this stage that initial conditions (operative efficiency and capital endowments) come to the forefront. Banks that are better off from this point of view and that have lower information costs are particularly well suited to lead this process of structural change. The latter is a consequence of competition, rather than the other way round, as implied in a typical structure-conduct-performance model.

The only conclusion that we can draw from the Italian experience, as far as European convergence is concerned, is that competition works quite slowly, not following a linear path as implied by traditional theory. On the other hand, it is obvious that a complete financial integration cannot be achieved until retail markets have been integrated.

It is important to stress at least two facts:

- European banks are still characterised by strong differences in terms of market conditions, operating efficiency, capital endowments
- the market share of European banks in foreign retail markets (their presence as external banks) is very small and in many cases practically non-existent

As has been recently pointed out (Dini 1992), the obstacles to entry in foreign markets seem to justify the cautious strategies followed by European intermediaries in entering other markets in the Community. For the most part they have chosen to acquire interests in banks with a sizeable market share rather than set up branch networks. Furthermore, in most cross-border purchases the acquiring bank has left its subsidiary to continue operations under its original name; this was the case when Deutsche Bank took over Banca d'America e d'Italia, one of the largest cross-border acquisitions of the last few years.

Mergers and acquisitions are the quickest way to integration (Vives 1991) but will prove to be very difficult for economic and political reasons (Revell 1988): the path to European integration will be quite difficult and will take much more time than is implied by a typical model of perfect competition.

LIST OF REFERENCES

Assbank (1990), *Manuale per il 1993 e oltre: Strutture, Sistemi e Strategie Bancarie* (G. Vaciago, ed.) (Milano: Edibank)

Baumol, W.; , J. Panzar and R. Willig (1982), *Contestable Markets and the Theory of Industry Structure* (New York: Harcourt Brace Jovanovich)

Cesari, Riccardo and Marco Villani (1989), 'Analisi della rischiosità degli impieghi del sistema bancario e dei settori industriali regionali: il caso dell'Emilia-Romagna', *Banca Impresa Società*, no. 3

Conti, Vittorio (1990), 'Concorrenza e redditività nell'industria bancaria: un confronto internazionale', Banca d'Italia Temi di Discussione del Servizio Studi, no. 149

Conti, Vittorio and Mario Noera (1988), 'Quale banca per il mercato o quale, mercato per la banca: le ragioni di una ricerca ancora aperta' in Francesco Cessarini *et al.* (eds), *Banca e Mercato* (Bologna: Il Mulino)

Di Battista, Maria Luisa and Michele Grillo (1988), 'La concorrenza nell'industria bancaria italiana', in Francesco Cessarini *et al.* (eds), *Banca e Mercato* (Bologna: Il Mulino)

Dini, Lamberto (1992), 'Financial aspects of European integration', Roma, Banca d'Italia, mimeo

Faini, Riccardo; Gianpaolo Galli and Curzio Giannini (1991), 'Finance and development: the case of Southern Italy', paper presented at the CEPR Conference, Santiago de Compostela, 13-15 December

Galli, Gianpaolo and Marco Onado (1990), 'Dualismo territoriale e sistema finanziario' in *Il Sistema Finanziario del Mezzogiorno*, Banca d'Italia, Roma

Giannini, C.; L. Papi and A. Prati (1991), 'Politica di offerta e riallocazione del credito bancario negli anni ottanta', Banca d'Italia Temi di Discussione del Servizio Studi, no. 151

Montgomery, John D. (1991), 'Market segmentation and 1992: toward a theory of trade in financial services', Board of Governors of the Federal Reserve System, International Finance Discussion Papers, no. 394 (April)

Onado, Marco (1992), 'Lo stato dell'unificazione dei mercati finanziari e creditizi alla vigilia del 1993', paper presented to the Conference 'Quale modello di banca per gli Stati Uniti d'Europa', Milano, Ciriec

Revell, Jack (1988), 'Come le banche si preparano al 1992: indicazioni e problemi' in *Banca Impresa Società*, no. 3

Sharpe, S.A. (1991), 'Asymmetric information, bank lending and implicit contracts: a stylized model of customer relationships', in Francesco Cesarini *et al.* (eds), *Banca e Mercato* (1991)

Vives, Xavier (1991), 'Banking competition and European integration', in Alberto Giovannini and Colin Mayer (eds), *European Financial Integration* (London: Cambridge University Press)

CHAPTER 3
NEW FORMS OF COMPETITION FACING THE SPANISH BANKING SYSTEM

Javier Quesada

INTRODUCTION

After the disruption caused by the 'deposit battle' fought in Spain by most banks, and to a lesser extent by savings banks, competing fiercely through vast increases in interest rates, the Spanish banking sector has seen in the last year and a half the emergence of new financial products that have caused a sharp shift in household portfolios. Pension plans, investment funds and the forthcoming Popular Savings Plans are three instruments aimed by the authorities to induce a higher saving rate. As is often the case, a special fiscal treatment gives rise to the explosion of an asset demand, which lasts until regulators change their objectives. In the meantime, the banking sector designs strategies to become a player in the new market situation so that it gets 'linked' to the disintermediation process.

PENSION PLANS

Although pension plans (PP) are not exactly new in Spain, it was not until 1987 that a new law was passed to set up a modern regime in order to organise existing plans and to encourage households to make their own retirement plans. In this way, it was thought, savings would be stimulated throughout the economy. In addition to new savings, the possibility of making contributions to a pension fund (basically an IRA or Individual Retirement Account) could divert funds away from banking products (savings and time deposits, for example). The law - changed twice in 1990 and 1991 - gave PP fiscal benefits that made their after-tax rate of return higher than the one given by regular saving assets. The fiscal benefits may be summarised as follows:

- The annual *per capita* contribution cannot exceed either 750,000 ptas (US $8,300) or 15 per cent of earned income (excluding capital income and all kinds of rents), whichever is less. These contributions are tax-exempt.

- Pension funds can reinvest their returns without paying any income taxes. Corporate tax rate is zero, and the participant does not have to pay any income tax until retirement arrives and withdrawals start. Furthermore, participants do not have to pay wealth taxes on accumulated contributions in the form of consolidated rights.
- A previously existing deduction (15 per cent) of part of the annual contribution[1] from the final tax was eliminated.
- Pension fund withdrawals are taxable at the time of accrual. Taxes become due during retirement and the government collects the funds it left untaxed at the time the contribution was made.

It is clear that banks can hardly compensate such tax benefits with a higher explicit rate of return. What has been the strategy followed by financial intermediaries to fight the new competition? The answer has been 'linked' disintermediation; that is to say, to act as a promoter organising a pension plan for their customers, acting with subsidiaries as managing firms of the fund and becoming also the depository of the assets held by the pension fund. The possibilities then open for banks to place some of their products in pension fund portfolios and lets them recapture part of the disintermediation pushed forward by the authorities. So banks offer pension funds as an extra service to their customers, not risking the loss of any customer for not having found such a service in the bank.

Quantitatively not many funds have as yet been directed towards pension plans, although this will still be a growing market as *per capita* income grows steadily.

INVESTMENT FUNDS

Investment funds (IF) have been active in Spain since the beginning of the 1970s. Most of them were variable income funds and experienced great losses during a very extended period of a bearish stock market, which made people cautious about their profitability as well as their risk. It was only recently that the new law on personal income tax substantially changed the tax treatment of IF so that they became the greatest competitive product for pension plans, as well as for banking products. Evidence on the popularity of the fixed-income investment funds (money market funds) is presented in Table 3.1.

Collective investment can take the form of (i) *Sociedades de Inversión Mobiliaria* (SIM) or Financial Investment Societies, and

Table 3.1 Progress of Spanish capital market (FIM) and money market (FIAMM) mutual funds, 1981-91

| | FIM | | | | | FIAMM | | | |
	Entities (numbers)	Participants (thousands)	Share value (ptas bn)	Per capita (ptas mn)	Total bank deposits (ptas bn)	Entities (numbers)	Participants (thousands)	Share value (ptas bn)	Per capita (ptas mn)
1981	23	123.1	16.1	130.4	11,977	-	-	-	-
1982	23	120.5	18.5	153.3	14,028	-	-	-	-
1983	23	117.6	28.7	224.1	15,655	-	-	-	-
1984	26	172.5	75.7	438.9	17,737	-	-	-	-
1985	30	286.2	128.5	449.1	19,945	-	-	-	-
1986	49	466.1	324.0	695.2	20,376	10	21.3	45.3	2,123.3
1987	89	514.6	307.4	597.3	21,868	13	27.8	73.0	3,012.0
1988.1	99	490.7	332.8	678.4	21,710	20	33.7	144.7	4,296.8
1988.2	111	496.7	381.5	768.0	22,300	23	37.7	166.3	4,415.9
1988.3	128	515.2	449.4	872.0	23,078	26	43.1	192.0	4,452.7
1988.4	144	518.2	450.4	869.0	23,461	31	42.7	198.0	4,633.5
1989.1	...	...	...	...	23,848	...	...	...	...
1989.2	...	...	...	...	24,456	...	...	...	...

continued

Table 3.1 (continued)

	FIM					FIAMM			
	Entities (numbers)	Participants (thousands)	Share value (ptas bn)	Per capita (ptas mn)	Total bank deposits (ptas bn)	Entities (numbers)	Participants (thousands)	Share value (ptas bn)	Per capita (ptas mn)
1989.3	161	454.6	383.5	843.7	25,398	40	79.0	235.0	2,975.3
1989.4	171	446.7	409.6	917.0	25,709	41	104.2	288.4	2,767.9
1990.1	179	...	402.9	...	26,301	46	...	379.9	...
1990.2	184	416.6	383.9	921.5	27,589	48	152.5	423.7	2,779.0
1990.3	195	401.1	386.7	964.1	28,687	51	166.2	481.9	2,899.3
1990.4	206	376.2	393.4	1,045.0	29,191	62	193.8	534.1	2,756.1
1991.1	206	379.3	495.7	1,306.0	30,336	68	245.5	694.8	2,830.0
1991.2	245	436.6	817.6	1,872.0	31,573	73	303.3	979.6	3,229.4
1991.3	267	488.7	1,051.0	2,150.0	32,720	80	370.4	1,287.5	3,476.4
1991.4	285	663.2	1,671.0	2,519.8	33,499	88	482.0	1,762.3	3,656.2
FIM+FIAMM									
1992.1	658	...	4,835.0	...	34,984	...	...	...	...

Source: Bank of Spain

(ii) *Fondos de Inversión Mobiliaria* (FIM) - Financial Investment Funds. FIM shares must be tradable in the stock market, and SIM can have fixed or variable capital, according to the possibility of issuing new shares to raise new capital. As shown in the table, it is the accelerating increase in FIM's share of the market that has caused a great change in household portfolios affecting the demand for bank deposits.

According to the share of fixed-income securities (X) in their portfolio fund they are called:

- FIAMM - *Fondo de Inversión en Activos del Mercado Monetario* (money market funds): 100 per cent invested in fixed-income assets: $X = 1$
- *Fondos de renta fija mixta* (mixed fixed-income funds): 70 per cent $< X < 100$ per cent
- *Fondos de renta variable mixta* (mixed variable income funds): 30 per cent $< X < 70$ per cent
- *Fondos de renta variable* (variable income funds): $X < 30$ per cent

It is argued, and available evidence confirms it[2], that risk increases with the portfolio share of variable income assets, so that customers may choose between different investment funds according to their preferences towards risk and return.

As is well known, investment funds offer the smallest investor the possibility to diversify his portfolio, benefiting from professional management and from economies of scale in transaction as well as information costs. Nevertheless, what has made them so popular in recent months is tax features of which the most appealing to households may be summarised as follows:

- Dividends on IF shares are tradable, but capital gains are taxable only when they are sold. Since almost all FIMs distribute no dividends, all income is generated in a capital gain form, in this way deferring tax payments. Since no personal income tax is paid during the holding period, funds may accumulate at a rate higher than if funds were reinvested individually by the investor. There are no tax withholdings either. This higher rate of accumulation ought to encourage savings since it is the market price for waiting.
- Capital gains receive special treatment under the new income tax law, namely, a scheme based upon the working of a finite memory. After holding an IF for two periods there is a linear reduction in the part of the capital gain that is taxable, so that after a fifteen-year period the system completely forgets the generated income. The 7.14 per cent annual reduction in taxable capital gain means a higher

after-tax rate of return for IFs than the one offered by a bank deposit.

- FIMs are subject to a very low corporate tax of only 1 per cent. This is almost a tax exemption for FIMs in order to be able to accumulate capital at the highest speed, probably passing over the return on to the participants.

This new investment fund market has become an area of interest for banks and savings banks, which have incorporated it into their product list and have also used their extensive network to reach effectively the whole market. The result has been very impressive, and concentration and specialisation have come after this process. Banks have pushed harder with investment funds closer to the variable income side of the product set, selling them to their richest customers who look for higher rates of return on their *supercuentas* (high interest rate cheque accounts). Investment funds have provided the bank with a product that satisfies customers' needs without having to incur a higher financial cost, such as occurred during the deposit war. In this way the bank does not see the customer leaving to open a new account at another bank and does not compromise financial margins with a rate increase.

Savings banks have concentrated on selling money market funds in smaller quantities but to a larger number of customers, thus avoiding the deposit leak towards banks that the interest rate battle brought about and without having to pay a higher interest rate that would reduce financial margins. Again, savings banks have had a late start in this new market but, once they moved, it has been with very significant consequences.

We should note that not only tax treatment is relevant for customers in deciding in favour of an investment fund. Liquidity and convenience are two key elements in customer demand for banking products. As for liquidity, investment funds must be sold to the market and have the money transferred within a 72-hour period, whereas money market funds face a 24-hour limit for the same purpose. Price variance - the other element of liquidity - depends on the portfolio composition, on the market, and on expectations about interest rates. As for convenience, some investors would rather see regular interest payments from a time account or a certificate of deposit than a steady increase in the value of their investment fund share. If the customer wants to reinvest earned interest, he will most likely find more convenient a product that does so automatically, the investment fund. As for maturity, if the individual buys a Treasury bill he has to keep track of its maturity and roll it over every year or every six months. This can be avoided if he holds an IF because its maturity is indefinite. So, the investment horizon is a crucial element for assets to fit household preferences.

Bank strategy is also a relevant factor in the success of the investment fund market. Fees incurred when purchasing the fund (and even ensuring the issue), at withdrawal, for the management of the fund portfolio and for having assets deposited at a financial intermediary can eat up the advantage on the rate of return brought in by fiscal benefits. It would not be surprising to see banking firms adjust all kinds of fees to position their products in the desired relative place. Investment fund management firms are under the umbrella of the Spanish financial intermediaries - respecting all conditions on separability and independence of management[3] - and transaction costs can be modified almost at their convenience. If a bank wants to push forward, say, time deposits, it can increase the withdrawal fee as a deterrent for customers to purchase investment funds in such a way that the net rates of return are equalised. The Stock Market Commission (Comisión Nacional del Mercado de Valores) sets the maximum rates for these fees, and competition between banks sets the effective rates.

The Spanish Treasury introduced an investment fund called Fondtesoro (Treasury Fund) with an aggressive advertising campaign. This is an investment fund with a portfolio formed 100 per cent of public debt, enjoying the guarantee of the State. Financial intermediaries may ask to become members of the Fondtesoro group if they satisfy certain conditions. The more relevant ones are stricter limits on fees that can be charged in an effort to reduce gross margins established by banking firms. The maximum fees that may be charged are shown in Table 3.2.

Another factor that may have contributed to the success of investment funds is that financial intermediaries like selling them more than Treasury bills and other public debt because, first, investment funds do not mature and, second, they produce stronger customer relationships. On the other hand, each bank has had to provide its customers with an investment fund similar to the one offered by other banks in the market. As for the near future, it seems likely that the banking system will continue to play a very important role in the investment funds market.

POPULAR PENSION PLANS

As mentioned earlier, these plans have not as yet been put forward by Spanish authorities, and we only know their general features as they appear in the new (1991) law on personal income tax. It is very likely

Table 3.2 Maximum fees charged on Spanish investment funds

Fees	FIM	FIM Fondtesoro	FIAMM	FIAMM Fondtesoro
Deposit	0.004	1.75%	0.0015	1%
Management	2.5%A 20.0%E 1.5%A+10%E		1.5%A 1.5%E 1.0%A+10%E	
Purchase	5.0%	0	1.0%	0
Withdrawal		2.0% p.a. until year 2		only on use of cheque

Key: A = on assets; E = on earnings

that the delay in introducing these plans may be due to the foreseeable transitory increase in the public deficit caused by them. The return on this account is tax free as long as the following (and any future) requirements are met:

- Funds must have been invested for five years or more in the PPP.
- There is a *per capita* limit on the total amount saved in this plan, namely, 10 million pesetas (US $110,000).
- The annual maximum contribution to this plan has to be under one million pesetas (US $11,000) and it has to be part of that period saving.
- Each individual can be a member of only one PPP.
- There will be no tax withholdings on the income derived from the investments made by the plan.
- If the member withdraws the funds before the five-year period, all tax benefits are lost and capital gains are treated as any other increase in wealth. Even tax withholdings are immediately restored.

Although more regulatory norms will be enacted before PPPs are introduced it is obvious that they will become an alternative to financial products supplied by the banking system. If a great share of loanable funds are diverted into PPPs, it is certain that the banking system will try again a 'linked' disintermediation process in which it will still have an important role to play.

CONCLUDING REMARKS

Two new forms of competition have challenged the Spanish banking system in the last few years, and a third one will also be a highly competitive instrument to attract household savings away from the banking system. In the past, a high degree of adaptation - the first requirement for survival - has been shown by banks and savings banks integrating these new products in their product list. Financial intermediaries have looked for a function to play in this disintermediation process, aimed also at making easier the financing of public deficits. In this process banks' own products have been pushed back towards more liquid liabilities - closer to the means of payment services - while on the asset side they must keep their loan portfolios as their basic activity of transforming risks at the lowest cost.

The gradual reduction in investment coefficients experienced in the banking sector during the last few years has liberated some of the 'captive demand' used by government to finance budgetary deficits. Investment funds, money market funds and Fondtesoro funds are alternative ways to ease public debt marketing. With these instruments the Treasury appeals more directly to the final lenders, the households. Still the role of financial intermediaries is crucial for the success of government debt policy.

The future introduction of Popular Savings Plans as well as the arrival of foreign investment funds will produce another wave of competition between financial intermediaries, which will require a cautious strategy by banking firms. Although all new forms of competition try to encourage national saving[4], they do give rise to a transitory increase in the public deficit that may affect the timing of these financial reforms. Even if a policy is sound in the long run, it has to be viable in the short and in the medium run otherwise political pressure will make the government back off its announced policies and lose its reputation.

NOTES

1. Before the new law on personal income taxes only up to 500,000 ptas could be deducted from the base, and 15 per cent of the remaining 250,000 pts from the final tax.
2. See García Vaquero (1991, 42-5).
3. The law wants the management firm and the depository institution to belong to different banking groups, so that the depository firm can exercise control on the management company.
4. On the effect of pension plans on public savings see Feldstein (1992) and Quesada (1992).

LIST OF REFERENCES

Albella S. and J.A. Mayorga (1991), 'Notas sobre el nuevo reglamento de la ley de instituciones de inversión colectiva', *Papeles de Economía Española, Suplementos sobre el Sistema Financiero*, no. 35

Azcoitita G. and J. Borque (1991), 'La actitud del ahorrador particular frente a las distintas opciones de inversión colectiva', *Papeles de Economía Española, Suplementos sobre el Sistema Financiero*, no. 35

Contreras, C. (1991), 'Las entidades de crédito ante la popularización de la   inversión colectiva', *Papeles de Economía Española, Suplementos sobre el Sistema Financiero*, no. 35

Domínguez, J.R. (1989), 'Régimen fiscal de los planes y fondos de pensiones y de las fórmulas alternativas de cobertura', *Papeles de Economía Española, Suplementos sobre el Sistema Financiero*, no. 26

Feenberg, D. and J. Skinner (1991), 'Sources of IRA saving', *Tax Policy and the Economy*, no. 3, 25-46

Feldstein, M. (1992), 'The effects of tax-based incentives on government revenues and national saving', National Bureau of Economic Research Working Paper, no. 4021

García, Vaquero (1991), 'Los fondos de inversión en España', *Boletín Económico*, Banco de España (December)

Herce, J.A. (1989), 'Planes y fondos de pensiones', *Papeles de Economía Española, Suplementos sobre el Sistema Financiero*, no. 26

Quesada, J. (1992), 'Ahorro, planes de pensiones y deficit público', *mimeo*, Valencia

PART II

BANK ORGANISATION AND STRATEGY

CHAPTER 4
BANK MARKETING, ORGANISATION AND PERFORMANCE

Edward P.M. Gardener

INTRODUCTION

European banks, like most other FSFs (financial services firms), have experienced major changes in their organisational designs, or structures, during the past two decades[1]. These changes have helped to fuel a number of questions (positive and normative) and related debates. Should banks be larger or smaller? Is the specialist model superior to the conglomerate or universal bank? How might organisational design changes be targeted strategically and managed to improve banking performance? These are just a sample of the kind of important questions that confront bankers, policymakers and students of banking.

This paper explores the impact of marketing-induced organisational design changes in banks on the respective performance of banks. Particular attention will be focused on retail banking as a case study in the later stages of the paper, but most of the paper is generalisable to the majority of banking functions in developed, free enterprise, financial systems. The paper refers to quite a wide range of banking in order to draw out relevant experiences and possibly related hypotheses. An early argument advanced is that the growth and managerial influence of the marketing function in banks are useful indicators of the extent of the overall 'demand-determination' of banking strategy. As such they are *inter alia* an important indicator of the impact of external, market forces on banking strategies. The author's interest in this area was stimulated through some related project research undertaken by the Institute of European Finance working with a major UK bank (see Clarke *et al.* 1988).

The impact of the marketing function in banking organisational design is important in its own right, but it is particularly interesting in the new, more competitive (deregulating) banking environment. The latter, for example, is apparently predicated in large part on the economic desirability of a strong market orientation, a demand-determined emphasis, in banking strategies. This paper is essentially an exploratory survey that seeks to generate relevant and useful, testable hypotheses and to locate a respective empirical testing framework. The first section is a selective background survey; the second section addresses more specifically our main area of concern.

59

ORGANISATIONAL CHANGE IN BANKING

Nature of organisational design

Changes in organisational design (or structure) have been an important and often much-publicised aspect of European banking strategies. The rise of so-called marketing-orientated organisational structures in retail banking and the rapid construction of banking financial conglomerates in the build-up to London's Big Bang are two examples. At its most basic level, organisational design focuses on the structuring of two fundamental tasks: specialisation and co-ordination. Organisational design is concerned with sub-dividing activities into different departments or divisions (specialisation) and then managing (co-ordinating) this portfolio so that the organisation meets its strategic objectives.

Organisational design, then, is concerned essentially with the people within the organisation; there has been an increasing recognition that the organisation of a bank's staff has a crucial bearing on the development and successful implementation of strategy. Traditional (historic) views[2] from the business strategy and management literature are associated with a top-down view of strategy making, which emphasised bureaucratic or mechanistic principles of control. This view of strategy and the appropriateness of respective mechanistic structures are now widely recognised as questionable. More recent strategic management views still accept the need for regulating the implementation of strategy, but this has to take account of many influences. The latter include, for example, whether the environment is complex and changing or, alternatively, simple and static.

Many different kinds of organisational structure have been identified: these include simple, functional, multidivisional, holding company and matrix structures[3]. Despite the apparent neatness of these classifications, in reality of course, many variations and hybrid forms exist. Other 'models' of organisational structure[4] focus on the degree of integration and control exercised. An important issue in organisational design for the implementation of strategy is whether (and to what extent) to centralise or decentralise. These latter policies must be internally consistent for each organisation: there is no 'right' or 'wrong' formula.

There are several important influences on a firm's organisational design; these include the major influences of strategy, technology, type of organisation and environment. In his historical studies, for example, Chandler (1962) found that firms with limited product markets and comparatively simple operations tended to be relatively centralised and to adopt functional structures. For present purposes, however, the influence of the environment is of particular interest.

The bank organisational changes of most direct concern to this paper (that is, changes associated with marketing operations) are in large part a product of a greater demand orientation in banking strategies. This phenomenon is a result of the increasing 'market orientation' associated with deregulation and other developments in financial markets. Viewed in this light, a bank's organisational structure may be seen simply as a kind of interchange system between the external (outside) environment and the internal resources of the bank.

Banking organisational structures have traditionally been bureaucratic and top down, but most banks' organisational structures have changed significantly during recent years; they are now in a virtually constant state of re-appraisal by management. No two banks are exactly alike, but a crucial factor that differentiates banks and shapes the success of strategy implementation appears to be the form of organisation adopted. During recent years the needs of particular customer segments or groupings have become a much more important influence on bank organisational design.

Organisational design and strategy

Throughout the 1980s European banking strategies responded *inter alia* to a number of external pressures. During this time there has been a general trend in banking systems towards a greater market-orientation in strategy; banking strategy has become more demand-determined. This should not be unexpected given the generalised progression towards more strongly market-orientated financial systems. The natural corollary has been that traditional, supply-led banking has been increasingly replaced by much more pro-active banking. However, there are respective costs and associated dangers of 'over shooting' towards an excessive demand orientation in strategy.

Investment banking in the run-up and beyond to Big Bang was a recent, good case study on the practical management problems of rapid banking expansion and responding quickly to perceived market demand[5]. After 1982 many banks in London moved rapidly into capital market products and de-emphasised syndicated lending. Many banking syndicated lending teams were disbanded and replaced by capital market groups; high premiums were paid for new managerial expertise. The rapid 'bolting together' of traditional banking and more trading-orientated cultures led to severe internal problems for many banks in London.

The destructive potential of the kind of culture clashes that often accompany the merger of banking and securities activities under the same corporate umbrella had already been an earlier feature of Wall Street after 1975[6]. In London, most banks that bought a stock market firm experienced problems absorbing it into their organisational structures; a recent international study summarised the views of many bankers that commercial bank-investment bank mergers ... 'do not work': see Smith (1992, p. 108). One very simple (almost trite) lesson from these experiences is that organisational design is a crucial issue in the successful implementation of any banking strategy. Another aftermath of the post-crash banking environment was an overall increased awareness of the human resource constraints in banking strategy; one tangible response in many banks has been the increased managerial emphasis of the HRM (human resource management) function.

Increased competition and a generally greater market orientation are economic targets of the Single European Market (SEM) proposals. The Cecchini study[7], for instance, assumed (at least implicitly) that banks will grow larger in order to exploit competitive opportunities and to achieve economies of scale. However, there have been many criticisms of Cecchini's assumptions and of the practical difficulties of locating, much less targeting, economies of scale in banking[8]. For present purposes, banks and other FSFs throughout Europe have given a much higher strategic emphasis towards designing more responsive and flexible organisational structures. In many FSFs organic (more informal) organisational design has been targeted, and traditional bureaucratic (or mechanistic) structures have become less popular and appropriate.

In this context the link between organisational design and financial innovation is interesting and relevant. The 'new environment' is characterised *inter alia* by high rates of financial innovation, at least over the medium to longer term. Indeed, the ability of financial systems to innovate effectively and quickly in response to rapidly changing market demand is apparently an objective of structural deregulation[9]. In this context states of organisational crisis (change) appear to have a high potential in generating innovation. It seems to follow that organisational structures may be changed to help induce innovation, and they may need to alter in order to respond to external innovation demands. Mottura (1986, p. 14), however, cautions about 'misguided attempts' to 'force' an operating organisation to generate innovation or even only change. In respect of financial innovation, organisation theory has no organisation solution to offer other than locating organisational differentiation[10]. In this general setting European banking strategies in the run-up to 1992 have raised some important organisational questions.

European banking strategies

There has been a great deal of speculation and debate on the best 'organisational model' for banking in the SEM. One key part of this debate is whether the specialist model of banking is 'better' than the universal bank or conglomerate. This debate ranges wider than our immediate concern, since it encompasses many other elements (beyond organisational design in the strictest sense) of bank strategy. Nevertheless, organisational design is a key part of this debate.

Even a cursory survey of recent European developments confirms the importance of organisational design within the competitive strategies of banks and other FSFs. One general trend until the early 1990s at least has been to consolidate or enhance the general organisational model of the financial services supermarket (FSSM). Typified in the Austrian, German and Swiss universal banks, the FSSM model of organisational design is very much a traditional European banking feature.

Five different types of bank 'merger activities' emerged in the run-up to 1992 (Gardener and Molyneux 1990): alliances (non-predatory minority interests), blocking/strategic minority interests, cross-border acquisitions, national mergers or acquisitions, and cross-border mergers to create a supra-national group. The majority of recent bank merger-type activity has related to cross-border acquisitions, mainly large banks purchasing much smaller ones. Nevertheless, the bulk of bank merger-type activity to date has involved national integration and/or product and distribution alliances; a recent study by Salomon Brothers (1990) confirmed this trend. These partnerships have often brought together a comparatively sophisticated product provider from Northern Europe with a partner distribution network in the South. Within these strategies the apparent advantages of the distribution of insurance products through branch networks have become an increasing strategic priority for many FSFs. Nevertheless, the kind of 'merger activity' envisaged by some in the often euphoric run-up to SEM has not really materialised yet, and many FSFs are now seriously re-appraising some of their earlier 'marriages'.

Recent bank strategic thinking appears to be towards re-emphasising the attractions of specialisation and concentration on a bank's traditional strengths, even within some modified form of universal bank or conglomerate structure. Post-crash strategic thinking in investment banking, for example, tended to de-emphasise the alleged advantages of synergy and to advocate so-called 'cluster strategies' (see Gardener 1990 and Smith 1992). A cluster strategy approach is one where a bank specialises in a number of different services, locations or kinds of customer; essentially it means playing to one's strengths.

In a wider context, Revell (1991) examines the recent criticisms of the universal bank as a monolithic organisation, and he explores the McKinsey 'federal bank' concept. The latter proposal is that the big universal banks should be effectively restructured into 'federal banks' or 'federated banks'; the basic objective is to break down the bank into a number of specialist units. Each of the latter is then conducted independently, as far as possible, in order to recapture the advantages of specialisation. This is a similar concept to the cluster strategy approach (also developed by McKinsey consultants) discussed above. Each federated bank is operated so far as possible as an independent business in order to recapture and exploit the advantages of specialisation. Suggested examples of FSFs pursuing this kind of strategy are Barclays Bank, Compagnie Bancaire in France and the network of German co-operative banks[11].

These new 'models' and the recent (at least up to 1990) European trends towards national integration and/or product and distribution alliances are interesting and relevant for present purposes. European banking in organisational terms is generally in a mature phase of its development. The latter growth-phase is characterised *inter alia* by a tendency to be more innovation-resisting[12]. This may be be seen at one level in the kinds of corporate culture clashes that have emerged in some banks, and the apparent desire of some FSFs at various times to replace (rather than re-train) existing staff. For larger organisations, growth through collaboration (see Figure 4.1) also becomes more important during the mature phase of their development.

MARKETING AND ORGANISATIONAL CHANGE

Demand-determined and supply-side strategies

It has been emphasised that the essence of demand-determined banking strategies is that they are market-orientated, essentially market-driven. One important objective is that they are flexible and at the limit are highly responsive, indeed proactive, towards market demand. This

Figure 4.1 The five phases of growth

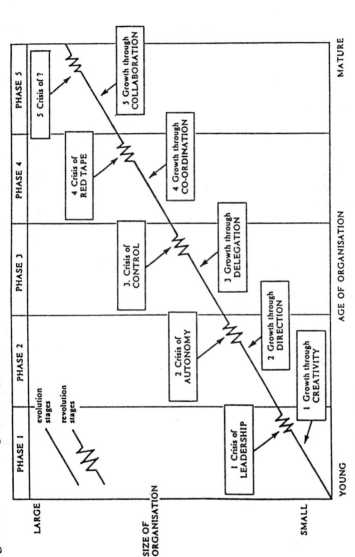

Source: Braddick (1987, p. 101)

raises the important question of how far or to what extent a high market-orientation of this kind is desirable. We have already seen that one of the lessons from London's bank financial conglomerates in the build-up to Big Bang might be that responding too quickly to perceived market needs - that is, strong demand-driven strategies - can produce negative results. The apparent, recent movement of some retail FSFs (like the TSB) towards an increased emphasis on their traditional core business is another sign of possible, renewed organisational reappraisal.

Industrial and microeconomists have produced an extensive literature on the importance of a firm's organisational structure, and much of this literature is in part a criticism of the assumption inherent in the traditional theory of the firm. The 'behavioural school', for example, argues that the behaviour of an organisation is not independent of its internal processes[13]. This organisational criticism of the traditional theory of the firm[14] argues that a firm's objectives should be seen as evolving from a process of internal bargaining between the individuals and groups comprising the firm, and these typically have conflicting interests. Another, relevant criticism of the traditional theory of the firm for present purposes is its static equilibrium framework. Penrose (1959) and others have argued convincingly that a firm is constrained in its behaviour not only through its absolute size but also its rate of growth.

In her work Penrose emphasised the importance of the managerial (internal) restraint to a firm's rate of growth. The collective experience and skills of a firm's existing managerial team will (given the firm's productive resources) help to shape the extent and nature of the productive services that are available for expansion. New management can be brought in, but it takes an outsider time to gain experience of the existing team and achieve full efficiency. Penrose (1959 p. 47) puts it:

> ... if a firm deliberately or inadvertently expands its organisation more rapidly than the individuals in the expanding organisation can obtain the experience with each other and with the firm that is necessary for the effective operation of the group, the efficiency of the firm will suffer, even if optimum adjustments are made in the administrative structure.

Although this managerial restraint may recede through time, it limits a firm's rate of growth in a particular period. Bringing in outsiders does not solve the problem since it takes time for them to work effectively within the firm, and, in the short term, they can even exacerbate the managerial restraint. Penrose largely employed business histories and biographies of individual businessmen in order to help support her theory.

The work of Penrose and other economists is relevant to the present, exploratory survey. If there is a managerial restraint to firm expansion, there is no *a priori* reason why banks should be exempted. Indeed, we have seen that recent banking experiences appear to support this managerial restraint to banking expansion, growth and/or increased diversification. More fundamentally it leads to questions about the desirability of an exclusive demand-orientation in banking strategy and organisational design. The question that follows is how far should strategy and respective organisational design be demand-determined or supply-led? When do the apparent benefits of a high (attempted at least) demand orientation begin to be outweighed by the respective costs?

Abraham and Lierman (1991) have explored these kinds of questions. In their paper they draw attention to a basic dilemma of banking strategy that is inherent in comparing the following views expressed by two distinguished bankers:

> Compared to a few years ago, and certainly to a decade ago, it is a new world - and the speed with which it is evolving makes it a riskier and more uncertain world. There is truly only one way that bankers can protect themselves within such an environment - that is to maintain as flexible a posture as possible to respond to and capitalise on changes and opportunities as they arise.

S. Mark Robinson, Vice President Financial Industry Management, Unisys, Detroit, *The World of Banking*, Nov.-Dec. 1989, p. 18.

and

> Strategy will be better built up from the banks' own existing position - size, franchise, strengths, weaknesses etc. - than down from the global changes in demography, markets, regulatory frameworks etc.

Sir Kit McMahon, (then) Chairman and Group Executive Midland Bank plc, London *The World of Banking*, Nov.-Dec. 1989, p. 6

These two views exemplify the differences between an almost exclusive emphasis on demand-orientation in strategy compared with the need to emphasise more strongly supply (internal) factors. They also indicate the apparent lack of consensus amongst bank strategists on what is the best approach.

Abraham and Lierman (1991), however, note a shift in European bank strategic thinking towards a supply-led approach away from an exclusive or very strong demand-determined philosophy.   They also explore *inter alia* the costs and benefits of internal and various forms of external re-structuring in banking.   Their main thesis is that (1991, p. 24) '... demand oriented bank strategies should be supplemented, in the Europe of the nineties, by a more supply-constrained approach, centred on internal and external restructuring'. Against this background, we may now focus on the nature and impact of the marketing function's role in banking organisational design.   Retail banking will be our 'laboratory' for the following two sections, but (as explained in the introduction) much of this has a more general applicability to most modern banking functions.

Marketing and organisational design

It has been emphasised that the bank marketing function may be regarded as a kind of linkage between the external market and the orientation, or focus, of overall banking strategy.   As we have seen, *a priori* reasoning at least suggests that deregulation, *de jure* or *de facto*, should mean an increased role for marketing activity within a bank's overall operations.   Although marketing management is comparatively new in banking, it now plays an increasingly important role in most banks and other FSFs; this is particularly evident and transparent in retail banking.

Increasingly retail banks have sought to emulate their counterparts in the consumer goods retailing industry through developing and implementing strategies tailored specifically to the demands of their customers.   This metamorphosis from a 'production orientation' (supply) to a 'marketing orientation' (demand) has not been a phenomenon confined to the 1980s and 1990s.   In the United Kingdom and other European retail banking segments it really started in the 1960s, but during the 1970s and 1980s the pace of change accelerated markedly.

Thompson *et al.* (1985) provide a useful evolutionary perspective of marketing in retail banking: see also Clarke *et al.* (1988).   They use Keith's (1960) model to illustrate the modern historical development of marketing in US banking.   Clarke *et al.* (1988) apply this descriptive model to UK banking, and it is generally applicable to European banking.   It is essentially a logical-historical order model, and the first stage is the 'production era' (probably up to the early 1960s).   During this period the banking emphasis was on production and selling; banks had a predominantly inward-looking orientation.

During the next stage (the early 1960s to the early 1970s), banks began to emphasise more strongly product quality and the impact of competition. During this so-called 'promotion era' banks began to focus more on areas like the impact of competition and product quality. There was increasing recognition of the potentials of marketing; banks began to recognise the need to identify customers and to advertise. Some time during the early 1970s banks entered the third stage, the 'marketing-orientated' or 'marketing department' era.

The early 1970s marked the beginning of the modern period of turbulence in banking characterised *inter alia* by deregulation, a more volatile financial environment and intensifying competition. It also witnessed the erosion of many historic traditions and long-standing ways of doing business in banks. During this period the selling concept was much more emphasised and banks made greater efforts to promote their products and services. This stage intensified during the 1980s in the United Kingdom with the growing competitive inroads into traditional banking made by building societies and other FSFs. Retail banks and other FSFs are now beginning to enter the fourth (and final) stage of Keith's model, the 'marketing control' era.

The marketing control era is simply an intensification of the marketing orientation phase. Marketing and associated profitability become the ultimate driving force of the firm and most of its organisational structure. Strategic marketing considerations influence more strongly and directly areas like finance and capital expenditure, traditionally outside the direct sphere of marketing. Within this stage, marketing becomes increasingly identified with senior management. The ultimate in marketing control is where marketing considerations drive the whole organisation.

Table 4.1 illustrates some of the differences between the marketing-orientated and marketing-control eras. The Keith model[15] then charts the modern, historical progression from a supply-led, inward-looking (production-orientated) approach towards (at the limit) a completely demand-led, marketing-driven organisation.

Clarke *et al.* (1988, p. 10) suggest that, because bank marketing has traditionally had a bias in favour of retail banking, the full implementation of marketing control may be easier in a more specialist, retail FSF than in larger and more diverse financial conglomerates. The main reason for this view is that the implementation of marketing control is a function of a FSF's organisational design and senior management's

Table 4.1   Market-orientated and market control eras

	Marketing-orientated era	Marketing-control era
Environment	(1) Relatively stable	(1) Uncertain and volatile
Structure	(1) Functional	(1) Adaptive
	(2) Determine strategy	(2) Determined by strategy
Mission of marketing	(1) Devise the bank's marketing plan	(1) Determine bank's strategic direction
	(2) Implement the bank's marketing plan	(2) Train bankers to be marketers
		(3) Turn bank into marketing institution
Target customers	(1) External customers	(1) External customers
		(2) Internal customers (a) line employees (b) management (c) executive staff
Assumed roles	(1) Develop customer services	(1) Develop customer-demanded services
	(2) Advertise these services	(2) Develop those services which the customer will predictably buy
		(3) Position the bank according to (1) and (2)
		(4) Use advertising to (a) market services (b) communicate with, train and inspire employees

Source: Clarke *et al.* (1988, p. 11, Figure 1)

commitment. In a more specialist, retail FSF intra-organisational conflicts between different power groups are likely to be less of a problem (or non-existent) than in a larger, more diverse FSF, where international, corporate and other specialist units are likely to be competing strongly for resources.

The operational impact of marketing has been one of the characteristic phenomena of banking from the 1970s. Increased emphasis towards marketing products and services, much greater customer awareness and stronger efforts to target products and services towards specific customer and market segments characterise the new environment. Integrated customer information files (CIFs) and market segmentation are *inter alia* especially important managerial considerations. Clarke *et al.* (1988, pp. 16-19) examine in some detail the kind of requirements needed for the effective implementation and control of marketing-orientated and market control strategies. Most Western European FSFs are now probably in the marketing-orientated era, and some in the more competitive financial sectors have begun to enter the market-control stage.

It is clear from the wide diversity of organisational structures in modern banking (even within the same market amongst specialist FSFs and in the same country financial sector) that the search for any kind of optimal organisational structure is likely to be a non-starter[16]. This view also seems to accord with the work of Abraham and Lierman (1991) and management theory. The premise underlying 'contingency theory' is that there is no one best organisational structure for an enterprise. This theory seeks to recognise explicitly the dependence (conditionality) of a firm's organisational structure on the dynamic interaction between such forces as external (environmental) factors, the kinds of organisational tasks and the composition of the management team. Many management specialists prefer the term 'situational' rather than conditional in this context. In short, what a bank or other FSF does should depend on the realities of the contemporary environment, both internal and external.

Impact on performance

Marketing-induced (demand-orientated) organisational design changes in banking clearly matter, and the main purpose of this paper is to consider broadly how and in what direction these might influence performance. The preliminary research conducted by the author was an exploratory (and very limited) case study on the strategic marketing orientation and respective organisational design changes of a large UK bank (Clarke *et al.* 1988); this study confirmed the importance of marketing-induced organisational changes in that particular bank.   An interesting and probably the most significant finding from this exercise was the (then during the late 1980s) commitment of the very senior management towards a marketing orientation.

Other relevant, recent research in this area has been conducted by Clode (1989) and Feeney (1989); both of these studies were for PhDs. Feeney's work was not concerned specifically with organisational design, but his research emphasised the market (demand) orientation of modern corporate banking; this research employed *inter alia* case study, participant observation and survey methods.   Clode's research is more relevant for present purposes.   He was concerned with measuring the impact of competition in UK retail banking, and he used *inter alia* a longitudinal case study approach on a specialised UK retail bank.   The Clarke *et al.* (1988) and Clode (1989) research appeared to provide support for the relevance of the Keith model in UK retail banking.   The work of other researchers, like Revell (1991) and Abraham and Lierman (1991) also seems to lend further, general support.

To date, however, no serious empirical research has been attempted in this field within the United Kingdom, with the exception of Ferguson and McKillop (1992) who have explored the impact of organisational structure changes on the performance of UK building societies.   Their study over the past decade found that significant shifts have occurred in the organisational designs of UK building societies.   The objective of building societies has been to develop more flexible and responsive organisational structures; intensifying competition in the marketplace has been the major strategic driver of these changes.

Our main concern in this paper is with the impact of marketing-induced organisational changes on banking performance[17]; a number of empirical lines of research are initially possible.   An obvious line of attack would be to start with a series of longitudinal case studies.   The author has begun preliminary work in this area with two UK banks: the initial sample comprises a large specialist in retail financial services and a (regional) universal bank.   These case studies will have two objectives. First, they will simply chart the type, extent and main strategic drivers of marketing-induced organisational changes during the past ten years (up to end-1991) and the kind of impact these have had on respective performance.   The way that marketing is organised and its influence on the bank's organisational culture will also be explored.

This case study exercise will be followed by a wider survey in order to help compile a relevant database.   The initial objective here will be to adapt and replicate a US study by Reidenbach, Moak and Pitts (1986) on

UK data. This study focused on the extent of the adoption of the marketing concept, the extent to which it is implemented in banking, and its relationship to bank profitability. Their approach was to score organisational features that represented (in their opinion) greater evidence of the adoption or implementation of the marketing concept. They identified - using earlier work by McNamara (1972) - four 'adoption items' and four 'implementation items': these are summarised, with their respective scores, in Table 4.2.

Table 4.2 Marketing concept scoring criteria

Adoption Items	Score (points)	Implementation Items	Score (points)
1. Training programs		**1. Title of top marketing executive**	
(a) University executive development programs	4	(a) Vice president or higher	5
(b) Special lectures (business consultants)	3	(b) Uses the word marketing in title	5
(c) Bank meetings and conferences	1	*Total possible points*	10
(d) On-the-job training	1	**2. Scope of responsiblility of marketing**	
Total possible points	9	(a) Three points if a functional area is very much the responsibility of the marketing executive	30
2. Committee and group membership of top marketing executive			
(a) Board of directors	5		
(b) Executive	4		
(c) Finance	3		
(d) Asset/liability management	2	(b) One point if a functional area is shared responsibility of the marketing executive	10
(e) New product/service planning	1		
Total possible points	15		

continued

Table 4.2 (continued)

Adoption Items	Score (points)	Implementation Items	Score (points)
3. **Level of reponsibility of marketing department in strategic planning process**		(c) No points if a functional area is not the responsibility of the marketing executive or if not applicable	0
(a) If marketing has equal or or greater responsibility than other functional departments	10	*Total possible points*	*30*
		3. **Interdepartmental coordination methods**	
(b) If marketing has responsibility but not as much as other departments	5	(a) Three points if a method is very frequently used	15
(c) If marketing has no responsibility	0	(b) One point if a method is not frequently used	5
Total possible points	*10*	(c) No points if a method is not used	0
4. **Background of key individuals**		*Total possible points*	*15*
(a) One point assigned for each marketing background indicated	5	4. **Communication methods**	
Total possible points	*5*	(a) Three points is a method is very frequently used	24
		(b) One point if a method is not frequently used	8
		(c) No points is a method is not used	0
		Total possible points	*24*
Total possible adoption points	*39*	*Total possible implementation points*	*79*

Source: Reidenbach, Moak and Pitts (1986, p. 20, Figure 2)

They tested the hypothesis that there is a positive and direct relationship between the degree of adoption and implementation of the marketing concept and a bank's profitability. Selected banking executives were asked to respond to a mailed questionnaire (based on Table 4.2); stepwise regression was used with operating profits as the dependent variable. Overall, they found that the degree of adoption and implementation of the marketing concept explained 42 per cent of the variance in operating profits in larger banks; they found no similar relationship in smaller banks. Within their larger bank results, they found that Implementation Item 3 (interdepartmental co-ordination methods) had the largest relative impact on a bank's operating profit.

CONCLUSIONS

This paper is an exploratory study that outlines some preliminary research that the author is conducting. One objective of the two-bank case study exercise will be to appraise the relevance of the McNamara (1972) model and its adaptation by Reidenbach *et al.* (1986) for the UK sample[18]. A related objective will be to compare specialist and universal bank marketing-induced organisational changes and their respective impact on performance. More recent empirical work by marketing, organisation and industrial economics specialists also needs to be examined in this context.

Marketing-induced organisational design changes clearly 'matter', and they are invariably made with performance objectives in mind. These changes are a product of the contemporary financial environment and the underlying market-based philosophy towards resource allocation. As such, they are one microfeature of structural deregulation and intensifying competition in modern financial systems. In this context, they operate on the allocative efficiency of banks and influence the future development path of banking systems. We know from the work of *inter alia* Penrose (1959) and Abraham and Lierman (1991), however, that too strong a demand-orientation in organisation design changes may produce negative results. What we need now is a clearer idea of the empirical impact and extent of these changes on banking performance. A wider, European comparative study would have obvious utility for strategists and policy makers.

NOTES

1. See, for example, Revell (1987), Gardener and Molyneux (1990), Abraham and Lierman (1991), Revell (1991), Mullineux (ed.) (1992) and Steinherr (1992).
2. Traced back to the early twentieth century management 'scientists' and beyond: see Johnson and Scholes (1989, p. 256).
3. Johnson and Scholes (1989, ch. 10) discuss these different structures.
4. Braddick (1987, pp. 106-10), for example, identifies four basic types: power-based organisations, bureaucratic, project-based organisations and people-based organisations.
5. See Gardener (1990).
6. See, for example, Auletta (1986).
7. Commission of the European Communities (1988).
8. For example, see Revell (1987), Centre for Business Strategy (1989) and Gardener and Teppett (1990 and 1992).
9. This is often stylised more formally as enhancing the capacity of the macroeconomy for risk-taking and more effective risk management.
10. See Mottura (1986, pp. 113-114).
11. See Revell (1991, p. 8).
12. See, for example, Mottura (1986, p. 110).
13. For example, Cyert and March (1963).
14. The traditional theory assumes that these kinds of internal processes and conflicts can be 'assumed away'.
15. In a kind of cross-sectional perspective, Channon (1986, pp. 200-204) distinguishes the following major organisation forms in banking: retail/commercial branch-based structure; customer/service-based structure; customer-based structure; centralised/international division structure.
16. The importance of regulation (for example, see Norton 1991) in shaping organisational and other strategies is also important in banking, but this paper does not explore this important influence. Our particular emphasis is on marketing, a kind of 'competition influence'.
17. Other, related hypotheses might be concerned with questions like the main determinants of organisational change and the kind and extent of change. One might also be concerned with the impact of organisational design on the culture of the organisation: for example, see Pettigrew, Ferlie and McKee (1992).
18. Another objective will be to try and locate any significant 'events' and time periods when the banks (and banks in general) changed the marketing orientation of their organisational structures.

LIST OF REFERENCES

Abraham, J.P. and F. Lierman (1991), 'European banking strategies in the nineties: a supply side approach', IEF Research Papers in Banking and Finance RP 91/8 (Bangor: Institute of European Finance)

Auletta, K. (1986), *Greed and Glory on Wall Street: the Fall of the House of Lehman* (Harmondsworth: Penguin)

Braddick, W.A.G. (1987), *Management for Bankers* (London: Butterworths)

Centre for Business Strategy (1989), *1992: Myths and Realities* (London: London Business School)

Chandler, A. (1962), *Strategy and Structure* (Cambridge, Ma: MIT Press)

Channon, D.F. (1986), *Bank Strategic Management and Marketing* (Chichester: John Wiley)

Clarke, P.D., E.P.M. Gardener, P. Feeney and P. Molyneux (1988), 'The genesis of strategic marketing control in British retail banking', *The International Journal of Bank Marketing*, **6**, 2, 5-19

Clode, S.C. (1989), *Competition for Retail Transactions Balances* (unpublished), PhD, University of Wales, Bangor

Commission of the European Communities (1988), *European Economy: the Economics of 1992* (Brussels: European Commission)

Cyert, R.M. and J.G. March (1963), *A Behavioural Theory of the Firm* (Englewood Cliffs: Prentice Hall)

Feeney, P. (1989), *Euronotes: Risk and Pricing* (unpublished), PhD, University of Wales, Bangor

Ferguson, C. and D.G. McKillop (1992), 'Internal performance features of UK building socieities and their effect on organisational structure', unpublished paper, Queen's University, Belfast

Gardener, E.P.M. (1990), 'A strategic perspective of bank financial conglomerates in London after the crash', *Journal of Management Studies*, **27**, 1 (January), 61-73

Gardener, E.P.M. and P. Molyneux (1990), *Changes In Western European Banking* (London: Routledge)

Gardener, E.P.M. and J. Teppett (1990 and 1992), *The Impact of 1992 on the Financial Services Sectors of the EFTA Countries*, EFTA Occasional Paper no. 33 (Geneva: EFTA)

Johnson, G. and K. Scholes (1989), *Exploring Corporate Strategy: Text and Cases* (London: Prentice/Hall)

Keith, R.J. (1960), 'The marketing revolution', *Journal of Marketing* (January), pp. 35-38

McNamara, C.P. (1972), 'The present status of the marketing concept', *Journal of Marketing*, **36** (January), 50-57

Mottura, P. (1986), 'Organisational aspects of financial innovation' *Economia Aziendale*, **5**, 2, 109-21

Mullineux, A. (1992), *European Banking* (Oxford: Blackwell)

Norton, J.J. (ed.) (1991), *Bank Regulation and Supervision in the 1990s* (London: Lloyd's of London Press)

Penrose, E.T. (1959), *The Theory of the Growth of the Firm* (Oxford: Blackwell)

Pettigrew, A.; E. Ferlie and L. McKee (1992), *Shaping Strategic Change* (London: SAGE publications)

Reidenbach, R.E.; D.L. Moak and R.E. Pitts (1986), 'The impact of marketing operations on bank performance: a structural investigation', *Journal of Bank Research* (Spring), pp. 18-27

Revell, J.R.S. (1987), *Mergers and the Role of Large Banks*, IEF Research Monographs in Banking and Finance, no. 2 (Bangor: Institute of European Finance)

Revell, J.R.S. (1991), 'Changes in universal banks and the effect on bank mergers', IEF Research Papers in Banking and Finance RP 91/15 (Bangor: Institute of European Finance)

Salomon Brothers (1990), *Multinational Money Center Banking: The Evaluation of a Single European Banking Market* (London: Salomon Brothers Stock Research)

Smith, A.D. (1992), *International Financial Markets: The Performance of Britain and its Rivals*, National Institute of Economic and Social Research (London: Cambridge University Press)

Steinherr, A. (ed.) (1992), *The New European Financial Marketplace* (London: Longman)

Thompson, T.W.; L.L. Berry and J.H. Donnelly, Jr. (1985), 'The marketing/ retail banking partnership: an evolutionary perspective', *Journal of Retail Banking*, **7**, 2 (Summer), 9-22

CHAPTER 5
ORGANISATIONAL CHANGE IN UK CLEARING BANKS: THE CAUSES AND CONSEQUENCES

Ian Morison

INTRODUCTION

The purpose of this chapter is to consider some of the causes and consequences of organisational change in the UK commercial banking industry. It examines how, and why, banks have moved in a relatively short space of time from simple - some would say simplistic - organisational forms to more complex structures, which attempt to reflect more faithfully the complexities of the markets in which they now operate. It identifies some of the main issues which the banks have had to face as they have sought to find the best fit between their chosen strategies on the one hand and their organisational structures and management processes on the other, with a view to maximising the extent of goal congruence within the organisation and minimising the risk of dysfunctionality.

The main conclusion of the chapter is that the rapid pace of change in the banks' strategic priorities and competitive environment has presented them with massive challenges in the ways in which they organise their business activities, and that they are still a long way from surmounting these challenges successfully. Organisational structures have been changed and changed again with disturbing frequency, in some cases overtly reversing moves which have proved too radical, complex or costly for the bank to accommodate, however appropriate they might have appeared in theory.

ORGANISATIONAL STRUCTURE

The theory of organisational structure

Structure follows strategy - so at least argued Chandler (1962) when showing how, as companies grew and diversified, so they needed to develop appropriate new organisational forms to allow them to manage their increasing diversity. Thus the vertically-integrated single-product firm would typically adopt a functional organisational form, separating out such diverse functions as research and development, production, marketing and sales; while the multi-product firm would be more likely to embrace the multi-divisional form. Subsequent researchers in the field extended and developed Chandler's original work in a number of important respects (Galbraith 1973, 1977 and 1983; Galbraith and Nathanson 1978; Lawrence and Lorsch 1967 and 1969). They explored the relationship between strategy, structure and performance, showing how an appropriate structure tends to correlate with superior profitability, especially in competitive market conditions (it is fairly easy to get away with the wrong structure if there are no competitors to worry about). They also stressed the importance of achieving the right fit, not just between strategy and structure, but between both of these and a company's people systems, information and decision-making processes, and corporate culture; and they extended the analysis to embrace more contemporary organisational forms and practices such as multinational corporations, strategic business units and systems of matrix management.

One common thread to this work has been the contingency theory of organisations (Lawrence and Lorsch 1967; Galbraith 1973 and 1977), which states that corporate structure is contingent on strategic and environmental factors and that, therefore, while there is no one best way to organise, not all ways of organising are going to be equally effective. Another common thread to this work is that organisational change tends by its nature to be discontinuous and therefore may well lag, or occasionally even lead, changes in the contingent variables. The most important work undertaken in the United Kingdom on the role of contextual variables on organisational form remains that of the 'Aston Group' in the 1960s (Pugh *et al.* 1963, 1968, 1969).

Empirical evidence to support some of the more recent theoretical advances in this area remains sketchy and the direction of causality between strategy, structure, process and performance remains contentious. For example, just because divisionalised multi-product firms perform well in competitive markets, which the evidence suggests they do, it cannot be assumed that it is the divisionalised structure that causes the superior performance; it may equally well be that strongly-performing multi-product firms feel more confident than their weaker competitors about decentralising their management authority to relatively autonomous divisions (Child 1974 and 1975). Few would deny, however, that structure matters and that an inappropriate structure will be a bar to superior performance in a competitive marketplace.

The evolution of the UK clearing banking sector

The starting point for any consideration of changing organisational structures in the banking industry must therefore be the changing market
environment in which the banks have been operating, given the well-
documented importance of environmental change as a driver of organisational change (Lawrence and Lorsch 1967; Child 1972; Aldrich and
Pfeffer 1976). It is not necessary in this paper to rehearse in any detail
the main change factors with which the banks have had to contend, all of
which have been copiously documented elsewhere. (For an overview of
the main developments and issues, see Llewellyn 1990 and 1991, and
Morison 1991). The most important of these are: changes in the regulatory environment, and in particular the elimination of previous barriers
to diversification by banks, non-bank financial institutions and other new
participants in the financial services industry; radical changes in the
technology of the industry, with the consequent reconfiguration of delivery and support systems, and the reduction of traditional entry barriers;
the ending of a wide range of restrictive practices and a general height-
ening of the competitive 'animal spirits' of the industry; and changing
patterns of final demand for financial services, reflected in a general
increase in customer sophistication and discrimination and a shift in
demand from traditional forms of financial intermediation to new services, often technology-driven, with higher added-value content.

These and other changes have been partially driven by, and partially
the cause of, increased pressures on industry profitability and increased
concern to enhance financial performance, where necessary by radically
reconfiguring the business being undertaken. In some cases, particularly
in the most recent past, this has involved the banks in cutting back on
services previously offered or withdrawing entirely from particular
markets, where adequate returns were being neither earned nor in pros-
pect. Over the wider span of time with which this paper is concerned,
however, the dominant trend has been the opposite one of substantial
diversification by the banks into new markets and products.

Until the 1970s the UK commercial banks provided an extremely
limited range of services to a largely undifferentiated customer base -
current accounts and associated money transmission facilities to personal
and corporate customers alike, savings accounts to persons and over-
drafts to companies. Such limited diversification as had occurred had
essentially taken one of two forms - organic diversification into a limited

range of ancillary activities, such as executor and trusteeship services for persons and export finance for companies; and diversification by acquisition into a few related but unintegrated activities such as hire purchase. Today the banks can best be regarded as financial services conglomerates, providing a vastly wider range of services to far more strongly differentiated groups of customers. Some of the new services, such as interest rate swaps and multi-option facilities, simply did not exist before. Others, such as mortgage loans and corporate finance, were previously the preserve of different institutions. Others still, such as interest-bearing current accounts or term loans for small firms, involved refining specifications in response to evolving market needs.

At the same time, the increasing internationalisation of economic life blurred the old boundaries between domestic and overseas banking. In some of their activities, such as foreign exchange dealing and euro-currency transactions, the banks now find themselves competing in a global marketplace. In others, such as the top end of their corporate lending business, the market is international, or at any rate European, rather than global. In others still, such as the bulk of their commercial and personal business, it remains essentially national, with in many cases a strong regional or local flavour.

The organisational development of UK clearing banks

In considering how the banks have responded organisationally to these and other market developments, this paper traces the organisational evolution of a typical clearing bank group through five phases.

Phase one is the unit bank, where the bank is the branch and the branch is the bank. This is how most banks started in the nineteenth century, and it is an organisational form which survives to this day, buttressed by regulation and tradition, in much of the United States. In Britain, like most other developed countries, it has long since been rendered obsolete by branch expansions, takeovers and mergers, yet it continues to cast a long shadow over banking law and practice. There is still a formal legal requirement, for example, that a collecting bank should present a cheque for payment at the branch on which it was drawn; while the foundation stone of the banks' accounting systems is in many respects still the branch's general ledger.

Phase two is the late nineteenth, early twentieth century model of the multi-branch bank, with each branch reporting directly to its head office, where administrative policies were laid down and larger lending decisions taken. Midland, with its highly centralised management style, conformed most closely to this model and Barclays least so, since it was in effect a federation of family banks, each of which retained its strong regional centre of authority.

Phase three witnessed the dawn of horizontal diversification through the establishment of trust companies, overseas branches and the like and the acquisition of some self-standing subsidiaries, notably in the areas of Scottish and Irish banking and instalment credit finance. Barclays was again distinctive in that it also had a major international affiliate, later to be acquired outright, in the shape of Barclays DCO.

Phase four was the period of reconfiguration following the mergers of the late 1960s, which saw the creation of National Westminster and the Royal Bank of Scotland group, and the liberalising measures of the early 1970s, notably 'Competition and credit control'. Most of the banks developed far more substantial international divisions through a mixture of organic development and acquisitions; while on the domestic front they established new regional and area offices, or reformed existing ones, in order to move effective decision-making closer to the branches and the customers. They also took their first faltering steps into merchant banking. At the same time they moved to increase the professionalism of their support functions in such areas as personnel management, finance and computer systems. Before considering the key characteristics of phase five, which is the one through which the banks are still passing, it is necessary to consider why radical structural change from the phase four model has been necessary.

Choices of organisational form

Like any other company, once a bank outgrows its initial unitary form it has to decide on which basis, or combination of bases, it will group its activities for organisational purposes. It has a choice of four dimensions: geography, customer, product and function. It can, if it wishes, emphasise one of these dimensions at one level of the management hierarchy and another one at another level. Alternatively, it can seek to adopt a new management style, such as matrix or strategic business unit (SBU) management, which allows it to manage along more than one dimension simultaneously. In this regard banks face the same basic organisational choices as any other type of company. Nevertheless, there are at least three features of the banking industry which make the choice of organisational form an unusually interesting and, in some respects, an unusually difficult one.

First, there is the traditional supremacy of geography as the primary organisational dimension, both domestically and internationally. It is only very recently that clearing banks have started to develop organisational structures which correspond at all closely to their key customer segments or product groups, rather than to their geographic regions. As the change factors summarised earlier in this paper made their impact increasingly felt, so the banks began first to embrace the concept of market segmentation (developing different products and services for different customer groups) and then, at least partially, matching this policy of segmentation with similarly differentiated organisational forms (distinct business units serving distinct customer groups or providing distinct product ranges). It was not exactly divisionalisation as an industrial company would recognise the term, but it was an important move away from the traditional unitary form nonetheless.

If divisionalisation is in some ways an alien concept for banks, the concept of functional specialisation along the traditional industrial lines of R & D, production, marketing and sales is perhaps even more so. The nature of the classic business of banking - taking deposits, arranging payments, making loans - long permitted what might be termed the total vertical integration of functions at the branch level and therefore militated against any such specialisation. More recently, however, all the banks have established substantial, self-standing departments in areas such as marketing and financial control, with responsibilities cutting right across the traditional geographic reporting lines of the branch banking structure.

Midland went further than most down the path of functional specialisation in the late 1980s when it established a group operations sector and thereby separated its operational activities from its revenue-generating activities at a high level within the organisational structure.

The second factor is the sheer pace of change that has rendered time-honoured organisational forms obsolete so quickly. After decades of virtual organisational stagnation, bank employees have had to inure themselves to frequent changes in organisational structure and reporting relationships. While not all of these changes have been directly driven by the needs of the marketplace, there is no doubt that the pace of environmental change is the main factor behind the organisational turbulence of the past decade. To take just one example, the new ability of the banks to diversify into securities trading in 1986 permitted (or arguably necessitated) a high degree of structural integration of their securities, treasury and merchant banking activities. Once the traditional institutional barriers between trading in short-dated gilt-edged securities and money market instruments had been removed, it scarcely made sense to manage them as discrete activities.

The third factor is the pervasive nature of the interdependencies between different parts of the business of banking, something which makes organisational design especially difficult for a bank. The problems of managing interdependencies have a well-established place in conventional organisation theory (see for example Galbraith 1973), which is concerned not only with how to group activities but also with how to manage the necessary flows of information and authority between the resulting groups. The latter challenge is particularly acute when, as in the case of banks, the different groups have complex reciprocal relationships with one another and make significant use of pooled corporate resources such as computer systems, financial capital and customer information. Indeed, the massive increase in the sheer volume of management information now available to the banks leads them inexorably in the direction of organisational complexity while providing them, it must be hoped, with some at least of the necessary tools for managing that complexity.

Thus it is almost inevitable that if a bank chooses to emphasise one of the four organisational dimensions - products, customers, geographical markets and functions - at any level of its organisational hierarchy, it is almost bound to face the need to manage significant and complex interdependencies along one or more of the remaining dimensions. One real-life example may be taken to illustrate this point. Consider an executive of a British bank who has the job of providing treasury products to multinational companies in Paris. Should he report along the product axis to the head of treasury sales in London, or along the customer axis to the relationship manager for the company concerned, or along the geographical axis to the country manager for France, or along the functional axis to, say, the group risk management department, or to any two, three or four of them? Clearly none of these axes can be totally ignored. Equally clearly, they cannot all be given equal weight, which is another way of saying that four-dimensional matrix management could never work. Essentially the challenge facing the banks has been that of finding the 'least bad' structural fit and then supplementing the resulting organisational structure with enabling mechanisms designed to manage the inter-group interdependencies effectively; and that has proved to be easier said than done.

CURRENT ORGANISATIONAL FORMS AND ISSUES

Progress

Faced with these difficulties, it is hardly surprising that the banks' progress into the fifth phase of their organisational evolution has been uneven and faltering.   On the positive side, they have all given more emphasis to customers and products and less to geography throughout their organisations.   At the top of a clearing bank group's organisational hierarchy, the primary basis of grouping is now typically products: commercial banking products on the one hand, capital market products on the other.   Within the commercial banking group, the second-order basis of grouping is customers: multinational, major corporates (often sub-grouped by industry rather than region), medium-sized companies, small firms and personal customers.   Within the capital markets area, however, the second-order basis of grouping typically remains products: for example, treasury products, securities dealing, venture capital, capital raising and advisory services.   This is for the good reason that capital market product characteristics are highly complex and specific, whereas the market for those products tends to comprise similar types of major corporate and institutional customers.

Geography is now of only third-order importance in commercial banking, as a basis for grouping retail branches.   One of the consequences of this has been the decline in the role of the traditional regional director, who used to represent all aspects of the business of the bank in his part of the country, and of the divisional general manager to whom he reported.   It should be noted, however, that Midland - which had previously moved as far as any bank towards a quasi-divisionalised organisational structure - has now started to reverse the process.   Under a policy described by its current group chief executive as 'putting the bank together again' it is reintegrating some of the previously separate personal and corporate business activities, eliminating some of the specialised central management functions and enhancing the previously downgraded roles of the regional directors.   The precise reasons for this reversal of policy remain to be researched, but are likely to include the difficulty of managing an increasingly complex nexus of reporting and communication lines under the previous structure.   The virtues of greater organisational simplicity have their natural appeal.

For obvious reasons, geography remains of greater importance when it comes to managing the banks' overseas operations, particularly where locally-incorporated subsidiaries are involved, though here too the authority of country managers has often been compromised in order to allow closer direct control from head office over particular commercial activities and management functions. It remains to be seen to what extent the creation of the Single European Market encourages the banks to integrate their European operations more closely across geographical boundaries.

Despite the problems caused by greater organisational complexity, the banks have gone some considerable way towards recognising the need to manage the interdependencies resulting from these new structures. For example, corporate customers which are large and important enough are allocated relationship managers with planning and liaison responsibilities designed to ensure that the efforts of the different product groups within the bank are properly co-ordinated. Huge investments have been made in management information systems in order to generate meaningful information about customers and products, in order to supplement the accounting information traditionally generated about branches and subsidiaries. (In this context the banks seem to have taken the point that there is little to be gained by organising along product or customer lines unless the management information exists to allow the organisation to plan and monitor its performance along those same lines.)

At the functional level, not only have marketing and other traditional support operations grown in size, sophistication and influence but powerful new functional specialisations have been introduced in the areas of risk management, balance sheet management and compliance. However, in order to ensure that these functional managers are fully responsive to the needs of the business, they have now typically been widely dispersed to the various business sectors, leaving behind at the corporate management level small teams whose task is mainly that of overall policy co-ordination.

Shortcomings

Against these achievements, however, must be set a considerable number of shortcomings. First, there is little evidence to suggest that the organisational changes themselves have been based on a clinical assessment of the strategic and environmental contingencies. Sometimes they seem to owe rather more to power-broking between rival executives or to trial and error. As a result, the changes have sometimes gone too far, have sometimes not gone far enough, and have sometimes proceeded in the wrong direction. Not infrequently, as already illustrated, they have had to be reversed.   In the process, banks have learnt that the destabilising consequences for their staff and customers of excessive organisational change are not inconsiderable.

Secondly, anecdotal evidence at least would suggest that there has been a preoccupation with what one might term the anatomy of the organisation (who is grouped with whom and who reports to whom) at the expense of the organisation's physiology (where real power resides within the organisation, how decisions are taken, how information flows both within and between groups, how the activities of different groups are co-ordinated, in short, how people actually get on with their work). It is central to the contingency theory of organisations that *all* the design variables must be in harmony, not just the strategy and structure but also the people systems, the distribution of power within the organisation, the planning and control mechanisms, the performance measurements and the reward systems.   This is a lesson which, on the available evidence, the banks do not seem yet to have taken fully on board.

Thirdly, there is a deep ambivalence within the banks about the role of what used to be termed the staff functions, the long-established ones like personnel and finance as well as the new-fangled ones like internal audit and compliance.   Is it their role to control line managers or merely to advise and assist them?   Wherein lies their authority, and how should that authority best be exercised?   There is increasing awareness within the banks of the need for greater clarity as to those matters where functional managers merely need to be advised, those where they need to be consulted, those where they can exercise authority concurrently with line management and those where they enjoy exclusive authority.

Approaches suggested by organisation theory

Because of the particular features of the banking industry which have been identified in this paper, it is not really surprising that the banks' organisational responses should have been less than fully adequate to the needs of the situation.   Nor does organisation theory or the experience of other industries provide cut-and-dried suggestions as to how they might do better.   Nevertheless, organisation theory does suggest a number of approaches to organisational change which could be of use the banks.

The first concerns the role of the chief executive.   Any form of complex organisational structure is bound to create tensions between the champions of particular customer, product, market or functional interests. It must be one of the key roles of the CEO not so much to take the difficult decisions himself but, in the words of Galbraith (1977), to orchestrate the decision-making process, channelling conflict wherever possible into the planning process and compensating for the inevitable imbalances of power which arise between his subordinates. The role of the chief executive of a clearing bank is still influenced to a considerable extent by the traditional duties of the old chief general manager, whose main role was that of first among equals when it came to taking major lending decisions.

The second approach concerns the role of strategic business units, though as a planning rather than as an operational entity. This would involve identifying particular constellations of products, customers and markets which lend themselves to an integrated planning effort because they share a common business mission in the face of common commercial threats and opportunities. There is no reason why these SBUs need to be coterminous with the bank's operational groupings. What is important is that the bank's information systems should allow operational performance to be translated into SBU performance for planning and monitoring purposes.

The third is to make effective use wherever appropriate of the techniques of matrix management. These have already been adopted by a number of banks, not entirely successfully, and indeed, some organisation theorists would go so far as to say that if it is not necessary to use matrix management, then it is necessary not to use it. Attempts to introduce it have often become bogged down in bureaucratic procedures, role ambiguity and internal conflict. Matrix management is a term which can cover a wide variety of organisational forms capable of being used in part or all of an organisation. At one extreme it may involve little more than institutionalised project teams or product groups, or the appointment of executives with specific responsibilities for co-ordination and integration across organisational boundaries. At the other extreme, in what has been termed its bipolar management form, a genuinely equal balance of power and responsibility is shared by two units for one activity.

As one moves towards the latter extreme, so one moves well beyond the concept of straight and dotted line reporting relationships familiar to the old staff/line dichotomy, to a situation where there are not only two or more line structures, but also two accounting systems, two bases of reward, two budgeting systems and so forth. Such an approach flies in the face of much conventional management theory and, badly executed, can certainly lead to lack of clarity in setting objectives and accountability, and thus, to general dysfunctionality within the company.

When, therefore, does it make sense to use matrix management? According to Lawrence and Davis (1978), three conditions need to be met. First, the external forces at work on the company must require a dual focus to the way the company operates. Secondly, the traditional organisational model must have outgrown its capacity to generate and process the information which the company needs in order to make decisions, which argues for the dispersal and sharing of decision-making responsibility. Finally, there must be pressure on the company to share resources of people, capital, technology and so forth across organisational boundaries.

Most would agree that all three conditions are met in the British banking industry at this time. The first of them may be emphasised in particular. The forces of competition, technology and customer needs mean that banks have found it increasingly hard to avoid adopting a dual, if not multiple, focus to the conduct of their business. Thus, to revert to an earlier example in this paper, the provision of sophisticated treasury market products to a sophisticated clientele requires a bank to organise itself simultaneously along both the product and the customer dimension. Matrix management is a way of helping it to do this - but that implies not just a matrix structure but matrix systems, matrix behaviour and indeed a matrix culture which allows conflicts to be resolved and scarce resources allocated within a bank in the face of diverse demands for them. Thus for any form of matrix management to be successful it is likely that managers within the organisation concerned will need to possess shared values, skills, experiences and attitudes to a very considerable extent, so that they are comfortable dealing with one another across conventional reporting lines. Some of the requisite skills can be inculcated by training and development programmes. Others may come only with time and experience.

Finally, the banks have found that rapid and radical organisational change can easily exacerbate rather than ameliorate the problems of goal displacement which arise when the immediate objectives pursued by individuals and groups within companies achieve a life of their own rather than being seen as the means to the end of achieving the company's ultimate objectives. One obvious and topical example of goal displacement in banking is the pursuit of lending and other business volumes with insufficient regard to the resulting risk profile of the business. Such problems may well have been exacerbated by the increasingly prevalent practice of linking the remuneration of key executives to the performance of their own divisions and departments, rather than to the overall performance of the company - a hazardous trend in what are necessarily highly interdependent organisations where it is both conceptually and practically very difficult to correlate effort with achievement.

Thus, the banks have discovered, rather painfully in some cases, that there are major risks involved in any attempt to disaggregate their business organisationally. A bank simply cannot be organised as a collection of little businesses, each with its own balance sheet, profit and loss account and employment terms and conditions. Attempts to treat it as such, while in some ways a commendable departure from the more centralised, bureaucratic and authoritarian practices of the past, seem on the basis of recent evidence all too likely to foster destructive internal rivalry and the sorts of excess of zeal which tend to result in multi-billion pound bad debt provisions. It is at least partly for this reason that the present (phase five) organisational structures of the major UK commercial banks are not yet in anything like steady state.

LIST OF REFERENCES

Aldrich, H. and J. Pfeffer (1976), 'Environments of organisations', *Annual Review of Sociology*, **2**, 79-105

Chandler, A.D. (1962), *Strategy and Structure* (Cambridge, Ma: MIT Press)

Child, J. (1972), 'Organisation structure, environment and performance: the role of strategic choice', *Sociology*, **6**, 1-22

Child, J. (1974), 'Managerial and organisational factors associated with company performance - part I', *Journal of Management Studies*, pp. 175-189

Child, J. (1975), 'Managerial and organisational factors associated with company performance - part II', *Journal of Management Studies*, pp. 12-27

Galbraith, J.R. (1973), *Designing Complex Organizations* (Reading MA: Addison-Wesley)

Galbraith, J.R. (1977), *Organisation Design* (Reading MA: Addison-Wesley)

Galbraith, J.R. (1983), 'Strategy and organisation planning', *Human Resource Management*, **22**, 63-77

Galbraith, J.R. and D. A. Nathanson (1978), *Strategy Implementation: the Role of Structure and Process* (St Paul: West)

Lawrence, P. and J. Lorsch (1967), *Organization and Environment*, Harvard Business School

Lawrence, P. and J. Lorsch (1969), *Developing Organizations: Diagnosis and Action* (Reading MA: Addison-Wesley)

Lawrence, P. and S. Davis (1978), *Matrix* (Reading MA: Addison-Wesley)

Llewellyn, D. (1990), 'Competition and structural development change in the British financial system' in E. Gardener (ed.), *The Future of Financial Systems and Services* (London: Macmillan)

Llewellyn, D. (1991), 'Structural change in the British financial system' in C. Green and D. Llewellyn, *Surveys of Monetary Economics*, 2 (Oxford: Blackwell)

Miles, R. and C. Snow (1978), *Environmental Strategy and Organisation Structure* (New York NY: McGraw-Hill)

Morison, I. (1991), 'Dynamics of competition in banking' in *Banking Operations in a Changing Environment: the Profitable Use of Resources* (London: Chartered Institute of Bankers)

Pugh, D.; D. Hickson and C. Hinings (1969), 'An empirical taxonomy of structures of work organisations', *Administration Science Quarterly*, 14, 115-26

Pugh, D.; D. Hickson; C. Hinings; K. Macdonald; C. Turner and T. Lupton (1963), 'A conceptual scheme for organizational analysis', *Administrative Science Quarterly*, 8, 289-315

Pugh, D. and T. Lupton (1968), 'Dimensions of organization structures', *Administrative Science Quarterly*, 13, 65-105

CHAPTER 6
STRATEGIES OF MAJOR BRITISH BANKS SINCE BIG BANG

Jack Revell

UNIVERSAL BANKS AND MAJOR BANKS

Preamble

For the first version of this paper I was given the task of analysing the strategies of 'universal banks', but that is not a very useful way of describing the large banks in any banking system because nowadays the term has a number of different meanings. It began as a description of the German banks, in which the holding of participations in the shares of corporate customers was a necessary element of the term, but now it seems to mean little more than unspecialised, thus including most banks that operate in several markets. With this usage the term can cover banks of any size, and the official Netherlands banking statistics go so far as to lump all commercial and savings banks together under the single heading of 'universal banks'. Very few people would naturally consider a small local bank, savings bank or building society as a universal bank, and it is therefore necessary to introduce additional criteria. The most important of these are (1) that it should undertake both retail and wholesale business and (2) that it should operate not only throughout its own country but in some other countries as well. In other words, the term implies both overall size and importance in particular markets.

Even though the concept of a universal bank is very little help in identifying the British banks to be included in this survey, it played a part in the strategies of large banks purely as a concept of the nature of a large bank. It became a sign of manhood among bankers, just as the term 'international bank' had been in the happier days of the late 1970s and very early 1980s. In this role it urged banks to expand their activities both geographically and into new services, such as the whole range of operations associated with investment banking and securities business at the time of Big Bang. This left them to face the excess capacity of the recent years in a state of over-expansion.

The upshot of this definitional discussion is that we should concentrate on a group of major banks and building societies. Fortunately there are two groups for which consistent statistics are available. The more important of the two is the group that the Bank of England calls 'large

93

British banks', for which it supplies aggregate statistics based on fully consolidated accounts in its annual *Banking Act Report*, together with a most useful commentary. The members are the four English clearing banks (Barclays, National Westminster, Midland and Lloyds), the two Scottish clearing banks (Royal Bank of Scotland and Bank of Scotland), Standard Chartered and TSB Group; some of the figures are for the 'four largest banks', which are the English clearing banks. The British Bankers' Association (BBA) category 'major British banking groups' has the same composition, except that Abbey National plc is included in the membership from 1989, although not yet in many of the tables. Most of the detailed BBA statistics include only those subsidiaries that are in the UK banking sector, but some of the tables in its *Annual Abstract of Banking Statistics* are sketchy summaries of the fully consolidated accounts, covering the business of member bank groups throughout the world.

Total assets of the major banks and building societies

Table 6.1 shows the total assets of the banks that are included as major banks and of the five largest building societies. The major groups are all British banks, and there are several banks that are excluded from these groups of major banks by reason of national origin or of size but appear in the Bank of England's main statistical category, 'retail banks'. Among these are the sizeable UK operations of the two Irish Banks (Bank of Ireland and Allied Irish Banks), Girobank (now owned by a building society) and the three banks recently acquired by National Australia Bank. Two of the banks that are grouped under Australian ownership are the former Midland subsidiaries Clydesdale Bank and Northern Bank, together with Yorkshire Bank acquired from a consortium of English clearing banks; although this 'National Australia Group' is the only group of banks that operates in all the three partly separate markets of the United Kingdom (England and Wales, Scotland, and Northern Ireland) as well as in the Republic of Ireland, its aggregate total assets in the United Kingdom were only £11.3 billion at the end of 1990 and around £12 billion if the Irish subsidiary, renamed National Irish, was included. None of the excluded banks is larger than any of the major banks.

There are considerable differences between the eight major banks. Only the two largest, Barclays and National Westminster, are truly universal in the sense that they have a large international presence. The next two, Midland and Lloyds, are mainly domestic in their business,

Table 6.1   Major British banks and building societies, end-1990

£ billion

	Banks	Total assets	Building societies	Total assets
1	Barclays	134.9		
2	National Westminster	121.1		
3	Midland	59.6		
4	Lloyds	55.2		
5			Halifax	54.2
6	Abbey National	45.5		
7	Royal Bank of Scotland	30.1		
8	TSB	27.5		
9			Nationwide Anglia	26.7
10	Standard Chartered	22.1		
11	Bank of Scotland	18.4		
11			Woolwich	18.2
12			Alliance & Leicester	16.1
13			Leeds	14.7

Sources: 1. British Bankers' Association, *Annual Abstract of Banking Statistics*, vol. 8, Table 2.12
2. Council of Mortgage Lenders, *Housing Finance Fact Book 1991*, Appendix to Chapter 5

although they both have some overseas subsidiary banks. The two Scottish banks are also mainly domestic, the term increasingly covering England and Wales as well as Scotland. Abbey National and TSB were respectively a building society and a group of savings banks only a few years ago; they are not only domestic but also predominantly retail in character.

The extent to which the five largest building societies fit within the size distribution of the major British banking groups, or are only just outside it, is noteworthy; the five largest building societies accounted for just under 60 per cent of aggregate building society assets at the end of 1991. (A few societies, as well as some banks other than the four largest, have end-year dates other than 31 December). The Building Societies Act of 1986 gave them some powers to carry on wider banking business, but they remain overwhelmingly retail in their business, specialising in the provision of house purchase finance, and would not fit within even a fairly wide definition of the term 'universal'.

Strategies and constraints

The period 1986-91 covers a phase of frantic competition in the retail sector, followed by a phase dominated by the effects of the general economic recession and the freezing of the house purchase and consumer credit markets. A corporate banking market buoyed up by large merger and acquisition activity was similarly followed by a phase of massive increases in provisions. In the international banking market there was a legacy of large provisions on Third World debt, leading to a general air of caution, and even retreat, throughout the period. Special features applied to the other institutions and markets, such as merchant banks, securities houses, and the two branches of insurance business, but the same split of the period into two parts was also found in all of them.

In the first phase the general strategy was that of expansion in all profitable markets, with the herd instinct being given full rein. The tighter capital adequacy requirements and general regulation that were a legacy of the recession and international debt crisis of the early 1980s provided the only brake. At the end of the phase, both companies and households were very highly geared, and the bubble burst when the economic recession began. The banking system as a whole became increasingly fragile and those banks that had not recovered from weak-ness caused by the earlier recession, or from events even further back, became putative targets for acquisition; the two prime candidates were Midland and Standard Chartered. In this second phase it became diffi-cult to talk of strategies because banks were battling to survive against the constraints, which generally became the dominant factor; it was a phase of restraint and retrenchment.

Method of discussion

The main object of discussion is the so-called universal banks, which I have equated to the eight major British banks, alongside which are the five largest building societies, whose powers of competing with the major banks are effectively limited to the retail banking market. In the early sections the major banks are examined in some detail through statistical tables, which bring most series up to the end of 1991. The only series for building societies readily available are for all societies. Up-to-date statistical information of the kind required is generally lacking for the other kinds of institution.

These features dictate a two-stage approach to the question of strategy. The statistics on major banks and building societies are examined in some depth, not just for their own sake but also for the light they throw on the position of other institutions and for the only reliable clues to what strategy the large banks may have had. In this stage the discussion is organised around the question of capital adequacy as the main constraint on bank strategy, showing how various stages in the operating account influence the total of capital and the effect of capital issues and asset reductions. In the second stage the main source of information is anecdotal evidence of the various markets in which both major banks and the other institutions, such as merchant banks, insurance companies and fund managers, operate. The overall conclusions about strategy appear in the final section.

The paper is devoted to an intensive examination of the strategy of banks in one country, and there is no attempt to extend the study to statistics of other European countries. On occasion it will be possible to draw rough parallels with what has been happening elsewhere, although the whole story could be repeated with minor amendments in most countries.

CAPITAL ADEQUACY

The significance of capital

Not so long ago the main objective of banks and most financial institutions was growth and, consequently, the size of the balance sheet total. Since the international debt crisis and the imposition of strict ratio requirements on the capital position of banks in most important banking countries, this objective has been replaced by profitability. Fulfilment of the capital ratios is an imperative, and profitability is a *sine qua non* for adding to reserves and keeping the cost of capital issues as low as possible. Capital and capital ratios are of great significance for the following

reasons (see Llewellyn 1992):
- they are a rigid requirement of the supervisory authorities
- they turn the attention of banks away from the pursuit of size to that of profitability
- they determine the ability of banks to expand by acquiring assets, mainly in the form of lending
- capital of all kinds must be serviced, in the form of either dividends or interest, and the cost of capital affects the pricing of bank services, thus helping to determine competitiveness with other banks and the capital market.

Additions to the level of capital can come from only two sources: retained earnings added to reserves and fresh capital injections raised by issues on the capital market. These two main sources are shown in the boxes immediately under 'Capital adequacy' in Figure 6.1. Of the boxes below these two, those on the left show how the operations of the bank build up to the figure of retained earnings, but those on the right are somewhat different because they are both means of raising a capital ratio without increasing the total amount of capital. Asset sales and adjustments to the rate of expansion modify the denominator of the capital ratio. The layout of Figure 6.1 is intended to portray the line of argument in the following sections; the captions in the boxes do little more than set out the section titles.

Capital ratios

The first step in the discussion is to see how far British banks have been able to comply with the capital requirements of the Bank of England; the figures are in Table 6.2.

In 1988 the Banking Supervision Division of the Bank of England issued a notice (BSD/1988/3) to all institutions authorised under the Banking Act 1987 on the 'Implementation of the Basle Convergence Agreement in the United Kingdom'. This imposed the obligation for all banks to switch over to the Basle scheme no later than the end of 1989; the 1988 figures in Table 6.2 are therefore only for comparative purposes. In the notice the Bank stated its expectation that the majority of British banks would be able to meet the minimum international standard of 8 per cent set by the Basle Committee. The Bank operates with two capital adequacy ratios for individual banks, both of which are considerably higher than the 8 per cent in most cases. The first is a target ratio to be attained under normal circumstances, and the second is a trigger ratio, below which the bank must take drastic action to rectify the position.

Figure 6.1   The determinants of capital adequacy

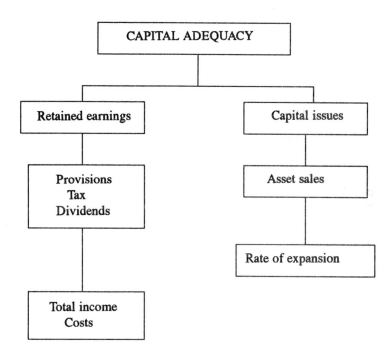

The ratios in Table 6.2 show no consistent pattern. Such a diversity should probably be expected, particularly at a time like the present, when retained earnings make a very small or negative contribution to capital. The banks are thus forced to use the capital market to maintain their ratios, and they are likely to do so for relatively large sums at irregular intervals. The only case of a ratio below 8 per cent was that of Lloyds Bank in the first year, 1989; it had to adjust by a sale of assets.

It is difficult to relate the historical pattern of ratios of the individual banks to specific circumstances. TSB Group is perhaps an exception because it was left with an excess of capital on flotation, some of which was spent on various acquisitions; a few of the institutions acquired have since been sold. Apart from this obvious point, it is noteworthy that the two largest banks, Barclays and National Westminster, have generally lower ratios than the smaller ones, and that the two banks under threat, Midland and Standard Chartered, have fairly high ratios. The four largest banks, the English clearing banks, obviously made a special

Table 6.2 Large British banks: risk asset ratios

Bank	1988	1989	1990	1991	1991 Tier 1
Barclays	9.3	9.0	8.3	8.7	5.9
National Westminster	9.8	9.1	9.1	9.6	5.5
Midland	11.8	10.0	9.8	10.3	5.5
Lloyds	10.1	7.4	8.5	9.7	6.2
TSB Group	14.9	12.4	11.1	12.2	8.5
Royal Bank of Scotland	13.0	12.8	11.6	11.0	6.9
Standard Chartered	10.4	9.2	10.7	10.0	5.0
Bank of Scotland	...	11.0	10.6	9.9	5.6
Large British banks	**10.0**	**9.2**	**9.2**	**9.7**	**9.7**
Abbey National	...	12.1	11.0	10.8	10.3

Sources: 1. British Bankers' Association, *Annual Abstract of Banking Statistics*, vol. 9, 1992, Table 2.14
2. Bank of England, *Banking Act Report for 1991/92*, Table IX

Notes: 1. There are certain adjustments in the figure for large British banks that are not in the figures for individual banks
2. Lloyds Bank sold assets early in 1990 to raise its ratio above 8 per cent

effort to raise their ratios in 1991; with the exception of Lloyds the increase was largely in the form of Tier 2 capital.

Building societies will have to move to the Basle scheme on 1 January 1993, but at the moment their ratios are calculated differently, so that no direct comparison is possible. The Building Societies Commission has calculated the ratios under the new scheme, and its report for 1991-92 said that the weighted ratios for 1990 and 1991 were 11.2 (fifty largest societies) and 11.8 per cent (all societies) respectively, higher than those of most large banks. Societies are allowed to issue subordinated debt (Tier 2) and, from 1991, permanent interest-bearing shares, or PIBS (Tier 1). At the end of 1991 these two items accounted for 17.5 per cent of gross capital.

Retained earnings

Between trading profits, the results of the operations of the period, and the retained earnings that can be added to capital there are several claimants to be satisfied. The most important of these is provision for possible losses, but tax and dividends are pressing. The amounts devoted to these headings are discretionary in the limited sense that the trading profits are known before the management sits down to decide on their distribution; each heading has its own constraints. Tax can be manipulated, but only to a small extent at this stage. Provisions are a recognition of possible losses before they occur; in the period under consideration these possible losses were recognised earlier than in the recession of the first part of the 1980s, and there have been cases of stronger banks trying to use provisions as a competitive weapon by making heavy provisions when weaker banks were not in a position to follow suit, action discouraged by the Bank of England. Dividends cannot be regarded as a mere residual because low dividends raise the cost of issuing new capital on the market. All three headings have one thing in common: funds devoted to them reduce capital, although tax implications mean that the reductions are not always *pro tanto*. In the circumstances of the period since 1986 decisions on provisions and dividends have assumed considerable importance. The figures are shown in Table 6.3, with a graphical portrayal in Figure 6.2.

The figures for retained earnings are considerably lower than they were in the ten years up to 1986. The average for the four largest banks in the earlier period was 33 per cent of trading profits, against 3 per cent for 1987-90 (Llewellyn 1992, p. 21). In the first four years of the period from 1986 there was an alternation of relatively good years and bad years for retained earnings. Since trading profits before bad debts were on a rising trend throughout this period, it is necessary to find culprits in the body of the table. Tax, as would be expected, largely accommodated itself to the trend of trading profits, and the culprits are the provisions and dividends. Provisions rose to 88 and 89 per cent of trading profits in the bad years and dropped to lower percentages in the good years; they are of such a magnitude that they will be examined separately below (see Table 6.4). Dividends, on the other hand, although of less import in the total picture, remained on a rising trend as

Table 6.3   Large British banks: earnings, provisions, tax and dividends

£ billion

	1986	1987	1988	1989	1990	1991
Trading profits						
before bad debts	5.58	6.02	6.86	7.72	7.29	8.28
Provisions	1.74	5.29	1.19	6.86	4.48	6.64
Pre-tax profits	3.84	0.73	5.67	0.86	2.81	1.64
Tax	1.36	0.64	1.99	0.36	1.45	0.59
Post-tax profits	2.48	0.09	3.68	0.50	1.36	1.05
Dividends	0.57	0.73	0.94	1.07	0.84	1.29
Retained earnings	1.91	-0.64	2.74	-0.57	0.52	-0.24

Source: Bank of England, *Banking Act Report for 1991/92*, Tables VI and VII (1986 from previous year's report)

Note: Provisions, tax and dividends are obtained by subtraction; they are portrayed in Chart 4 of the source

Figure 6.2   Large British banks: distribution of trading profits

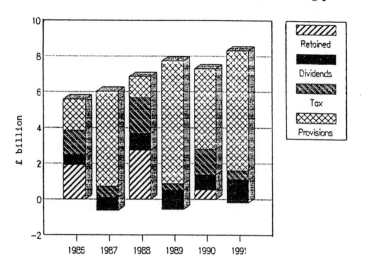

a proportion of trading profits until 1989; after a drop in 1990 the percentage rose sharply again in 1991.

Banks are in a dilemma over their dividend policy during bad times that are thought unlikely to persist. The role of shareholders, actual and potential, as providers of new capital to bolster capital ratios tends to dominate in the eyes of management in such periods until things get so bad that they must be viewed in their original role, that of bearing the burden of losses. Nevertheless, banks should bear in mind that poor earnings will eventually make the shareholders fearful of a future drop in dividends.

Table 6.4 analyses the bad debt provisions. Throughout the period up to 1990 the provisions on loans to problem countries remained above those for domestic commercial loans, both on the net amounts added to provisions each year and even more so in terms of outstanding provisions as a percentage of loans outstanding. The problem country loans date from the 1970s, and the level of provisions demanded by central banks rose steadily. The development of a secondary market for these loans and swap deals alleviated the position for many banks, which sold the loans at heavily discounted prices to other banks not so deeply committed ; some were able to reduce the total of their provisions when the price obtained on secondary market sales exceeded the previous provisions. The 'other' category includes all the lending to households that turned bad in 1990 and 1991.

The effects of specific and general provisions on tax and additions to capital and reserves are quite different. Specific provisions, those recognising the possibility of loss on specific loans, do not count as capital, but they are allowable against taxable income. This means that effectively a sum equal to the tax that would otherwise have been paid is available as an offset to the reduction of capital that would be caused by making the provision; with a 35 per cent rate of tax, capital is only 65 per cent lower than if no provision had been made. General provisions, on the other hand, are not allowable against taxable income but count as Tier 2 capital. General provisions do not relate to any specific loans but take account of the fact that in any portfolio of loans a certain proportion that are not yet recognised as problems will turn bad before the end of the year. If they had a free hand, it would obviously be to the advantage of banks to maximise general provisions at the expense of specific ones, but the allowable amount of general provisions is calculated by a formula that averages the loss experience over the past five years. Banks have no choice in the matter, and it takes a few years before past losses are fully reflected.

Table 6.4   Large British banks: bad debt provisions

Type of loan	1986	1987	1988	1989	1990	1991
Amounts outstanding (£ billion)						
Domestic commercial	2.2	2.2	2.3	2.7	4.1	6.8
Problem country	...	5.0	5.1	9.2	6.5	6.0
Other	...	1.5	1.3	1.7	2.1	2.1
Total	**...**	**8.7**	**8.7**	**13.6**	**12.7**	**14.9**
Specific	4.0	7.4	7.7	12.3	11.0	13.2
General	...	1.3	1.1	1.3	1.7	1.7
Percentages of loans outstanding						
Domestic commercial	1.9	1.6	1.3	1.3	1.9	3.4
Problem country	...	30.5	32.3	60.3	56.5	59.6

Sources: 1. Bank of England, *Banking Act Report for 1991/92*, Tables
V and X
2. British Bankers' Association, *Annual Abstract of Banking Statistics*, vol. 9, Table 2.15

Note: Domestic commercial and Problem country are from source
(1); Total is from source (2), with Other as a residual

There was a pattern in the timing of provisions and the possible bad debts that they reflect. In the early stages the provisions tended to concern large numbers of loans to small businesses, which are generally the first to suffer, some because they have not had time to establish themselves and others because they receive the effects of financial difficulties in the larger businesses, either through the drop in orders for their sole output or through delay by the larger businesses in paying their bills. By the middle of the period, larger and larger companies were running into difficulties, although small businesses continued to fail. A new feature occurred in the last period: the ramifications of the crisis in the property market, both commercial and residential.

A graph, attributed to the Bank of England, in *The Banker* article (Blanden and Shreeve 1992, p. 11) shows that UK bank lending to property companies climbed steadily from 1985 to reach around 9 per cent of total bank lending by 1991, a figure only marginally below that of 1975; lending to construction companies, at around 4 per cent of the total, was much lower than in the crisis period of the mid-1970s. The article cites estimates that these figures are a considerable understatement, largely because lending to property and construction subsidiaries of conglomerates such as P&O is often classified to the sector of the holding company. Two additional factors increased the effects of the difficulties experienced from the property market: the first was the freezing of the residential property market, and the second was the fact that a considerable amount of lending to other sectors was secured on land and buildings. The article suggests that between 50 and 70 per cent of the total loans of UK banks was related in one way or another to property values.

This particular aspect of provisions for bad debts throws into sharper focus the general problem behind the lending by banks in the earlier part of the period. Banks generally acknowledge that some, at least, of the lending was carried out without sufficient analysis of the creditworthiness of the borrowers. The consumer spending spree and the willingness of the household sector to be tempted into increasing its borrowing to a figure above current income set the herd galloping without too much regard for the soundness of the lending. The property boom had the same impetus. There are some who say that this time bankers have learnt their lesson and will be much more cautious next time round, but there is no evidence in banking history to support this view.

In most banking crises property lending has played a large part in bank failures. It was a major cause of the fringe banking crisis in Britain in the mid-1970s. In the past three or four years there have been banking crises in many countries. Those in the Scandinavian countries and in Australia and New Zealand having been among the most severe. In reports on Norway, Sweden, Finland and Denmark, property loans are mentioned time and time again as one of the main causes of the troubles experienced by commercial banks, savings banks and public banks, banks in the last two categories having been egged on by governments to behave like private banks in the search for efficiency and having done so rather too enthusiastically.

This is not surprising because property development is one of those industries that follow what economists call the 'hog cycle': a shortage of accommodation followed after a few years by a superfluity. In the original hog cycle an over-production of hogs in one year leads to sharply lower prices and causes some farmers to withdraw from the market in the next year. The resulting high prices bring them all back into the market, a profitable year being followed by an unprofitable one. In property the cycle is of much longer duration and causes correspondingly more havoc, but the main cause is the same, imperfect information on the market as a whole and on the intentions of other developers. Shipbuilding and other industries with a long time-lag between investment decisions and completion have similar characteristics.

These cyclical industries have been the cause of banking difficulties for so long that it is surely an important policy issue to limit the cyclical nature and to restrict bank involvement. Most of the big developers can probably acquire market information easily enough, even at the stage of application for planning permission, so that wider dissemination of such information would not be sufficient to overcome the speculative attraction that property seems to have for banks and even the most conservative elements in society - witness the recent £500 million losses on property investments by the Church Commissioners of the Church of England. Since property investment is such a speculative venture, it should be financed mainly by equity, or at least by the capital market in various forms, even in the early stages. This could be achieved if bank lending to property developers and construction companies were limited to a relatively small proportion of risk assets, the regulation being enforced by penal increases in the risk weighting of property lending or by the requirement to raise large provisions beyond the limit.

Even building societies cannot be absolved from the charge of overenthusiastic lending. Their provisions against mortgage losses are relatively so small that they needed too many decimal places to include in Table 6.4, but they have risen considerably nevertheless. From 0.0021 per cent of mortgage loans in 1980, the figure rose to 0.0307 per cent in 1988 and to 0.24 per cent in 1990 (Council of Mortgage Lenders 1989 and 1991), a rise of 115 times in ten years. Banks and building societies have repossessed many houses whose owners were in arrears on their mortgage repayments, but with the larger commercial property developments banks are still nursing empty properties until the market picks up, preferring to appoint an administrator to realising a loss.

EARNINGS

Income

The progress of the total income of banks and building societies is best viewed later, when we consider individual banking markets, and the immediate concern is the split between interest and non-interest income and the margins at which interest-bearing business was undertaken. These are shown in Table 6.5. The outstanding feature of the statistics is the steady climb of non-interest income to 40 per cent of the total. The first reaction might be to see in this the growing importance of off-balance sheet business, which was such a marked feature of the discussions after 1986, but there are many other factors involved.

For the large British banks the climb during the six years in the proportion of total income that is not received in the form of interest is remarkable, roughly from one-third to two-fifths. Fees and commission have always been levied on business accounts, and these have no doubt been raised as fast as the market will bear, but a large part of the increase in fees is on retail business. A boost was given by the successful marketing of life insurance, pensions and unit trusts. Pensions business has been hit to some extent by the recession, but the large commissions earned on the endowment policies associated with house purchase loans have fallen badly with the freezing of the housing market. A large part of the fee income now comes from the fees charged on personal payment accounts.

The banks are now boxed in a corner by the policy of offering current accounts that are free of charges as long as they remain in credit. This is a good example of the dangers of allowing marketing considerations, which are by their nature short term or, at best, medium term, to dominate retail banking policy. This is a strategy that cannot be reversed without causing discontent among the customers, as was shown by the reaction to a spate of press reports in September 1992 that they were about to charge commission on accounts with small balances. For many of the large banks, non-interest-bearing sterling deposits have dropped from around 50 per cent of total deposits in 1980 to around 15 per cent today. This has considerably reduced the 'endowment effect'.

The only strategy that the large banks have been able to follow is that of increasing fees for special services associated with personal current accounts, either by raising existing fees considerably or, more often, by imposing fees for services that were formerly provided free.

Table 6.5   Large British banks and building societies: non-interest income and interest margins

Type of institution	1986	1987	1988	1989	1990	1991
£ billion						
Large British banks						
Net interest	10.40	11.06	12.32	13.92	13.97	14.45
Non-interest	5.23	6.02	7.02	8.44	8.95	10.42
Total income	**15.63**	**17.08**	**19.34**	**22.36**	**22.92**	**24.87**
Percentages of mean assets						
Building societies						
Net interest	2.00	2.00	2.11	2.14	2.09	2.09
Non-interest	0.28	0.33	0.37	0.43	0.40	0.46
Non-interest income as percentages of total income						
Large British banks	33.46	35.25	36.30	37.75	39.05	41.90
Building societies	12.28	14.16	14.92	16.73	16.06	18.18
Interest margins						
Four largest banks						
Domestic	5.60	5.50	5.00	4.70	4.30	4.00
International	2.00	1.80	1.80	1.80	1.90	2.10
Overall	3.60	3.60	3.60	3.40	3.30	3.30

Sources: 1. Bank of England, *Banking Act Report for 1991/92*, Tables II and III
2. Building Societies Commission, *Annual Report 1991-92*, Table G

Among the latter are charges for the safe custody of securities and documents, which have risen to between £50 and £100 a year for even a few items. A particular target is an overdraft that is incurred without the prior agreement of the bank, which attracts not only a fee but a specially high rate of interest, often as high as 37 per cent. A feature of many of the interest-bearing current accounts is a fee for the ability to overdraw up to a certain limit without prior notice.

In the four years up to 1989 the building societies also managed to increase their fee income. The largest element of this has always been insurance commissions, both on the endowment policies that eventually repay the mortgage loans and on buildings insurance on the house that serves as security for the loan; since 1986 building societies have been able to offer other life insurance and pensions services, which probably made a modest contribution to commission income.

The domestic interest margins have narrowed considerably during the period. The interest margins on personal lending, such as those on personal loans and credit cards, have widened and banks have tried to widen the margins on lending to small business, pleading increased risk as justification. The large banks made a determined effort to widen their margins in 1991 by not allowing their rates to fall as fast as base rates; the evidence from these figures is either that they were unsuccessful, leaving increased fees to bear the whole burden, or that wider margins on personal lending were more than offset by lower margins in other parts of the domestic sector. Personal lending accounts for only about 30 per cent of bank lending, half of it on house purchase, and both that and other consumer credit slumped badly in 1991.

The margins on international business began to narrow before the beginning of the period, remained fairly steady during the period and then rose sharply in 1991. In terms of basis points the group net interest margins of the four banks changed between 1989 and 1991 as follows:

Barclays	- 20
National Westminster	- 20
Midland	+ 17
Lloyds	+ 50

The two banks that have a large international presence seem to have come out of that period considerably worse than the two mainly domestic banks.

Costs

The banks could have weathered the period of narrowing interest margins, aided to some extent by the increase in fee income, if they had been successful in moving to their long-proclaimed goal of drastically reducing costs. The figures in Table 6.6 show that the cost-income ratio of large British banks remained on a rising trend up to 1990, and that it was only in 1991 that there was some improvement. In the building society figures the marked worsening of the ratio in 1990 and 1991, despite drops in the cost/mean assets ratio, is evidence of a factor that applies also to the banks: a cost-income ratio can rise as much from a drop on the side of total income as from an increase in costs. When bank activity and income drop, there is therefore an automatic mechanism that tends to raise the cost-income ratio and *vice versa*. The 1991 drop in the ratio seems to have been a compound of the two factors: income rose, but the cost-cutting programmes of the banks began to take effect. The Bank of England (1992, p. 9) comments that the changing structure of the UK banking industry and increased competition mean that 'the heavy cost structures supported by the large banks are no longer viable'.

Of the individual banks shown in Table 6.6 Barclays has the worst performance, as the ratio is on a rising trend in the three years; it ends up with the second highest ratio. National Westminster slipped badly in 1990, and its ratio in 1991 is higher than it was in 1989; it emerges as number 3. The 1989 and 1990 figures for Midland are very poor, but there is a dramatic improvement in 1991, the rate of fall in the ratio being the highest among the four banks. Lloyds is clearly number 1, but even this bank slipped in 1990.

There are two main lessons to be learnt from Table 6.6. The first is that the banks have failed to bring their costs under anything like full control. The second is that the building societies have cost-income ratios considerably lower than those of the banks. At first sight this is a peculiar result to emerge because building societies are still almost pure retail banks, and the received doctrine is that retail banking has higher cost-income ratios because of its relatively labour-intensive nature. There are several possible answers to this conundrum. The first is that building society customers make less use of cheques in payments. The second is that even the largest building societies have fewer branches than banks of comparable size; they make considerable, though diminishing, use of agents to handle the simple, and relatively more expensive, services in the field of money transmission. The third is the possibility suggested by Robbie and de Hoest (1992, p. 15) in an analysis of this general question that cost-income ratios may be higher in some of the fee-earning services on which banks are more dependent than building societies. The fourth is that building societies have been much more successful

Table 6.6 **Large British banks and building societies: cost-income ratios**
Percentages

Type of institution	1986	1987	1988	1989	1990	1991
Large British banks						
Barclays	...	...	...	64.0	65.7	67.8
National Westminster	...	...	...	66.6	70.0	67.5
Midland	...	...	...	70.4	74.6	68.6
Lloyds	...	...	...	63.8	64.3	61.8
All 8 large banks	**66.2**	**66.4**	**66.5**	**67.0**	**68.0**	**66.7**
Building societies	47.7	47.6	48.2	47.6	51.4	56.1

Sources: 1. Bank of England, *Banking Act Report for 1991/92*, Table IV
          2. *The Banker*, March 1992, p. 10
          3. Building Societies Commission, *Annual Report 1991-92*, Table J
Note: The ratios for Midland Bank exclude Thomas Cook

than banks in bringing technology into 'front-office' operations: on-line counter terminals have been commonplace in building society branches and in banks on the Continent for years.

The key points that determine the costs of both types of institution are the numbers of staff and branches, and the effectiveness of investment in information technology. These are the points on which banks lay emphasis when they declare their determination to reduce costs. Table 6.7 sets out the available information. One difference between the figures for staff and those for branches stands out: whereas the overall number of staff for all major banks is higher in 1991 than it was in 1986, the reverse is true for the number of branches. The staff numbers of individual banks show several drops that are followed by further increases, and a substantial number of redundancies does not occur until

Table 6.7   Large British banks and building societies: staff and branches

Thousands

Institutions	1986	1987	1988	1989	1990	1991
Staff						
Large British banks						
Barclays	82.2	84.6	88.3	85.9	84.7	81.6
National Westminster	75.1	81.4	86.3	86.6	85.9	81.7
Midland	47.5	47.0	46.5	47.5	47.1	43.7
Lloyds	49.4	52.1	56.7	62.4	58.6	52.5
Total major banks of which:	**307.4**	**322.9**	**338.3**	**342.1**	**334.8**	**331.8**
Male	121.8	127.0	131.4	130.9	125.3	121.6
Female total	185.7	195.9	206.9	211.3	209.5	210.2
Female part-time	36.6	38.7	41.1	43.5	46.1	49.3
Building societies	62.5	66.8	72.0	67.3	68.8	...
of which: Part-time	13.4	15.0	16.2	14.6	15.1	15.2
Abbey National	...	...	...	13.6	16.7	...
Branches						
Four largest banks						
Barclays	2.8	2.8	2.7	2.6	2.6	2.5
National Westminster	3.1	3.1	3.1	3.1	2.8	2.7
Midland	2.2	2.1	2.1	2.0	2.0	1.8
Lloyds	2.2	2.2	2.2	2.2	2.1	1.9
Total	**10.3**	**10.2**	**10.1**	**9.9**	**9.6**	**8.9**
Building societies	7.0	7.0	6.9	6.2	6.1	5.9
Abbey National	...	...	...	0.7	0.7	0.7

continued

Table 6.7 (continued)

Sources: 1. British Bankers' Association, *Annual Abstract of Banking Statistics*, Tables 6.21 and 6.22
 2. Building Societies Commission, *Annual Report 1991-92*, Table 1, p. 56
Notes: 1. The staff figures are for full-time equivalents, counting part-time staff in the totals as one-half
 2. The staff figures for banks are for Great Britain only and include staff of certain subsidiaries
 3. Abbey National staff is included in the bank total for 1991

1991, a reduction in numbers that was not sufficient in some cases to bring the figures below those for 1986. (It is worth remembering that some changes could have come from the sale of subsidiaries.) The numbers of branches for individual banks fell steadily throughout the period, but the pace was staid and majestic rather than ruthless. In neither field was the progress achieved what one was led to expect from the cost-cutting noises of the banks. Despite the signal given by negative retained earnings in 1987, the magnitude of the problem was not realised by the banks until the last three years of the period, but the question is why it was not until 1991 that anything approaching ruthless action seems to have been taken. Part of the answer lies in the fact that, paradoxically, cutting costs is an expensive business. The decisions that determine the pace are akin to investment decisions, with a calculation of the pay-back period for the expenditure involved.

In the case of staff the redundancy payments for senior staff are likely to extend the pay-back period into a second year, and longer if the person has to be replaced. There was a time when turnover among female staff on marriage or child-bearing could be relied on as a cheap means of reducing total numbers, but social habits have changed. With branches the problem is slightly different between branches of which the bank owns the freehold and leased premises. In the former case the calculation involves very conservative estimations of the price likely to be realised for the premises in the present market for commercial properties, of the time taken to sell and of the cost of maintaining the building until it is sold. Since the kind of branches that are being sold is not particularly attractive to potential buyers or leasers, the period before sale or the end of the lease is likely to be long. Because banks are not making the retained earnings to cover the expenditure and since property prices are not rising, calculations of this kind impose a brake on cost-cutting exercises, which must sometimes be abandoned temporarily for these 'accounting' reasons.

One notable feature of the staff figures is the extent to which banking, or at least branch banking, has become a female profession, women acounting for 63 per cent of the total staff of large British banks. Whereas the number of men was about the same in 1991 as it was in 1986, with one or two small jumps in between, the number of women rose by 13 per cent over the period, and of women working part time by 35 per cent. (The numbers of part-time staff are of individuals, although they figure in the totals as full-time equivalents.) This analysis shows that total numbers are often misleading. The significance of the overall changes in the composition of staff is probably a fall in the salaries/number of employees ratio even though men and women are paid equally for the same job.

The overall figures for the number of branches also disguise at least two trends. The first is the conversion of many full branches into sub-branches, with a saving of managerial staff. The second is the move of clerical work away from branches to regional processing centres, a move that has been responsible for some part of the switch to women and to part-time women. The branches merely parcel up cheques and credit vouchers for transport to the processing centres, where the work is carried out under factory conditions with economies of scale.

The use of information technology and computers has obvious implications for costs, but it is a field in which statistics of capital expenditure are hard to come by. There is no doubt that the major banks have spent vast sums on ATMs (automated teller machines) and computers, but the technology is spoken of more often as adding to cost than as reducing it. One hypothesis is that some part of the expenditure has been misdirected. It has gone in certain directions: the maintenance of account records on large mainframe computers; progress in setting up customer information files; the 'do-it-yourself' delivery of banking services to customers; and the design and operation of complicated services that would have been impossible without the use of computers. The concentration on these aspects of information technology has left one important gap, which is only now in the process of being filled, that of handling the paper documents that customers hand into their branches. This gap can be filled if each counter clerk has a counter terminal on-line to the main bank computers, the use of which can enable much of the 'back-office' clerical work to be taken out of branches altogether.

The building societies have been much quicker to realise the importance of this missing link.

There are also glimmerings of a new approach to cutting costs. Except in innocuous fields like the partial sharing of ATMs and the clearing of interbank payments, banks are always loath to co-operate to reduce the costs of all of them; the break-up of the Access group of credit card issuers shows that they will even dissolve existing forms of co-operation in the name of competition. They are thus unlikely to countenance a co-operative sharing of facilities when an alternative solution is available, but they are beginning to realise that they can gain access to economies of scale in some services by farming them out to specialist suppliers, usually in the computer field. This is called 'outsourcing' or, rather more elegantly, 'facilities management', and there are signs of bank interest in this concept (see *The Banker*, April 1992). Both Barclays and the Bank of England have recently transferred large parts of their computer operations to specialist service companies; in the latter case the original staff was transferred from the Bank of England to the service company.

NEW CAPITAL AND ASSET REDUCTIONS

Capital issues

There is a clear alternation of good years and bad ones in the figures of Table 6.8. In 1987, even before the onset of the recession, retained earnings resulting from the operations of the banks were negative, and after an exceptionally good year in 1988, it was only in 1990 that there was a relatively small need to go to the capital market to maintain capital ratios. One item of capital that does not come into the figures of Table 6.8 is general provisions, which have risen steadily over the period from £1.09 billion to £1.72 billion, in line with the formula that relates them to an average of losses over previous years; they must not exceed 1.5 per cent of weighted risk assets, a figure to be reduced to 1.25 per cent at the end of 1992.

Apart from two fairly large issues of perpetual debt in 1986 and 1989, the main burden of new capital has been met by share issues, both rights issues and perpetual preference shares, both of which are classified as Tier 1 (core) capital. Banks had issued subordinated term debt earlier in the 1980s; as the debt was up to the limit of 50 per cent of Tier 1 elements, they have been able to add to this debt only in line with rises

Table 6.8   Large British banks: new capital and dividends

Source	1986	1987	1988	1989	1990	1991
			£ billion			
Retained earnings	1.91	-0.64	2.74	-0.57	0.52	-0.24
Perpetual debt	1.25	0.09	0.01	0.93	0.10	-
Term subordinated debt	-0.29	0.44	1.56	0.11	0.18	1.19
Share issues	1.42	1.96	1.33	0.33	0.23	0.51
Total new capital	**4.29**	**1.85**	**5.64**	**0.80**	**1.03**	**1.46**
Total capital issues	**2.38**	**2.49**	**2.90**	**1.37**	**0.51**	**1.70**
Dividends	0.57	0.73	0.94	1.07	0.84	1.29
Net capital issues	**1.81**	**1.76**	**1.96**	**0.30**	**-0.33**	**0.41**
			Percentages			
Capital issues/total new capital	55.48	134.59	51.42	171.25	49.51	116.44
Dividends/total new capital	13.29	39.46	16.67	133.75	81.55	88.36
Dividends/capital issues	42.02	29.32	32.41	78.10	164.71	75.88

Source: Bank of England, *Banking Act Report for 1991/92*, Table VII

in Tier 1 capital and to replace matured debt. A particular example of efforts to increase Tier 1 capital occurred in 1990. Banks issued scrip issues to capitalise property revaluation reserves, thus converting the reserves (Tier 2) into shareholders' equity (Tier 1). This move was supported by the Bank of England but objected to by several other countries. Such moves to redefine the BIS/EC rules on capital adequacy are to be expected from most countries, and it will probably be necessary to tighten them before long if the situation is not to get out of hand.

Table 6.8 goes beyond the figures of sources of new capital by relating capital issues to dividends. One symptom of difficulty in maintaining the new capital ratios that has been noted in some countries is that banks have sometimes found it necessary to raise fresh capital just in order to pay the desired level of dividends on shareholders' capital. The row entitled 'Net capital issues' is designed to show the position of the major British banks in this respect. In both 1989 and 1991 more than three-quarters of the fresh capital raised went to cover dividends, and in 1991 some of the retained earnings had to be used for this purpose. This is a situation akin to Ponzi finance, in which debtors have to incur further borrowing to service the existing debt. Figure 6.3 provides a graph of the values of capital issues and dividends from Table 6.8.

Figure 6.3   Large British banks: capital issues and dividends

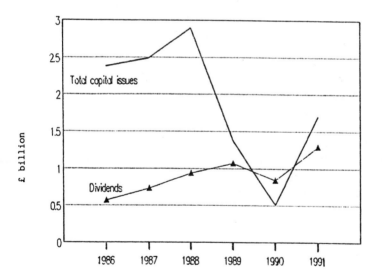

Asset reductions

The capital ratio in operation is a ratio of closely defined capital to a total of risk-weighted assets. This ratio can be increased just as well by reducing the weighted total of assets (the denominator) as by increasing capital (the numerator). The most straightforward way of reducing total assets is by the sale of anything from a few branches to a sizeable subsidiary, and the example that springs to mind is the sale by Midland Bank of its subsidiaries in Scotland, Northern Ireland and the Republic of Ireland, Clydesdale Bank and Northern Bank, to National Australia Bank at the end of 1987. These sales were of a size to make a considerable difference to Midland's capital figure, but there have been many others of banks in the United States, head office buildings in London and assets in the Far East. These transactions had something in common with the retreat to their core business by many industrial companies, but in the case of banks there was the imperative need to fulfil capital adequacy requirements, and the core was often defined in geographical terms.

The next method was the sale of parcels of assets such as house mortgages, hire purchase loans on cars and credit card revolving credit. These were usually sales to independent companies, which issued securities to finance the purchase; the latest form of asset to be securitised in this way is part of the commercial loan book. In all cases the Bank of England has to be satisfied that the bank has divested itself of all risk on the assets. As yet these are new markets, but they could well ease the problems of bank capital in the future. They would have the effect of partially transforming banks from financial intermediaries into little more than brokers and providers of services on the assets that they have sold to third parties. The Bank of England (*Banking Act Report for 1991/92*, p. 10) commented that merchant banks 'continued to shift towards arranging rather than advancing loans', a slightly different method of achieving the same end.

The third main method of reducing the balance sheet total, and hence capital requirements, is to cease to grow, or even to contract. This has been happening to some extent in the last years of the period because banks have reacted to the great increase in provisions and losses by imposing more stringent creditworthiness criteria on their lending. There is another side to this question. Those of us who learned our banking theory in the 1950s or earlier started with the banking multiplier, which related a required reserve ratio to the balance sheet total or to total deposits. In those days the reserves in question were either balances with the central bank or holdings of specified liquid assets, but the multiplier mechanism works with any imposed or conventional ratio between balance sheet items. Capital adequacy has thus replaced the former banking multiplier as the controller of bank growth, and it can also be used by a bank with a given amount of capital to manipulate its capital ratio by varying its rate of growth. It has one considerable disadvantage as a policy weapon in this respect: fresh capital can be obtained from capital issues, so that a bank can continue growing even when its operations do not yield sufficient retained earnings. There is a parallel here with an obligatory liquid assets ratio, under which a bank used to be able to avoid contracting by buying liquid assets from non-bank holders.

There is also another method of improving capital adequacy without increasing the total amount of capital: this consists of increasing holdings of assets with low risk weights at the expense of those with high weights. The most profitable moves for this purpose are from advances, with 100 per cent weighting, into various forms of government bond, which carry zero or very low weighting. Such moves could be only at the margin because no self-respecting bank wants to convert itself into an investment trust holding risk-free assets. Much more promising is an increase of lending for house purchase, which has a weighting of only 50 per cent. We shall see shortly that, in fact, the major banks have tended to move away from the residential mortgage market at the end of the period; the freezing of the housing market provided strong disincentives against following this method of 'capital adequacy without tears'.

OTHER INSTITUTIONS AND MARKETS

The statistics of the major banks have now been milked of virtually all the clues that they offer on the strategy followed by these banks, but further clues can be found in the various lines of business in which they and building societies compete. Some statistics are available, but not sufficient to tell the whole story.

Personal sector

To a great extent the personal sector provided the engine of expansion of the major banks and several others within the Bank of England category of retail banks during the first part of the period, and it was this sector that caused many of the troubles during the second half. The most striking event was the collapse of the housing market, bringing with it mortgage losses and repossessions for the primary lenders, banks and building societies; it also reduced business for insurance companies on the endowment policies and brought losses on many of the mortgage indemnity policies.   Alongside this was the move to repayment of existing consumer debt of other kinds as households tried to reduce the excessive gearing that they had accepted in the previous period of euphoria.   This also affected instalment credit, personal loans and credit cards of both the smaller banks and independent finance houses.

Table 6.9 shows some interesting points concerning the strategy of the major banks.   Their attack to destroy the near-monopoly held by building societies of house purchase finance began in 1982, and they quickly attained a strong position.   In 1987 the banks as a whole provided 40 per cent of the net lending; while remembering that the deduction from gross lending for repayments and redemptions must have been smaller than that of the building societies, we can regard this as an impressive offensive.   Of the 40 per cent provided by banks 68 per cent came from the major banks and about 13 per cent from specialist subsidiaries of banks set up to hold mortgage loans; banks other than the major ones were responsible for 18.5 per cent of the bank total.   In 1988 the total net lending was considerably larger, but the bank proportion fell to 33 per cent.   Thereafter the lending by the major banks and their subsidiaries declined in absolute terms, and by 1990 the other banks (foreign banks and other British banks in the 'retail' category for the most part) actually lent more than the major banks and all bank subsidiaries.   The major banks have not pulled out of the market completely but they have been content to see the building societies regain their dominant position.

Of the other lenders, the miscellaneous institutions, which finance themselves exclusively with wholesale money, dropped out of the market as the retail funds used by the building societies became a cheaper source of finance, and some of them were in difficulties.   The insurance companies and pension funds, which have never been large direct providers of house purchase funds, behaved in much the same way as the major banks.   The largest element in the public sector is local authorities, whose lending was curbed by the government so that they became little more than passive recipients of the repayments of mortgage loans advanced in the 1970s and early 1980s.

In the circumstances of a regime of high interest rates and a declining demand for loans the building societies have indeed bounced back, but in different circumstances the banks may resume their offensive.

Table 6.9   **Net lending for house purchase**

£ billion

Institutions	1986	1987	1988	1989	1990	1991
Building societies	19.43	14.81	23.70	24.00	24.14	20.57
Banks	6.80	11.68	13.24	9.52	7.58	5.51
Major bank groups	4.10	7.94	10.31	4.40	2.44	1.62
Subsidiaries of banks	1.60	1.57	2.33	0.76	1.11	0.60
Other	1.10	2.17	0.60	4.36	3.88	3.29
Misc. institutions	0.97	2.38	2.68	1.78	0.61	1.75
Insurance and pension	0.44	0.77	0.60	0.03	0.15	-0.33
Public sector	-0.46	-0.38	-0.19	-0.53	-0.35	-0.87
Total	**27.18**	**29.26**	**40.03**	**34.80**	**32.02**	**26.63**
Building societies as % of total	*71.49*	*50.62*	*59.21*	*68.97*	*75.05*	*77.24*

Source: British Bankers' Association, *Annual Abstract of Banking Statistics*, vol. 9, Table 6.41 (based on *Financial Statistics*, Table 9.4)

Notes: 1. Miscellaneous financial institutions are mainly mortgage companies, but some lending by bank subsidiaries in the Channel Islands and the Isle of Man that are not in the UK banks sector is included under this heading

2. In the source various adjustments have been made so that the total is slightly different from that shown here

They were first tempted to compete in this and other retail markets in the early 1980s because the international debt crisis robbed them of the booming market in the 1970s for syndicated international loans. The lesson to be drawn about the strategy of the banks is that they are prepared to enter and leave markets in search of quick profits. This mobility is possible because of their large dependence on wholesale funds; the action in the house mortgage market is to some extent a retreat to their core business and core funds in difficult times.

There are no obvious large competitors in the market for other forms of consumer lending because all the big finance houses are subsidiaries of the major banks, and a very high proportion of credit card business (over 80 per cent of the number of cards in issue in 1991) is conducted by them. In the past two years consumers have been more concerned to build up their wealth by saving than in any form of borrowing. Credit cards are a good example of the constant optimism with which the major banks have leapt into forms of competition in a zero-sum game. First of all the four banks that had joined together to issue Access cards broke up the scheme in favour of each bank's issuing both Access (Mastercard) and Visa cards as a prelude to competing by what is known as 'merchant acquiring', in which banks acquire all kinds of cards from retailers instead of just those issued by themselves. Credit cards are also another example of fee income. The first cards were posted broadcast by Barclays Bank in the mid-1970s to customers and non-customers alike, with no charges to holders who paid the full amount outstanding at the end of the month, and the other major banks eventually followed suit. Hesitantly, in 1991 nearly all the bank issuers began to charge an annual fee of between £8 and £12 to cardholders.

Corporate and international banking

What the banks would regard as corporate lending is nowhere distinguished in the statistics, and Table 6.10 depends on certain assumptions about the nature of the lending of the different groups of banks. All the lending of the major British bank groups to industrial and commercial companies is assumed to be corporate, whereas in reality the lending to small and medium-sized companies is partly balanced by 'corporate' lending to some other sectors. The assumption that the lending to the UK private sector of British merchants banks and overseas banks is predominantly corporate is nearer the mark.

There were really no drastic changes in the shares of the various groups of banks in the UK corporate banking market. The share of British banks fell from 57 per cent to 53 per cent, the sharper fall of the major British banks being partly offset by the slight gain of British merchant banks. Within the overseas banks, the share of American banks fell while those of Japanese banks and other overseas banks rose. There is no means of identifying these other overseas banks, but it is a fair bet that they come from countries that have been slow in experiencing the recession.

Table 6.10   Bank advances in sterling to UK corporate borrowers

Type of bank	1986	1987	1988	1989	1990	1991
£ billion						
Major bank groups	33.6	40.2	52.0	64.0	71.8	70.5
British merchant banks	4.9	5.9	7.7	11.5	14.3	14.5
American banks	8.3	9.2	9.8	10.0	10.2	8.3
Japanese banks	3.3	5.0	8.1	13.4	15.7	15.1
Other overseas banks	17.5	25.6	35.5	46.0	53.2	51.7
Total	**67.6**	**85.9**	**113.1**	**144.9**	**165.2**	**160.1**
Percentages of total						
Major bank groups	49.7	46.8	46.0	44.2	43.5	44.0
Total overseas banks	43.0	46.3	47.2	47.9	47.9	46.9

Sources: 1. *Bank of England Quarterly Bulletin*, February issues, Tables 3.2-3.7
2. British Bankers' Association, *Annual Abstract of Banking Statistics*, vol. 9, Table 1.31

Notes: 1. For major bank groups sterling advances to industrial and commercial companies from source (2); for other groups sterling advances to UK private sector from source (1)
2. 1991 figures for major bank groups are for February 1992 from Bank of England press release

   Domestic corporate banking and international banking overlap considerably, and many general trends affect both markets. One such trend is the drop in mergers and acquisitions in the past few years, which had been a strong source of activity in both markets at the end of the 1980s. In 1991 international banking activity fell to a low level, although the international securities market (eurobonds) made up for the drop in banking activity (see Figure 6.4). It seems quite likely that international banking will be the last market to pick up after the end of the recession because it has been suffering a *crise de confiance* ever since the international debt crisis at the beginning of the 1980s. The major British banks may have gone to extreme lengths to retreat back to their core business, the weaker ones selling branches and subsidiaries in foreign countries, but banks everywhere have been very cautious in international banking for a long time. One other factor has been that banks in many countries have been experiencing difficulties at home, those in Scandinavia and Australia having been particularly severe. This has led them to cease encouraging overseas branches and subsidiaries to expand, something that explains some of the trends in Table 6.10, because to the overseas banks the UK corporate banking market represents international banking.

Within the framework of corporate banking one can encompass much of the business of merchant banks. They can be viewed as smaller versions of the major banks because they cover most of the same activities outside retail banking; their fund management business in unit trusts even brings them into the retail financial services market. More of their income comes from fees, and the drop in mergers and acquisitions activity has hit them harder. They are also concerned with securities business, the fees for which depend on turnover and prices in the stock exchange. There are no readily available statistics beyond those shown earlier.

Figure 6.4 presents the information that is available on the international banking and capital markets as a whole, given in an article in the *Bank of England Quarterly Bulletin* (Bank of England 1992, Table A). This covers the whole world, and it remains to disentangle from other information given in the text of the article the part played by banks in the United Kingdom, and particularly by British banks.

The statistics that lie behind Figure 6.4 come fom the Bank for International Settlements and Euroclear as well as from the Bank of England itself. The banking flows are adjusted to exclude the estimated exchange rate effect, and the net total shown by the line in the graph is net of double counting, which ranges from $35 billion in 1991 to $79 billion in 1990. The outstanding feature of the graph is the huge drop in bank lending in 1991, to a point at which it was only around one-half as large as bond issues.

Figure 6.4 Estimated net lending in international markets, 1987-91

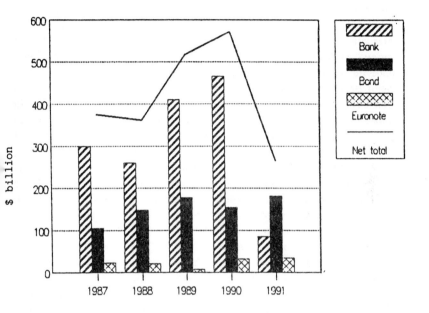

The United Kingdom remains the leading centre for cross-border bank lending (including interbank flows), with 16.3 per cent of the outstanding stock in 1991, a figure which is considerably lower than the 21.8 per cent in 1986. Japan is in second place, with 10.5 per cent in 1986 and 15.1 per cent in 1991, and the United States comes third, dropping from 14.4 per cent in 1986 to 9.4 per cent in 1991. International banking business in London increased up to 1990, but there was a drop of around 3 per cent in 1991.

In terms of international market share of major bank groups in London the British banks, of which the large British banks form a major part, have suffered a fall from 20.6 per cent in 1985 to 15.6 per cent in 1991, after a marginal rise during that year. The Japanese banks remain by far the largest individual nationality group in London; they had a 28.5 per cent share, a slight fall from 32.2 per cent in 1990. The share of American banks in London appeared to grow during 1991, but this was largely because some banks included in their balance sheets the notional principal of cross-country interest rate swaps; excluding these brought the American bank share down from 15 per cent to 10 per cent.

CONCLUSIONS

General

The shape of events during the six years of the period could be described, without too much exaggeration, as a typical 'boom-and-bust' banking cycle. What made it different from earlier periods of this kind was that the events of previous crises overhung this one. The international debt crisis that started in 1982 was the result of a previous banking boom, depending on the delusion that the ability of the Third World not only to absorb syndicated loans but also to service and repay them on time was limitless. Remnants of this debt are still in the portfolios of the banks, although debt swaps and a secondary market have reduced the burden on the major banks. More important was the impetus given to demands for higher capital ratios, culminating in the Basle scheme of 1988. The need to bring these ratios to a higher level and to maintain the level was made more difficult by the heavy domestic provisions caused by the recession of the early 1990s. Because of the previous experience of the recession in the 1980s the provisions were made earlier this time and probably anticipated the losses more fully.

The banking systems of most countries were already fragile when the present recession arrived, but the effects on British banks were particularly great because the recession started earlier than in many other countries, was deeper, and was slower to show signs of ending. If strategy is conceived as a series of plans to conquer new markets and to increase market share in existing ones, no strategy was possible in these circumstances; because of their weakness banks found themselves responding to events instead of taking a leading role. Occasionally the stronger ones made some aggressive gestures, but for the most part it was a strategy of survival. The design of this paper has therefore been to follow each stage of bank operations and to see what response the banks have made.

The future

January 1993 is supposed to be the date on which all hell will break loose and EC banks will scurry busily into each other's countries. The slowness of preparations so far indicates that nothing dramatic is likely to happen; the small and medium countries have concentrated on defence against foreign aggressors by merging their large commercial banks in some cases and by strengthening public sector banks as a bulwark immune to hostile acquisition in others. The large banks in large countries eye each other warily but have not gone much further than forming some tentative alliances. This is not quite what the proposers of the single European market had in mind.

The main reason why no major moves are likely in 1993, or even when the present phase of recovery gives way to a definite upturn in activity, is the undoubted excess capacity in European banking. There are no pockets of excess profitability anywhere to tempt banks to cross borders in a big way; there is no great incentive to invest heavily to enter markets that are already overcrowded, with very narrow margins. Since excess capacity is rarely eliminated in prosperous times, it begins to look as if the boat has been missed for some time ahead: the present troubled times are a period in which excess capacity could have been reduced in the traditional way, by the stronger banks gobbling up those banks that were particularly weak. Midland Bank springs to mind in this context.

This brings us back to the beginning of this paper, where the concept of the universal bank was discussed. The doctrine that large banks must be universal in the sense that they should be in all markets, classified in terms both of services and of geography, has proved to be a pernicious one, and it was largely responsible for the difficulties chronicled here. It was responsible for the over-extension of banks at a time when they were facing an unprecedented level of competition, and many of the new ventures, as well as some old ones, have been pruned in the last few years.

It is not only the concept of the universal bank that is disappearing but also several other fashions of the 1980s, including the dominance of marketing in strategic decisions. In the summer of 1992 many executives and chief executives left the large banks that are retail in their orientation: the two most prominent were marketing experts. There is also a tendency to replace those in high positions with people who have long experience of banking. I have never believed that chief executives are completely transferable from one industry to another. No doubt, there is something that can be called general management ability, but it cannot completely replace knowledge of the particular conditions of each industry, and this is especially true of banking.

The last conclusion of the trends analysed in this paper is that banks are becoming less like financial intermediaries and more like brokers of services, what with asset sales, securitisation, off-balance sheet activities and 'outsourcing'. There is an analogy here with the Cheshire cat of Lewis Carroll's *Alice's Adventures in Wonderland*, which had a huge grin. The body of the cat was wont to disappear, beginning with the end of the tail and leaving the grin for a long while.

> 'Well! I've often seen a cat without a grin', thought Alice; 'but a grin without a cat! It's the most curious thing I ever saw in all my life.'

Even a cursory study of banking history warns of the dangers of assuming that innovations will persist. The present period is beginning to take on some of the characteristics of the 1930s, when the banking crisis came after a bout of competition in the 1920s. As we all know, it was succeeded by a period of strict regulation and enforced specialisation. Even if there is a reaction to the excesses of the past decade, it is unlikely to take exactly the same form, but it may well lead to the disappearance for a while of many of the features charted here; the corporeal cat may reappear, partially at least, until something like the present situation is repeated in the years preceding the next general banking crisis.

LIST OF REFERENCES

Statistical sources

Association of British Insurers, *Insurance Statistics* (annual)

Bank of England, *Banking Act Report* (annual)

Bank of England, *Bank of England Quarterly Bulletin* (quarterly; many banking series now available only in press releases)

British Bankers' Association, *Annual Abstract of Banking Statistics* (annual)

Building Societies Commission, *Annual Report* (annual)

Council of Mortgage Lenders, *Housing Finance Fact Book* (annual)

Other

Bank of England (1992), 'Developments in international banking and capital markets in 1991, *Bank of England Quarterly Bulletin*, **32**, 2 (May), 190-96

Blanden, Michael and Gavin Shreeve (1992), 'UK bank results: all at sea', *The Banker*, **142**, 793 (March), 7-11

Llewellyn, David (1992), 'Bank capital: the strategic issues of the 1990s', *Banking World*, January, pp. 20-25

'Outsourcing grows up' (1992), *The Banker*, 142, 794 (April), 14-17

Robbie, Malcolm and Paul de Hoest (1992), 'Bank profits in the 1990s', *Banking World*, April, pp. 14-15

PART III

BANK REGULATION AND CRISES

CHAPTER 7
LIQUIDITY MANAGEMENT AND LENDER-OF-LAST-RESORT FUNCTIONS: RECENT DEVELOPMENTS IN THE ITALIAN BANKING SYSTEM

Francesco Cesarini

INTRODUCTION

In a paper presented in March 1989 at a meeting held in Perugia in which the instruments for safeguarding the stability of the financial system were debated[1], I expressed the view that, while the functioning of money markets and the precision of tools for monetary control had been greatly ameliorated, paradoxically no significant improvement had been achieved in instruments aimed at direct channelling of lender-of-last-resort funds to banks which experience temporary and intense liquidity stresses. This situation, which appears to be particularly harmful in the case of banks which are submitted to reorganisation procedures under the supervision of regulatory authorities, was to be attributed to the survival of an outdated and rigid legislation governing the eligibility of assets to be acquired by the Bank of Italy as collateral to refinancing operations on a bilateral basis, and it was sharply in contrast with the continuous refinement of the instruments which monetary authorities can negotiate in open markets for purposes of monetary control.

In my contribution to this seminar, I will argue that the process through which bilateral relationships between individual banks and the central bank are diverted into impersonal market dealings has continued, notwithstanding the fact that some additional important modifications have been made to the traditional instruments. In reviewing such changes, I will also suggest that it would be dangerous if benefits thereupon accruing, from the point of view of the accuracy and the autonomy of monetary management at the macroeconomic level, should be obtained at the cost of reducing the ability of the system to safeguard the viability of otherwise solvent individual credit institutions, which do not hold in their portfolios sufficient eligible assets to sell or pledge to the central bank.

CENTRAL BANK REFINANCING OPERATIONS

Changes in reserve requirement regulations

The nature and importance of Bank of Italy loans to credit institutions that can be considered to come under the heading of 'refinancing operations' are shown in Table 7.1 in terms of outstanding loans at year-end and as average daily figures in Table 7.2.

As a background to the discussion, I will recall that since 1985 outstanding loans of Italian banks have increased at a pace significantly faster than customer deposits.   The phenomenon has become more pronounced during the last three years, when the growth of loans was two to three times larger than the corresponding increase in deposits and, thus, the loan-to-deposits ratio went up by five percentage points

Table 7.1 Refinancing operations of the Bank of Italy: year-end data

Billion lire

	1986	1987	1988	1989	1990
Rediscounting of agricultural bills	238.1	306.6	426.2	351.7	352.1
Current account advances on securities	1,857.7	3,612.9	4,005.7	3,609.8	3,977.1
. ordinary	1,857.7	1,561.1	1,924.2	2,154.8	2,522.1
. according to Treasury Decree 27 Sept. 1974	-	2,051.8	2,081.5	1,455.0	1,455.0
Fixed-maturity advances on securities	1,534.3	-	10.0	1,388.5	2,637.9
	3,730.1	3,919.5	4,441.9	5,350.0	6,967.1

Source: Banca d'Italia, *Relazione Anno 1987*, p. 23; (1988) p. 24; (1989) p. 24; (1990) p. 24

Table 7.2 Refinancing operations of the Bank of Italy: daily averages

Billion lire

	1987	1988	1989	1990
Rediscounting of agricultural bills	303	324	315	347
Current account advances	1,117	1,242	1,119	1,041
Fixed-maturity advances				
. daily average	300	419	367	444
. aggregate number in the year	...	...	158	136
. aggregate amount	...	...	45,692	48,815

Source: Banca d'Italia

each year, reaching a peak level of 63 per cent at the end of 1990[2]. The expansion of customer loans was partially financed by a concomitant reduction in the aggregate amount of the securities portfolio held by banks, which went down by 2.1 and 5.6 per cent in 1989 and in 1990; the ratio of investment securities to aggregate credit assets has thus diminished from 44.8 per cent at the end of 1987 to 30.1 per cent at the end of 1990, and its reduction was much more substantial - over sixteen percentage points - in the group of the largest banks[3].

The evolution of customer deposits has produced a marked increase in the amount of compulsory reserves that banks keep with the Bank of Italy: for the entire banking system at the end of 1990, they amounted to 18.12 per cent of total deposits as against 17.4 per cent at the end of 1986. Notwithstanding the large expansion of capital funds, which act in the sense of reducing required reserves, a large number of banks must at present meet their reserve requirements at the average rate of 22.5 per cent of monthly increases in their deposits. On account of these developments, the implicit cost of compulsory reserve requirements has remained high and banks are striving to reduce it, either by better liquidity management or by collecting funds in forms which may lessen the burden of such reserves such as certificates of deposit, repurchase agreements and also the issue of convertible bonds and subordinated debentures, which were recently authorised and exempted from reserve requirements.

The concern for the economic impact of reserve requirements, and for the consequent cost disadvantage that Italian banks must face in respect of their EC competitors in the Single European Market, is one of the reasons which have brought monetary authorities to innovate their regulations in the sense of permitting banks to mobilise a small percentage of required reserves during the reference period. As is known, the mobilisation is allowed up to a maximum of 3 per cent of aggregate required reserves of each bank - a percentage which will be pushed up to the legally authorised ceiling of 5 per cent as from 15 October 1991 - and it is technically conceived in such a way as to allow the bank to compensate deficit with excess reserves held at the central bank, provided that it fully meets its obligation, computed as an average of daily data, for the whole one-month reference period. On the other hand, a deficiency in reserves is heavily discouraged by imposing the payment of a penalty rate of interest (official rediscount rate plus 5 points) for a period of thirty days; excess reserves, however, cannot be carried over to the following reference period and would earn a bare 0.5 per cent interest rate.

The mobilisation of required reserves - as well as the creation of the wholesale market for government securities and of the more recent telematic market for interbank transactions - is aimed at strengthening two of the three traditional functions of central bank refinancing activity: namely, to aid the implementation of monetary policy and to ensure the smooth functioning of the payments system. As a matter of fact, the reform of the mechanisms of compulsory reserve requirements has undoubtedly increased the number and the volume of transactions in the market for interbank deposits, and particularly it has favoured a sharp reduction in the volatility of the corresponding interest rates, which have consequently become a better indicator of liquidity conditions for the entire banking system. From the point of view of individual banks, the innovation has increased the ability of facing short-lived tensions in their liquidity position by increasing the number and quality of alternative choices available to bank treasurers and may even lessen, although in a very marginal way, the economic burden connected with compulsory reserve requirements[4], provided that the treasurer anticipates correctly short-term interest rate movements during the reference period.

Such favourable effects are enhanced by the circumstance that the credit-debit relationships of an individual bank with the Bank of Italy are now channelled into a single account, on which movements can be imputed through telematic techniques and on which registration is made also of credit and debit movements generated by the participation to a more generalised and efficient clearing system operated by the Bank of Italy itself. More specifically the refinancing account, the deposit account and the compulsory reserve account have been merged so that, at each moment in time, a single debit or credit balance synthesises the position of an individual bank with the Bank of Italy. Other things being equal, economies in the use of central bank money can be obtained both at the microeconomic and at the macroeconomic level.

However, the beneficial effects of the above-mentioned changes in reserve requirement regulations, from the point of view of the management of the liquidity position of banks, will be partially offset by a concomitant reduction in the aggregate amount of central bank funds that are made available to most banks through the current account advances that the Bank of Italy usually grants (and renews regularly at the expiration of each four-month maturity) upon pledge of eligible government securities. It is perhaps useful to remember that the technical nature of this instrument is strictly similar to the refinancing potential intrinsically connected with the mobilisation of required reserves, in that the initiative of drawing funds from the Bank of Italy - obviously within the limits of the agreed maximum amount - is fully under the control of each bank. The amounts involved are also closely similar: the credit facilities granted by the Bank of Italy in the form of current account advances averaged around 4,000 billion lire in the period 1986-1990, while the refinancing potential of the reserve mobilisation scheme (at the present level of 3 per cent) is estimated at about 3,600 billion lire.

In order to keep largely unaltered the aggregate amount of central bank credit immediately and unconditionally available to banks - a policy goal which was made explicit when the changes in reserve requirement regulations were first announced[5] - the Bank of Italy, with a decision taking effect on 1 September 1991, has doubled - lifting it from 0.15 to 0.30 per cent - the amount of the front-end fee, calculated on a flat basis on the entire amount of the agreed line of credit, which banks must pay every four months at the time of renewal of the advance. Given the economic impact of this particular cost element of the operation[6], it can be easily expected that banks will not ask for increases, and possibly will negotiate reductions, of the advances outstanding; concomitantly, the central bank will probably use its totally discretionary powers in the management of this instrument for refusing applications, if any, for higher amounts of financing[7]. The importance of this refinancing instrument is thus bound to decrease, and we may also consider it a realistic forecast that in the future the Bank of Italy will discourage the use of this instrument, while not entirely cancelling it from its formal set of policy instruments.

If the above developments are considered from the point of view of their impact on the third function of central bank refinancing instruments - namely, the provision of funds to individual banks hit by a financial crisis - they would *prima facie* appear quantitatively neutral. I would underline, however, that a bilateral instrument involving a negotiated relationship between an individual bank and the Bank of Italy will be gradually replaced by a more impersonal, less informative and somewhat automatic link, which may turn out to be less conducive to an efficient management of central bank functions in coping with crisis situations.

Fixed-maturity advances

Significant innovations have been recently introduced also with reference to fixed-maturity advances, the other important bilateral refinancing instrument at present adopted by Italian monetary authorities but, once again, their impact is to be found exclusively in the area of liquidity management and of monetary policy tools without any noticeable effect from the point of view of the lender-of-last-resort functions *sensu stricto* considered.

As is known, such operations, which are also to be collateralised by the pledge of eligible government securities having a large and deep secondary market, are granted by the Bank of Italy on a wholly discretionary basis for very short maturities (usually agreed upon with the applicant bank), and only when it has been ascertained that the applicant bank has exploited fully any other fund-raising possibilities existing in the market at the time of the application (usually just before the closing of daily compensations at the interbank clearing system supervised by the Bank of Italy). Given their nature and functions, fixed-maturity advances are usually granted to large banks and for relatively large amounts (their minimum size is 25 billion) exclusively in tight money situations: it may be recalled, for instance (Tables 7.1 and 7.2), that in 1990 the Bank of Italy extended 136 refinancing operations of this type for a cumulative amount of 48,815 billion lire and an average daily amount of 444 billion; at the end of the year they stood at 2,637.9 billion lire as against current account advances outstanding for 2,522.1 billion. (The corresponding figures at the end of 1989 were 2,154.8 and 1,388.5 billion respectively[8].)

The innovations introduced with the Decree of the Ministry of the Treasury of 12 May 1991 allow for a more frequent, flexible and cheaper use of this facility since it abolished the penalty rates imposed on banks which resort to this operation within a short interval of the reimbursement of the advance previously obtained (+2.25, +1.25, and +0.5 percentage points over the official discount rate when the above mentioned interval was respectively less than 5, 15 or 30 days).

In addition, and more importantly, the interest rate to be applied to this type of advance will be established autonomously by the Bank of Italy, which has been granted discretionary powers to exceed the official rediscount rate by an amount no higher than 1.75 percentage points. As such a rate must be applied to all applicant banks, irrespective of the frequency with which they resort to fixed-maturity advances, the innovation entails the elimination of the penalty nature of the rate itself and an actual cost advantage for the banks which are more dependent on central bank financing in the management of their daily liquidity position. At the same time, the rate becomes an instrument that can be used more readily, precisely and continuously by the central bank in order to influence monetary conditions and the evolution of market interest rates, thus partially offsetting the rigidities resulting from the procedures which the law requires for the modification of the official rediscount rate[9]. It may be added that the possibility of establishing and changing the rate on fixed maturity advances in a substantially autonomous way may increase the efficiency of open market operations which the Bank of Italy usually conducts in the form of repurchase agreements or reverse repos allotted to financial and credit institutions through auctions.

The increasing sophistication of refinancing operations must not lead to the neglect of the fact that the volume of assets eligible as collateral for such operations - that is government securities - is gradually becoming scarce, and that such assets are usually not available for banks which are facing financial difficulties. In fact, a bank which is confronted with this sort of problem will probably have exhausted its portfolio of eligible paper and will hold only less marketable and non-eligible assets; consequently it will not technically be in the position to apply for financial assistance from the Bank of Italy through the standard refinancing operations.

Paradoxically, the ability of such a bank to buy needed liquidity flows in the interbank market may have been weakened by the application and the enforcement of minimum capital ratios, and by the more refined disclosure and reporting rules imposed on banks in the new regulatory climate. As a matter of fact, the non-compliance with minimum capital ratios or the impairment of the position of the bank in respect of them is information (or an implicit rating) which is likely to become promptly known to the market and which might reduce or completely cancel the possibility of obtaining interbank credit - which is usually unsecured - or of obtaining it on reasonable conditions. This situation can be considered a collateral consequence of the otherwise positive influence engendered by the market discipline which has been fostered by the introduction of capital ratios. Such consequences may prove to be of vital importance, especially for smaller banks, in a period in which the increasing competition and the liberalisation of structural regulations (for example, rules on branching) are likely to combine in taxing their ability to remain in the market.

LENDER-OF-LAST-RESORT OPERATIONS

Interbank Deposit Guarantee Fund

Apart from the availability of eligible assets - which may become a problem in itself, if the present trends in the level and composition of bank portfolios persist - the severance of direct bilateral credit relationships between the Bank of Italy and individual banks or, more precisely, their increasing degree of impersonality and automatism, needs to be taken into proper consideration by regulatory authorities and by the legislator in order to avoid a loss of efficiency in the management of crisis situations.

The intervention of the recently formed Interbank Deposit Guarantee Fund is, in my opinion, only a partial and scarcely efficient answer to the kind of liquidity problems that I have tried to illustrate. The institutional purpose of the Fund is, in fact, to pay off the depositors of an insolvent bank according to an established set of rules and, by so doing, to co-operate with the central bank in preventing the spread of panic and any loss of confidence in the banking system on the part of bank customers.

The possibility of granting financial assistance to banks which have been submitted to a reorganisation procedure under the control of regulatory authorities must be considered as an ancillary instrument which has been attributed to the Fund probably because the institutional and legal setting of central bank refinancing operations was considered to be inadequate to such situations but could not be amended easily and rapidly.

As a matter of fact, the Interbank Deposit Guarantee Fund has been called upon to give rather important financial aid to Cassa di Risparmio di Prato, but the credit operation has had to be transformed into an acquisition from which the Fund finds it hard to disentangle itself, partly on account of conflicts of interest arising from its peculiar position.

Even when the bank involved is smaller in size, the Fund may be at a disadvantage in providing prompt assistance because it does not hold directly a large amount of liquid funds but has to procure them from its member banks by calling on the unused portion of their commitments. The procedure is time-consuming and may turn out to be inconsistent with the urgency of the liquidity needs of the bank involved.

Finally, it goes without saying that it would not be legitimate for the Fund to grant financial assistance to banks which, although illiquid, continue to operate in the market. The only institution which can independently decide to give lender-of-last-resort assistance in such cases is, in my opinion, the central bank and it must do so only if such assistance is consistent with, and conducive to, important policy goals such as the stability of the banking system, the prevention of financial panic and, eventually, the preservation of a financial institution which can be considered both solvent and important to a particular area. If these public policy goals are not relevant in the specific case, the alternative course of action which the central bank should follow would be to steer the problem bank into control by another bank, either through a merger *sensu stricto* or through the sale of its assets and liabilities, a procedure specifically contemplated by the Italian banking law and widely used in practice. In either case it usually takes some time for the deal to be negotiated, and, therefore, the system needs readily usable and efficient lender-of-last-resort instruments which may prevent the illiquidity situation from deteriorating into insolvency.

Need for legislation

As I illustrated at length in my 1989 paper, the legal and technical rules governing lender-of-last-resort operations of the Bank of Italy considered *sensu stricto* are outdated and wholly inadequate. Not only have the rediscounting facilities changed into a mechanism designed to transmit interest rate subsidies to farmers, but the list of eligible assets, which dates back to legislation approved in 1910, comprises *de facto* only government securities, an asset that typically will already have been depleted when a bank is facing serious liquidity problems.

In the past, the lack of flexible official central bank instruments made it necessary to find *ad hoc* solutions in order to inject important liquidity flows into large banks: for example, the intervention of a government-controlled financial institution to rescue IMI in 1981[10] and the provision of long-term funds to Banca Nazionale del Lavoro in 1989, which was effected by having subordinated bonds placed in the portfolio of an insurance company under government control. More frequently, regulatory authorities had to resort to advances extended at a low rate of interest according to Ministerial Decree 27 September 1974 (the so-called Sindona decree)[11], an *ex post* intervention which compensates for the losses incurred by the institutions called upon by the Bank of Italy in the rescue operation and which entails the liquidation of the bank. Any change towards making lender-of-last-resort techniques less rigid and more adequate to the actual conditions of the banking market requires a change in legislation.

In my opinion there are at least two opportunities of which regulatory authorities should try to avail themselves in an effort to push new legislative rules through Parliament. The first one is the preparation of a unified text of banking legislation which the Governor of the Bank of Italy considers necessary upon introduction of the Second Banking Co-ordination Directive[12]; the second opportunity, and perhaps the one technically more appropriate and nearer in time, is the presentation of the bill designed to give the Bank of Italy full and direct authority over the official rediscount rate.

As for the content of such legislative reform, I am still of the opinion that it should consistently enlarge the list of eligible assets to be pledged or sold to the central bank; that it should reinforce bilateral relationships, thus counteracting their gradual transformation into impersonal and automatic market dealings; and that it should give the Bank of Italy specific discretionary powers to mobilise in full the required reserves held with it by illiquid banks. I consider that the prudential aspects of this instrument of monetary control - given its high quantitative importance and its economic burden to banks - would deserve a reconsideration and could be appropriately used as a first line of defence in the event of a liquidity crisis, which is to be managed under the supervision of regulatory authorities.

NOTES

1. F. Cesarini, 'Crisi e strumenti di intervento finanziario: il credito di ultima istanza' in M.T. Cirenei and G.C.De Martin, *Il Sistema Creditizio nella Prospettiva del Mercato Unico Europeo*, Milano 1990, pp. 141-56.
2. Banca d'Italia, *Relazione Annuale 1990*, p. 165.
3. Banca d'Italia, *Relazione Annuale 1990*, pp. 192-93.
4. A more substantial reduction in the economic impact of reserve requirements is expected to occur via a reduction of the amount of required reserves following the addition to bank capital funds, contemplated by Law Amato and Law Formica, of large revaluation reserves.
5. Banca d'Italia, *La Mobilizzazione della Riserva Obbligatoria: Motivazioni e Implicazioni*, Roma, ottobre 1988.
6. A. Patarnello, 'Obiettivi monetari ed aspetti aziendali della nuova anticipazione ordinaria' in *Banche e Banchieri*, no. 7-8, luglio-agosto 1985, discusses at length the structure of the current account advance and the impact of the commission fee.
7. It is interesting to note that recently special credit institutions have been granted access to this form of refinancing in concomitance with their admission to the clearing mechanisms operated by the Bank of Italy, a development which confirms that the prominent function of current account advances is that of smoothing temporary liquidity imbalances.
8. Banca d'Italia, *Relazione Annuale 1990*, pp. 4 & 24.
9. A bill aimed at attributing directly and exclusively to the Bank of Italy the power of modifying the official rediscount rate was approved by the government in July 1991, and was subsequently enacted as Law no. 82 of 7 February 1992.
10. Being a special credit institution, IMI (Istituto Mobiliare Italiano) was not (and is not) entitled to have access to central bank loan facilities which the legislation in force restricts to banks. Only recently, as a collateral effect of their admission to Bank of Italy clearing facilities, special credit institutions have been given the possibility of applying for current account advances.
11. The outstanding figure at the end of 1990 amounts to about three-fifths of ordinary current account advances (Table 7.1).
12. C.A. Ciampi, *Considerazioni Finali Anno 1990*, p. 28.

CHAPTER 8
ECONOMIES OF DIVERSIFICATION AND CONFLICTS OF INTEREST: THE EFFECTS OF THE NEW REGULATION IN ITALY

Elisabetta Gualandri and Andrea Landi

INTRODUCTION

No-one would deny that the diversification of the activities of the commercial banks was one of the most important processes which marked the development of the main financial and banking systems during the 1980s. It can be considered as the result of a convergence, which has matured during the last few years, between the aims of supervisory authorities and the objectives pursued by the commercial banks themselves. In the banks' view, the diversification of their activities was the strategy which would allow them to increase their intermediation volumes and convert the resulting enlargement of the range of products offered into a reduction in costs and an increase in profitability. This was the policy which the commercial banks in the leading countries were virtually forced to adopt in a situation which has seen a rapid growth in the securities markets and a drop in traditional intermediation. For the authorities, functional despecialisation and competition between the various categories of intermediaries seemed to be the essential preconditions for a reduction in the rents in the various markets of the financial system and for an increase in the welfare of the consumers of financial services.

At the same time, the awareness that the diversification of commercial banks into the securities industry was bound to accentuate the problems relating to the concentration and stability of banking institutions and of the financial system led to a rapid adaptation of the regulations covering the operation of the markets, the rules governing banking conduct, and control of the credit and financial risks at the level of both individual operators and financial conglomerates. The authorities in the main European systems (the United Kingdom and France first of all) have been moving in this direction for some time.

In Italy the laws introduced during the last years have established a new set of regulations for the activity of commercial banks, bringing in new rules on the following subjects:
- the functioning of the securities market and the operations of financial intermediaries which operate on these markets (law no. 1/91)

144

- supervision at the level of bank holding companies (law no. 218/90 and decree-law no. 356/90)
- acquisition of dominant positions by banks or financial conglomerates (law no. 297/90 - Antitrust Law)
- relations between banking and commerce (Antitrust Law)

The combination of these laws will have important effects on the contents and methods of the diversification programmes of Italian commercial banks. The extent to which the banks and securities markets may come to complement each other in financing the Italian economy, the existence of an optimal organisational model for the management of this complementarity, and the economic importance which financial conglomerates may assume in our financial system are some of the main questions brought up by the changes in Italian legislation. Naturally, the aim of this paper is not to provide an exhaustive answer to questions of such theoretical and institutional importance. Our more limited aim is to focus our attention on the aspects concerning the question of information flows from the point of view of the intermediaries, factors which are dealt with explicitly in the measures to regulate the markets and financial conglomerates and which are also indirectly affected by the rules governing the relations between banking and industry.

The initial assumption of our analysis is that the scope economies which banks achieve in the management of information may be even more important than economies in operating costs, constituting the factor of greatest competitive advantage for the financial conglomerate which combines credit activity with operations in the various sectors of the securities industry. At the same time, economies on the information side and, thus, the exploitation by the intermediary of an asymmetry of information between the issuer and the investor, create the situation where an abuse of this position at the client's expense is possible.

The economies which can be made in the management of information and the conflicts of interest which may arise from a situation of information asymmetry must, therefore, be interpreted as opposing extremes; the task of ensuring an equilibrium between them is related to the combination of the efficiency and the stability of the intermediaries and the financial system chosen by authorities. The result is that the solutions offered by the authorities with a view to striking a balance between economies of scale concerning information and investor protection are destined to have a large degree of influence on the operational and organisational decisions of the various financial intermediaries, and on the competitive advantages of the financial conglomerate over the specialised intermediary.

This paper is divided into three parts. The first part specifies the advantages of information deriving from the combination of traditional intermediation with activities of the securities industry: in view of these advantages, we then identify the types of conflicts of interest which may arise within services typical of the securities industry, whether offered by securities operators or commercial banks dealing in securities. The second part provides an assessment of the philosophy of intervention by authorities in other countries (with special reference to the United Kingdom) on the subject of the conflict of interest, highlighting the implications of a management nature which these measures involve. The third section specifies the way in which the Italian authorities have tackled the problem of the trade-off between economies of information and conflicts of interest in the legislation introduced in 1991. Special attention is paid to the contents of the law which regulates the new securities operators, *società di intermediazione mobiliare*, or Sim, with the aim of defining the degrees of independence granted to them in the management of information flows.

The conclusions point out some probable effects of these measures on the operational and organisational strategies of the various financial intermediaries, and on the potential competitive advantages deriving from the diversification of the activity of commercial banks into securities industry services.

ECONOMIES OF INFORMATION AND CONFLICTS OF INTEREST

The advantages in terms of information

Economies of information are referred to in the literature on the existence and the role of financial intermediaries as one of the main factors which motivates diversification and the establishment of large financial conglomerates (see Herring and Santomero 1991; Landi 1991). The advantage of diversification derives in this case from the fact that information on clients collected within the conglomerate's individual operating areas (divisions or affiliates) is distributed to the bank's other divisions or affiliates, resulting in a lower unit cost for the acquisition of information compared to an independent company specialising in a single activity.

As far as the commercial bank operating in the securities industry is concerned, the types of economies of information can be classified in relation to the category of customers with which the bank is dealing:

companies on the one hand and investors or depositors on the other. In the financing and consultancy services which it provides to firms the bank could use the information acquired through the assessment and monitoring procedures related to loan operations or its work as a consultant for operations of corporate finance, either directly or through securities affiliates. The asymmetry of information between the issuer and new investors would be reduced by the guarantee provided by a third party, the bank, that the value of the securities is a true reflection of the company's soundness and the quality of its investment projects. The costs incurred by the bank for the acquisition of information as part of the credit operation would also be distributed to the department which manages the placement of securities, with a favourable effect on the prices of issue. The function of guaranteeing the quality of the issuer could also be reinforced, not only by the undertaking with regard to the bank loan, but also by the existence of a shareholding relationship between the bank and the issuing company. In this sense, the problem of the equity separation between banking and commerce interlinks with that concerning economies of information and the risk of conflicts of interest.

Generally, a correspondence can be established between the intensity of the asymmetry of information and the bank's involvement as lender or securities broker. The stronger the demand for a guarantee offered by a third party about the quality of the issuer, the more the investors will appreciate the function of assessment and monitoring provided by the bank through the bank loan or direct holdings in the company's equity (see Stiglitz and Weiss 1988; Stiglitz 1985; Cable 1985).

In the relationships with the clientele of investors and depositors, the main advantages in terms of information which arise from the diversification of commercial banks into the securities industry include the possibility of offering depositors a consultancy service about the securities handled or sold by the bank itself for one of its affiliates. To this advisory service we may add the asset management service. In this case the acquisition of information in the relationship with the issuing company also works to the advantage of the company or division which operates in the advisory or asset management activity.

The above comments on the bank's role as guarantor of the quality of securities allow us to emphasise the existence of two types of asymmetry of information. The first type concerns the issuers and the investors, specifically the fact that the former have more information about the degree of correspondence between the value of the security and the value of the firm than the latter. The second type concerns the information acquired by the bank. The fact that the bank is entrusted with assessing the quality of the firm and the securities which it issues implies the acquisition of information to which the investor does not have direct access. For the latter, the need therefore arises for a system of incentives and controls which induce the bank to give priority to the interests of the client, thus reducing the area of possible conflicts of interest between the agent and the investor, or between clients of the same bank.

As we will see in greater depth during our examination of the regulations governing the markets and securities markets, the distinction between the two types of information asymmetries also becomes important in classifying the type of measures which the authorities can introduce to reduce the asymmetry of information working against the investors. Thus, while for the first type of asymmetry, the authorities' measures are intended to aid investors by ensuring more access to relevant information, in the second type, the authorities are concerned not so much with the investor's access to information as with the behaviour of the agent and the elimination of a conflict of interest between the two parties.

The types of conflicts of interest

The appearance of conflicts of interest and the consequent need to safeguard investors derives from the special agency relationship established between the agent (financial intermediary) and the principal (investor). The existence of imbalances of information on the financial markets allows the agent, whose objective function differs from that of the principal, to exploit his position and take advantage of the latter.

One definition of conflicts which we consider especially succinct is that provided by R. Pennington (1986):

> The underlying principle of equity is that a person who acts as a representative of another is in a conflict of interest situation if, either at the time when he accepts appointments or subsequently while he acts as a representative, there is a material interest of his own or a third person for whom he also acts, and the pursuit or protection of that interest would create a substantial risk that he might not act in the best way to pursue or protect the interest of the person he represents.

This provides an exhaustive definition of the main cause of the development of conflicts of interest, and thus of behaviour damaging to clients, on the part of financial intermediaries working in the securities industry. It is clear, however, that both the clients of the securities house and the clients/depositors of commercial banks which extend their fields of activity into the securities industry are at risk, either directly or indirectly through subsidiaries. It is important to emphasise that in this case the potential damage to the depositor derives not only from impartial consultancy activities, but also from the risk that the bank may engage in activities which endanger its own safety and soundness. Therefore, in this case, the appearance of conflicts of interest not only concerns the problem of safeguarding the principal, but also involves the need to safeguard the depositor as such, thus also bringing in the problem of bank stability.

Passing on to an analysis of the specific field of operations of the securities industry, various types of conflicts of interest emerge, each tending to increase as the numbers of types of activity engaged in rise, and in proportion to the presence of a commercial bank as holding company parent or affiliate. If we apply a classification on the basis of the types of operators involved, we can identify the following five categories, to which all kinds of conflicts of interest belong (see Saunders 1985; Goode 1986; Robertson 1987; Cavazzuti 1989; Sabani and Sapienza 1990):

1. shareholders versus clients
2. client versus client
3. client versus house
4. client versus staff
5. staff versus house

1. *Shareholders versus clients.* In this case, the conflicts of interest emerge when the intermediary is a captive of its controlling shareholder(s) and this situation therefore gives rise, at an operational level, to behaviour damaging to clients and possibly also to the other shareholders. One example is the case where, as part of client investment management, or even as part of the management of its own portfolio, the bank places securities issued by its own majority shareholders, or its subsidiaries, at prices not favourable to those who underwrite them. The same possibility also arises in consultancy services.

2. *Client versus client.* This type of conflict refers, for example, to the case in which the intermediary is required to act as consultant for two clients with conflicting interests. We might take the case where

the corporate finance sector is acting, on behalf of a client, as consultant in a takeover operation at the expense of a company for which another sector is acting as stockbroker adviser. In this case we have a clear problem of professional deontology, the solution to which must depend on the bank's decision about the client for which it intends to continue to act as adviser on the basis of considerations about the customer relationship.

3. *Client versus house.* There is no doubt that this category of conflicts of interest is the largest. First of all, this type of conflict arises when a group section or company works in an agency capacity on behalf of a client, while another section works in a principal capacity, that is on behalf of the bank itself. Note that in some cases, in contrast with the usual situation, the conflict of interest which arises may damage the agent to the client's advantage. We may consider the case when the fund management arm or broking section knows values in the firm's market-making books which can work to the client's advantage at the intermediary's expense. It is clear that in this case the objective function of the fund management arm predominates over the global objective of the house. This may arise in a situation where there is a strong corporate spirit and a high level of competition between the teams in the various sectors, especially where high revenue targets are set for the various areas.

The opposite case occurs when the market-maker takes advantage of confidential information obtained from the corporate finance department, thus positioning its portfolio, in terms of the type of securities held and the prices, in such a way as to influence the market trend. Depending on whether the market-maker is buying or selling, and the size of the transaction, this may be damaging to the corporate finance client or to investors in general. It is also clear that this type of behaviour may lead to the crime of insider trading. Another typical case is when conflict arises from the agent's role as fund management adviser, which may be used to his own advantage instead of on the client's benefit. There are various possibilities of this kind: first of all, securities may be added to the fund under management (or the client may be advised to purchase them) not because they are considered advantageous for the client on the basis of the issuer's performance, but because the market-maker holds large numbers of these securities and it is difficult to place them on the market. Another case is where the commercial banks use the placing power of one of their subsidiaries for debt restructuring operations, in other words, in order to convert risky loans into securities issues, thus transferring the risk to the issuer's present and future shareholders or bondholders. The appearance of the conflict of interest is linked to the risk that the pricing of the issues may not take into consideration important financial information about the issuer.

So far we have considered examples where the conflict of interest arises from asymmetries of information, mainly between the investor/client and the issuer. We must not overlook the conflict which arises from non-competitive markets which, in this case, takes the form of the so-called economic 'ties-in', in other words, the joint sale of a number of services. In this case the client cannot take advantage of more favourable terms offered by other houses for some of these services. We should also remember the possibility that in asset management activity the tendency is to increase the turnover of operations in order to increase commissions, rather than to exploit the opportunities offered by the market to the client's advantage. This practice is known as 'churning'.

Other types of conflict of interest are those which involve the depositor in relation to the increased level of risk and/or reduced profitability of the commercial bank, as a result of the bank's involvement in the securities industry. We can take the example of loans granted at low interest rates in order to support the prices of securities which a subsidiary is responsible for placing. In another scenario loans are granted in order to shore up the poor financial situation of a company whose securities have been placed. Finally, the bank may increase the degree of leverage of affiliates working in the securities industry by granting loans at favourable interest rates.

4. *Client versus staff.* This type of conflict emerges if the staff do not give top priority to the clients' orders but make use of their information on the size and direction of these orders. This type of conflict may lead to the abuse of price-sensitive information and, thus, give rise to insider trading. Another example of this type of conflict of interest is the possibility of staff taking precedence over clients in the underwriting of securities placed by the house.

5. *Staff versus house.* This occurs when the staff use information, for example, about the market-maker books, to their own advantage at the expense, not of the clients, but of the house itself.

In short, from the above analysis it can be seen that the potential victims of the most important category of conflicts are clients in the asset management arm. However, we should not underestimate the fact that conflicts of interest may also arise within the area of corporate finance when the agent is required to act as adviser for two companies with opposing interests. Finally, it should be remembered that if a commercial bank is also active in the securities industry, the depositor is potentially at risk from damaging behaviour, both in his capacity as client/investor and because of the special relationship which links him to the bank with respect to its soundness.

CONFLICTS OF INTEREST AND INVESTOR SAFEGUARDS IN SOME FOREIGN CONTEXTS

The importance of conflicts of interest

Deregulation during the 1980s contributed to an increase in the attention paid to conflicts of interest by the regulatory bodies with reference to the problem of investor safeguards, even if a different emphasis was given in the various institutional contexts with regard to the degree of development of the financial industry, the structure of the systems and the operating practices adopted. It therefore seems appropriate, before illustrating the Italian situation, to provide a brief analysis of the development of this theme in other contexts, with special reference to the United Kingdom, which is certainly the most interesting and important case.

From a general point of view, the strategy of diversification pursued by various banks during the last decade, and especially the entry of the commercial banks into the securities industry, are the factors which have most accentuated the problem of conflicts of interest. In fact, the risk of such conflicts is greater in financial conglomerates than in a specialised bank since the behaviour damaging to the client by a single operating arm may arise, not only from the direct benefits to the latter, but also from an advantage to the house as a whole. In this case, we are faced with a complex target function to which the aims of the individual operating sections are subordinated (see Sabani and Sapienza 1990).

The problem of safeguarding investors against conflicts of interest has very strong historical roots in countries where for years the most noticeable feature has been the separation between various types of financial intermediaries. We are referring to the cases of the United Kingdom and the United States, where the aim of safeguarding consumers has been interlinked historically with regulations governing the specialisation of intermediaries. In the United Kingdom the formulation of the principle of single capacity, meaning the rigid separation between the roles of dealer and broker, at the beginning of this century arose in part from the need to introduce elements which would safeguard investors against the emergence of conflicts of interest[1]. Moreover, in the United Kingdom merchant banking has traditionally been separate from commercial banking. It was only in the 1970s that the clearing banks started to dabble in merchant banking, and they still maintained separate management by establishing *ad hoc* companies or taking over existing operators, thus forming the core of today's financial conglomerates.

In the United States, one of the aims of Congress in launching the Glass Steagall Act, which introduced the separation between commercial banking and investment banking in 1933, was to safeguard clients' interests. We should not forget the large amount of fact-finding activity carried out in the early 1930s in the US Congress on this subject, including the Pecora Hearings in 1933 and 1934, in preparation for the Glass Steagall Act (see Benston 1990). The same type of concern also led to the 1956 Bank Holding Act, which established the separation between investment banking and commerce.

In the United Kingdom itself the interest in this subject has been reinforced in recent years, giving rise to a much wider debate than in other European countries. The reason definitely lies first of all with the abolition of single capacity with the 1986 Big Bang, and the accompanying introduction of dual capacity, which permits securities firms to work as both brokers and dealers. A second factor is the general process of deregulation which has affected the financial markets, as well as the extension of the area of activity of agents, leading to the combination under one roof of activities which were formerly strictly separated (see Gualandri 1991). Coinciding with the process of deregulation and the reform of the financial markets came the introduction of the Financial Services Act 1986, one of whose main aims is investor protection. The wide-ranging legislation known as the Financial Services Act includes, amongst other things, the definition of the rules of professional conduct: this must comply with a number of guiding principles, including the rule that the agent must 'subordinate his own interest to those of his clients and ... act fairly between his clients'.

In effect, codes of conduct established by the various professional categories were already in operation before this; they were intended to discipline the behaviour of the various groups of operators, in line with the tradition of self-regulation (see Lobuono 1990). Moreover, the beginning of the 1980s saw the coming into operation of the first Chinese walls, of which more will be said later, whose main *raison d'être* was to protect the reputation of the intermediary. It was, however, clear that in a financial context which was undergoing deep changes and with the presence of a growing number of operators, including many foreigners, on the London market, it was no longer possible to trust in self-regulation alone[2]. The aim of the Financial Services Act was, therefore, to safeguard self-regulation, but within a statutory framework. It was thus left to the controlling bodies of the first level, the Securities and Investments Board (SIB), or second level, the self-regulating organisations (SROs), to prepare the necessary regulations, by drawing up rulebooks.

With the implementation of the Financial Services Act and the Companies Act 1989, the regulatory structure currently consists of three levels[3]. Protection against conflicts of interest was therefore placed, at the first level, amongst the ten statements of principles established by the SIB, the body responsible for control in the first instance (see The Securities Association 1990a):

A firm should either avoid any conflict of interest arising or, where conflicts arise, should ensure fair treatment to all its customers by disclosures, internal rules of confidentiality, declining to act or otherwise. A firm should not unfairly place its interest above those of its customers and, where a properly informed customer would reasonably expect that the firm would place his interest above its own, the firm should live up to that expectation.

At the second level there are the core rules, again established by the SIB, which provide a detailed identification of all the fields of regulation to be implemented to ensure the application of the statements of principles. These include the rules relating to the conduct of business and transparency in transactions. Finally, it is left to the self-regulatory bodies, the third level, to establish detailed rules for the conduct of business.

Awareness of the problem of conflicts of interest, only from the point of view of conduct of business rules, is currently on the increase in France, even if less urgently than in the United Kingdom, no doubt because the process of despecialisation is much more remote and the system has already been operating for some time with a number of mixed functions, in particular as far as commercial banking and investment banking are concerned (see Anderloni 1991). The theme of professional deontology, and thus of safeguards against conflicts of interest, has been tackled by the various professions, leading to the definition of a number of principles, with the drafting of the 'Rapporteur M. Brac de

La Perrière', in March 1988, later codified by regulatory and self-regulatory bodies (see Anderloni 1991): transparency; information; the principle of the best execution; the prevention of conflicts of interest; and organisational measures to prevent the circulation of confidential information. In particular, principles of professional deontology were introduced for intermediaries carrying out operations in a dealing capacity, in order to safeguard the clientele, who must be informed, at the outset, of this possibility and, if appropriate, of the position assumed by the intermediary in the specific transaction. As already observed in the case of the United Kingdom, the need to safeguard the financial intermediary's reputation seems to play an important role in guiding the professional behaviour of the intermediaries themselves. This regulatory work was accompanied by Loi no. 89-531, 2 août 1989, which extended the powers, including the capacities to inspect and investigate, of the Commission des Opérations de Bourse.

We find little awareness of this subject in other countries, above all in Germany. At the end of the 1970s the theme of conflicts of interest in the universal type banking system was dealt with in the report of the Gessler Commission, which reached the conclusion that the problem was theoretically possible but was, in fact, of little importance, and generally without negative effects on clients (see Gessler 1979). Since the 1970s, however, self-regulation rules on insider trading have been in force on the conduct of business, referring to trading and advisory activities by banks (see Jarc 1991). The launch of regulations on insider trading is scheduled during 1992. The deep-seated differences which emerge both in the level of awareness of the problem and in the stage reached in regulatory and legislative activities, in the various contexts, make it clear why the proposed EC directive on investment services does not include Conduct of Business Rules. In fact, this area should be covered by an *ad hoc* directive in the future because of the large differences between the various Community countries, which make even minimal harmonisation difficult. In the meantime, investment companies benefiting from mutual recognition must comply with the rules of conduct in force in the countries where they operate.

In short, our brief analysis shows that the problem of conflicts of interest has been found more urgent in the case of the development of financial conglomerates, as in the United Kingdom, than in situations where the various activities are all carried on within the same bank, as found above all in Germany. There is no doubt that the greater awareness of the subject of conflict of interest in the United Kingdom, compared with Germany, and even with France, can be related to the fact that, in the first case, a situation of rigid separation has now changed to the point where previously segregated activities are now collected under the same roof. The problem is probably emerging more slowly in other countries because there it is more usual to find a blending of various activities.

Instruments for safeguarding the clientele

The instruments which can be implemented to safeguard the clientele of financial intermediaries against the risk of conflicts of interest are of various kinds and imply different degrees of rigidity. They include a ban on engaging in certain kinds of activity, the introduction of juridical and/or organisational separation between different activities, and lastly, the imposition of rules for the conduct of business (see Wood 1986; Hall 1987; Cavazzuti 1989; The Securities Association 1990a and 1990b). We will now provide a brief illustration of the various kinds of instruments, concentrating our attention on barriers, or 'fire-walls', of an organisational nature, the so-called Chinese walls; these are of special interest in view of the new Italian law, since these instruments represent an absolute novelty in Italy's regulatory and organisational practice. Attention will be focused on the British experience, which is without doubt the most important on this subject.

The strongest tool for protecting investors against conflicts of interest is the separation between different activities, established by law. As we have already said, the separation between commercial banking and investment banking established by the Glass Steagall Act in the United States and the principle of single capacity in the United Kingdom are emblematic here. The separation between different activities may also be guaranteed by the obligation to establish juridically separate companies, or by introducing real fire-walls of an organisational nature, in order to prevent the passage of information between activities whose joint management is considered to generate conflicts of interest. In this case the intermediary is not prevented from engaging in one or more activities, but there is a requirement for measures which guarantee their organisational, administrative and accounting separation. The most interesting example is provided by Chinese walls, which may be introduced voluntarily (that is in order to protect the intermediary's reputation) or in accordance with specific regulations.

Conduct of business rules, on the other hand, are concerned with the behaviour of operators. They mainly concentrate on the following fields:

- transparency, with special reference to the obligation to inform the client if the intermediary has any interest in the specific transaction; one interesting example is so-called polarisation, introduced in the United Kingdom, for the marketing of financial products, under which operators must assume the role either of independent consultant or of exclusive agent, and then inform their clients accordingly
- limitation of flows of information which it is believed may give rise to abuses
- rules for the execution of orders that guarantee the client's interest, such as customer order priority, which requires the subordination of interest in the client's favour, and best execution, which requires that orders must be executed in such a way as to give the client the greatest possible advantage.

The widest-ranging case history is provided by the so-called SIB core rules in the United Kingdom. For example, Table 8.1 shows the proposals for rules of conduct, most important for the purpose of safeguards against conflicts of interest, prepared by the Securities Association (TSA), the self-regulating body of the securities operators, on the basis of the core rules published by the SIB. Another means of investor protection is provided by the principle of the reversal of proof, under which if a claim is made it is up to the intermediary to prove that he has acted with due diligence and has not caused damage to the client. Finally, it is important to remember the importance of the legislation on insider trading with reference to the problem of abuses in the management of information flows.

The British experience: Chinese walls and the role of the compliance function

The main system introduced to avoid improper use of confidential information, which may give rise to conflicts of interest, consists of the so-called Chinese walls which are defined by the Licensed Dealers (Conduct of Business) Rules 1983 as

> an established arrangement whereby information known to persons in one part of business is not available (directly or indirectly) to those involved in another part of the business, and it is accepted that in each of the parts of the business so divided decisions will be taken without reference to any interest which any other such part or any person in any such part of the business may have in the matter

> (see Hall 1987).

Table 8.1   UK: revised conduct of business rules: The Securities
           Association

Polarisation   A firm, which is not a tied firm and which pro-
                        vides investment services in respect of packaged
                        products, must act as an independent adviser in
                        respect of those products. A tied firm must ensure
                        that: a) a private customer to whom it or anyone
                        acting on its behalf provides investment services is
                        informed of its and that person's status; and b)
                        neither it nor anyone acting on its behalf promotes
                        a packaged product of (or arranged by) a person
                        outside the marketing group of the tied firm

Material interest   When a firm has a material interest in the subject
                        matter of a possible transaction, or a relationship
                        which gives rise to a conflict of interest in relation
                        to that transaction, it must not advise or deal in
                        that exercise of discretion in relation to that trans-
                        action unless it has observed such requirements as
                        may be imposed by its regulator in order to ensure
                        fair treatment for all the firms's customers. Dis-
                        closure of a material interest or conflict of interest
                        is required

Customer order   When a firm has accepted an order to deal in an
priority   investment, or has decided to effect a discretionary
                        transaction in an investment, the firm must not
                        deal for its own account or the account of an
                        associate in that investment or in any related in-
                        vestment before the execution or withdrawal of the
                        order or decision

Timely execution   Once a firm has agreed or decided to enter into a
                        transaction for a customer, it must do so as soon
                        as reasonably practicable in the circumstances

Best execution   Where a firm deals with or for a customer it must
                        take all reasonable steps to deal on the terms
                        which are best available for the customer in the
                        circumstances

continued

Table 8.1   (continued)

Churning	A firm must not arrange or recommend a deal if the dealing would be regarded by a reasonable investment manager or adviser as too frequent in the circumstances for that customer

Source: The Securities Association (1990a and b) (only proposed rules relevant to conflicts of interest have been quoted)

Therefore, in substance, Chinese walls work in such a way that the circulation of information is limited to those who 'have to' know, and that the decisions taken in one line of business will be in the interest of the client of that area, even if this conflicts with the interest of clients in another area, or of the house itself. Chinese walls consist mainly of the physical separation of various operational sectors, departments or companies, and a ban on exchanges of information between colleagues of different sectors. It is clear that this also reduces the risk of insider trading.

Chinese walls have in fact been developed mainly in the British context and at present they are not found, at least in such an advanced stage of development, in other countries. They are implemented as a means of preventing conflicts of interest from arising, in accordance with the Financial Services Act and on the basis of the rule books of the self-regulating organisations. However, it is important not to underestimate the fact that houses also implement them in order to provide the maximum safeguards for their reputations, to which great importance is given on the British market. Generally, a large number of Chinese walls are in operation in British financial conglomerates, first and foremost between the commercial banking and securities industry activities. The asset management and corporate finance areas are both separated from the rest of the group, while sales and analysis activities are in turn separated from the market-making activities. In view of the conglomerate's organisational structure, the various operating areas generally form separate companies.

If, on the one side, Chinese walls are created in order to protect clients of the financial conglomerate, on the other side they may howev-

er prevent the emergence of advantages, in terms of management efficiency, deriving from the passage of information flows, not harmful to
the clientele, between the various sections of the group. In this way they
limit economies of scale within the group. In the search for a delicate
equilibrium between two targets which may sometimes appear conflicting within the securities industry (we are referring to the protection of
consumers/investors and the pursuance of information advantages for the
agents themselves) it is clear that the British government, and thus the
controlling and self-regulatory bodies of the market operators, opted to
give priority to the former. It is, therefore, up to the function responsible for co-ordination within the group in disciplining access to information in accordance with current law to avoid the duplication of information processes where possible.

One attempt to strike a balance between client protection, which in
effect is given priority under current regulations, and the management
requirement of optimising resources, has led to the development of a
procedure known as 'bringing someone over a Chinese wall'. When a
group company or division starts a specific operation which involves a
particular client, for example advisory services for a merger or takeover,
the team of experts appointed for the operation may request permission
to co-opt an operator from another sector, for example, a research division analyst, who works on the company in question as part of his or her
research activities. This analyst, therefore, crosses the Chinese walls
and remains on the staff of the new team throughout the operation, no
longer having contacts with colleagues in the original sector.

It is clear that an effective system of rules, which limit the action of
the agent in order to safeguard the client, requires a reinforcement of the
internal auditing function, defined in the British context as the compliance function. As we will see later, the new Italian law works in the
same direction.

If we take the British case as our point of reference, we will see
that, although this is not specifically envisaged by the Financial Services
Act, the compliance function has been found indispensable in view of the
new laws and regulations. Its function is to ensure that houses working
in the securities industry comply with the requirements of the rule books
of the control and self-regulatory bodies, with reference both to the
conduct of business rules and to precautionary measures. It is up to the
individual banks to provide a clear definition of the responsibilities and
tasks of this function (see Nicoll 1989). With reference to the rules of
significance for investor protection, in general the compliance division is
required to develop and implement the measures concerning Chinese

walls and the conduct of business rules, on the basis of the guidelines issued by the respective regulatory bodies, and then to check that they are complied with. Generally, the compliance function is responsible for:

- making a check, normally annually, on compliance with the rules imposed by the controlling body
- making a check on the advertising leaflets and publications issued by the company in order to ensure that the contents are not misleading for investors
- ensuring correct execution of all procedures relating to clients' orders, the keeping of the necessary books, and execution and settlement times
- maintaining a dossier of all claims from clients
- keeping staff informed about the laws and regulations to be observed, providing any updates needed
- making a sampling check on transactions performed for clients in order to monitor the procedures for conducting business and to highlight any cases in which the current rules are not applied, such as those relating to conflicts of interest, execution times, the principles of best execution and insider trading
- conducting relations with inspectors in the case of inspections by the controlling body.

The compliance function becomes more complex as the number of activities undertaken increases. For British banks an additional factor which adds to the workload of this function is the specific regulatory structure of the investment business, which involves a large number of authorisations, and the existence of several self-regulating bodies, depending on the different activities engaged in. This has led to a considerable increase in the costs relating to internal auditing, especially for the largest financial conglomerates. In an integrated securities house, the compliance division generally has an overall view of the various activities and the operations in progress with regard to various clients within the group. It is therefore able to assess the risk of conflicts of interest amongst clients of the company or the group. However, it is up to top management to assess how best to avoid such conflicts. The final responsibility for all the house's activities obviously lies with the board of directors, but it is normally the job of the compliance officer and the compliance division to act as go-between with the regulatory authorities and to inform the staff about the regulations to be followed with regard to Chinese walls, as well as any modifications or updates to the same. In the final analysis, therefore, the compliance function can be considered to all intents and purposes as an additional level in the control structure, inspired by the principle of self-regulation.

MANAGEMENT OF INFORMATION AND CONFLICTS OF INTEREST IN THE REGULATION OF THE SECURITIES MARKET AND FINANCIAL CONGLOMERATES: THE CASE OF ITALY

The subject of the management of information flows and conflicts of interest is dealt with specifically in the recent legislation governing the activities of securities operators and the organisation of the financial markets. Fundamentally, law no. 1/91 reflects the government's effort to adapt the Italian financial system to those of other countries, with a view to the liberalisation of the supply of financial services at an EC level. The main contents of the law concern the identification of the activities typical of securities industry and the financial intermediaries authorised to engage in these operations[4]. This takes the form of a large body of regulations which establish the principles behind the exercise of such activities, and the rules governing the behaviour of authorised operators. It is in this context that the aim of protecting investors against the risk of conflicts of interest becomes important.

The law attempts to prevent potential conflicts of interest by means of a combination of regulations derived from the dual principle of the transparency of dealings and the reputation of the financial intermediaries in conducting such business. In this law the purpose of stating the principle of transparency does seem aimed primarily at ensuring that the activities of the financial intermediary do not come into conflict with the interests of the clientele. In other words, the intention is to guarantee that the fact that the investor has less information at his disposal about the quality of the securities invested in or negotiated is compensated either by the agent's services as an investment adviser or in direct management of the customer's assets; or, in any case, is not made even more to his disadvantage by activities on the agent's side which are damaging to the customer's interests.

Rather than making more information available to the investor about the real safety and soundness of the issuer and the quality of the securities, transparency in operations implies the maximum investor access to information about the nature and risks of the operations (Section e, art. 6), the type of services supplied by the securities firm, the way in which the services themselves are provided, and the size and method of calculation of the remuneration (Section c, art. 6).

As specified by the law, the maximum transparency in operations is ensured by the obligation to provide informative documentation and the obligation to supply information about the existence of conflicts of interest.

i)   *The informative and contract documentation required from agents consists of:*

- An informative document identifying and specifying the activities engaged in, as well as the list of companies in the group to which it belongs (Section 1 art. 1 Consob regulations and Section b, art. 6 law no. 1/1991) to be given to the customer before the contract is signed.

- The securities services must be offered on the basis of a written contract which specifies the type and features of the services supplied, indicates the instructions of a general nature given by the customer, states the remuneration of the securities firm or the objective criteria for its calculation, and contains a warning to the customer about the nature of the risks of liquidity and variation in value related to operations involving securities not issued by the state or not quoted on the stock market (or quoted in the Unlisted Securities Market) or futures contracts (art. 9 Sections 2 and 4, Consob regulations). The structure of the contract required for the management of clients' assets is more detailed and demanding, since it indicates any limits to the total value and composition of investments and mentions any authorisation to purchase securities issued by the authorised financial intermediary or companies in its group, or to effect operations concerning securities which it trades on its own account (art. 33 Section 1, Consob regulations).

- Moreover, for each operation executed authorised intermediaries are required to send a note relating to the operation itself, clearly specifying all the information regarding the procedures and contents of the operation, to the customer's address within the third working day after the date when the operation is effected (art. 12 Section 1, Consob regulations).

ii) *The transparency of the operation is also guaranteed by the obligation on the securities firm to inform the client of a potential conflict of interest*

The authorised intermediaries are not permitted to effect operations with or on behalf of clients if they have direct or indirect conflicts of interest in the operation, even with regard to group relationships, unless they have previously informed the customer in writing about the nature and extent of their interest in the operation and the customer has expressly consented to its execution also in writing.

A second group of regulations, which limit the emergence of conflicts of interest, are the rules of conduct for securities firms. These consist of an initial body of rules of conduct of a general nature, a second group concerning the compatibility and rules for execution of the various securities activities, and, finally, a set of rules governing the organisational structure required for engaging in the activity.

i) The principles of a general nature require the securities firm to carry out its activities with diligence, integrity and care, safeguarding its client's interest. To this end, as well as meeting the obligations to inform set out above, it must comply with the rules of operation of the markets on which it works and abstain from any actions which may favour one client at the expense of another or which favour the house at the expense of its customers (art. 6 law no 1/91 and articles 3 and 4 of the Consob regulations).

ii) Turning to the specific regulations governing the securities firm's conduct of business, one possible distinction arises between the rules for the conduct of operations on the primary and secondary securities market on the one hand and the restrictions placed on asset management on the other.

- The principle of the objectivity and certainty of prices and quantities negotiated lies behind the rules for the execution of orders to buy and sell securities. For the negotiation of securities quoted on the official markets, authorised intermediaries must buy and sell solely on these markets and using the negotiation procedures established for them (art. 11 Section 1 law no 1/1991). For securities quoted on unregulated markets, the securities firm may act in a dealing capacity, stating in advance the price conditions at which it is prepared to buy or sell the securities concerned (art. 26 Section 1, Consob regulations).

    When engaged in the placing and distribution of securities, authorised intermediaries may offer the securities to their own clients, after providing the information document, solely within the period, under the procedures and on the terms indicated in the placing programme. The obligations to note orders to underwrite or purchase (with enough information to identify the operation) and to record the quantities underwritten by each individual client within the day after the conclusion of the placing, are intended to reduce actions which discriminate against customers (art. 32 Sections 1 and 2, Consob regulations). There are similar obligations to keep records of orders to negotiate on behalf of the clientele (art. 35 Section 4, law no 1/91). Moreover, in order to limit conflicts in assets management, securities firms are not permitted to accept orders for the underwriting or purchase of securities from the group division or company involved in assets management which are received after the fifth working day from the start of placing (art. 32 Section 4, Consob regulations).

- Special attention is paid to the conflicts which may arise from the behaviour of intermediaries as asset managers. The regulations cover the inclusion in the trust accounts of securities issued by the authorised intermediary, or by companies in its group, or of securities in the intermediary's portfolio or in which it has preferential dealings. In the case of securities issued by any one issuer, there are limits to the composition of portfolios which reach a maximum of 10 per cent: in no case over 50 per cent of the value of the portfolio for the total of securities issued with reference to any one group (see art. 32, Section 2) - unless this limit is exceeded with the customer's approval, in accordance with art. 4, Section 2.

Securities firms combining asset management with securities trading are not permitted to act in any way which limits the composition of trust accounts to the securities which they handle or which form part of their own investment portfolios (art. 35 Section 3, Consob regulations).

iii) The rules of conduct extend to the definition of the organisational structures capable of avoiding exchanges of information with regard to the various activities engaged in (art. 15 Section 1, Consob regulations). To this end, the securities firms are required to have an internal structure which limits the joint production of activities (see Table 8.2). Each separate structure must have its own head, who is granted decision-making and operative autonomy in the management of an individual separate structure. The regulations also introduce criteria for separate accounting, which do not prevent the organisational and administrative centralisation of general services, provided the files of each structure and the accounts allowing the individual allocation of costs and revenues are strictly protected.

The regulations governing authorised intermediaries have a dual aim as far as the problem of the management of the flows of information which originate in the context of the various securities activities, and the closely related problem of conflicts of interest, are concerned. On the

Table 8.2   Italy: organisational separation between activities of securities industry imposed by the new law

	A	B	C	D	E	F
A) Trading		X¹		X		
B) Placement	X¹			X		
C) Asset management					X	
D) Orders collection	X	X				X
E) Advisory on securities			X			
F) Promotion of investment				X		

Note: 1. If the securities firm gives advisory services about corporate finance

one hand, the principle of transparency requires the securities operator to state publicly the emergence of conflicts of interest which concern the entire group to which the securities operator belongs and its investment customers. On the other hand, by preventing the circulation of information between the various divisions working in the securities field, the very conditions for the use of information flows at the expense of the investor client are eliminated. The elimination of the joint use of information also eliminates a number of the advantages (from an information point of view) deriving from diversification into a number of securities industry activities.

However, the regulations governing the management of information do allow two circumstances in which information may be exchanged inside the company structure. First of all, the economic-financial research and analysis function may provide 'neutral' back-up information to the other sectors of activity (art. 12 of Bank of Italy regulations). The costs which the intermediary incurs in acquiring information regarding the quality of securities can therefore be distributed across all securities market activities.

Moreover, the Consob regulations govern the behaviour of the administrative and management structures, as well as the individuals directly above the heads of the various operating structures in the hierarchy, requiring that the instructions concerning individual relationships with customers or individual operations and business to be concluded on the customer's account must be given in writing (art. 15 Section 2 of Consob regulations).

The reference to the management structures therefore gives the impression that the separation between the various activities does not conflict with the need for combined management of the various activities, and therefore single management of all the information flows in combination, while those responsible can still be traced if information is used against the customer's interests. It is therefore possible that, for example, assessment of a customer's creditworthiness might be handled singly for the entire organisation.

In so far as it provides specific regulations for securities firms, law 1/91 does not give measures to govern the entire range of situations of conflicts of interest listed in the first part of this paper. In other words, there appear to be no regulations for the area of the relations existing within the financial conglomerate, between the activities of the commercial bank and the activities of the securities industry, and especially the potential conflicts which may arise from lending to customers. For example, the law on securities firms does not fully protect the investor against a debt restructuring situation which has a detrimental effect on the value of the company's bonds and shares.

The conflicts of interest which arise from the combined management of banking and securities activity are, however, affected by the regulations which govern bank holding companies. Unlike the law on securities firms, this legislation does not intervene directly in the conglomerate's conduct of business[5] but, in attempting to ensure stability, the authorities reserve the right to monitor and intervene on the assumption and transfer of risks (concentration of the conglomerate's risk with regard to single debtors, debt rescheduling, exchange rate and market risks, and internal flows of financing), on their capital adequacy, and on the acquisition of external holdings, reaching the point where they indicate the criteria for internal controls and the reliability of the administrative/accounting organisation of the financial conglomerate (see Banca d'Italia 1989).

Remembering that the legislation governing bank holding companies gives the parent holding company large management powers in order to ensure the implementation of supervisory instructions concerning stability, it seems important to emphasise the principles concerning the supervision of information introduced by the new law and their repercussions on the management of information within the conglomerate. Decree 356/90 actually introduces specific rules governing the circulation of information:

> the parent holding company shall issue instructions to the members of the bank holding company for the implementation of the instructions given by the Bank of Italy in the interests of the stability of the conglomerate. The directors of member companies shall be obliged to supply all data and information for the issue of the regulation and the collaboration required for compliance with the regulations on consolidated supervision
>
> (art. 25, Section 4).

The parent holding company is thus attributed a function of co-ordinating the information flows within the conglomerate, in order to contain the risk accumulated in the various activities. Therefore it seems that at the level of the financial conglomerate we are not faced with the dominance of a criterion based on the separation of information flows originating in the various operating branches; the authorities give more importance to ensuring that the assumption of combined risks does not jeopardise the stability of the group.

The contents of the two items of legislation therefore seem to complement each other in pursuing the aim of safeguarding the saver, whether investor or depositor, while they are only apparently conflicting with regard to the degree of complementarity envisaged for the various activities engaged in[6]. The law on securities firms establishes the separate management of the various securities activities, requiring that this separation should be controlled by a 'specific manager' inside the organisation who has access to the administrative and accounts information of the various operational divisions but does not interact with the division's operating structure. However, a point at which information about customers is combined at higher management level is envisaged.

In the law governing financial conglomerates, the internal control function with regard to the implementation of regulatory instructions does not seem to be separated from the management functions. The same internal control structure which seems intended to limit the level of risk, in all its various configurations, and to prevent it from increasing as a result of the accumulation of lending granted by any division presupposes the combination of information about the positions assumed by the financial conglomerate's operating divisions in relation to the same customer. This reinforces the impression that while at the level of individual operating units, whether juridically separate companies or just divisions, the horizontal separation of information prevails, at the level of company and group management a degree of access to information capable of reaping the benefits of diversification is permitted both in practice and formally.

CONCLUSIONS

The economies in information achieved by banking organisations and conflict of interest are both phenomena which can be traced back to an asymmetry of information between operators within the system. These phenomena may also be considered as the opposite extremes of the more general problem of the trade-off between efficiency and stability in the financial system. If, on the one hand, the single management of flows of information about customers' quality and financial decisions may lead to increased efficiency in the allocation of flows of finance within the economy, on the other hand, the bank's advantage in terms of information may result in the abuse of this position, to the disadvantage of the customer, with implications in terms of damage to the bank's reputation and the resulting loss of confidence by the public. It thus appears clear that both the policies of the supervisory authorities and the operational and organisational decisions of the banks themselves, in their respective spheres of activity, must be inspired by the need to achieve a balance between economies of scale and investor protection.

Of recent years, in the various institutional contexts, special attention has been focused on the theme of conflicts of interest. This attention has been most noticeable in those countries where there has been a move away from a high degree of specialisation in the various banking sectors towards the formation of large financial conglomerates with widely diversified activities. The problem has been especially obvious in the case of commercial banks starting to operate in the securities industry.

If we assess the characteristics of the legislation and/or regulations in a number of important financial systems, it can be seen that the degree of intervention on the specific theme of conflicts of interest is related to the process of despecialisation of banks, being more intensive in those contexts where there was formerly a large amount of specialisation. In Germany there are very few controls based on self-regulation. The opposite extreme is represented by the United Kingdom where, after the definition of legislative guidelines (Financial Services Act), there has been a great deal of intervention on the rules of conduct by the supervisory and self-regulatory bodies. France comes somewhere between the two; in the most recent years we have seen the introduction of rules of conduct for banks based on the codification of principles of professional deontology. The case of Italy would seem to contradict the line of interpretation which links the degree of intervention by the authorities on the subject of conflicts of interest to the extent of deregulation in banking activities. The new Italian legislation is comparable to the British law in terms of its intensity and sweep, although Italy's banks operate in a manner more like that of their German equivalents, since they have traditionally engaged in a wide range of activities typical of the securities industry. This implies that Italian banks find themselves in the difficult situation of having to separate activities which were previously managed in combination.

In identifying some indicators about the effects of the new legislation on the operations of Italian banks, we should first of all underline that the new regulations on investor protection and the rules of conduct (separation of the organisation and information of the various activities) imply a considerable increase in administrative and organisational costs. The problems of adapting the organisational structure and staff to the new operating procedures must also be emphasised.

In terms of economies of information, it is clear that the new laws considerably reduce the possibilities of reaping the advantages of diversification. As well as eliminating the possibility of combined management of securities industry activities, organisational separation also reduces the horizontal transmission of the flow of information amongst the various operating areas. From the points made above, it would thus seem that the legislative framework penalised Italian banks excessively. In effect, when making an overall assessment of the law, we must not lose sight of its priority objective, investor protection, and the characteristics of this in terms of access to information. These concern first and foremost the limited level of institutional saving, with the resulting weakness of the investor in terms of information within the financial system. This disadvantage was made more serious by the lack of regulations governing the operation of the markets and the conduct of investment business. In this context, investor protection can only be fully guaranteed by a large programme of legislation and regulations, covering both transparency in customer relations and rules of conduct for securities and banking institutions.

Finally, it should be noted that the law does not prevent the bank from enjoying some advantages of diversification relating to information flows. On the one hand the centralisation of a research function may provide advantages in the acquisition of information on the securities markets, while on the other intermediaries, be they specialised securities firms, banks or financial conglomerates, are still allowed to implement combined management of information flows at the decision-making level.

NOTES

1. The principle of single capacity, already operating in the nineteenth century, was definitively introduced in 1909 (see Wormell 1985).
2. The inadequacy of traditional instruments and the need to define a clear set of regulations to ensure investor protection and the proper operation of the financial markets are underlined by the Gower Report (1984).
3. The regulatory structure initially defined by the SIB, on the basis of the Financial Services Act, was found especially burdensome in terms both of costs and bureaucratic procedures. Because of this, the Companies Act revised the regulatory system with the aim of increased simplicity and clarity.
4. *Società di intermediazione mobiliare* (Sim) and banks.
5. Note that the activities engaged in by Sim, as defined in art. 1 of law 1/91, come into the category of those of companies included in the definition of a bank holding company (art. 27 and annexed list).
6. P. Marchetti (1991) is also of this opinion, pointing out that 'the circulation of information about risks assumed on the bank's account, the aggregates of the dimensions and risks of the various activities, and the exercise of management powers over the Sim belonging to the financial conglomerate to the extent required to ensure compliance with instructions on the subject of equity stability required by the regulations governing the financial conglomerate are not in conflict with the system of separation of the activities (and functions) of the Sim.'

LIST OF REFERENCES

Anderloni, L. (1991), 'Banche e mercati mobiliari Francia' in G. Forestieri and M. Onado (eds), *Banche e Mercati Mobiliari* (Milano, Egea)

Banca d'Italia (Bank of Italy) (1989), *Intermediazione finanziaria non Bancaria e Gruppi Bancari Plurifunzioanli: le Esigenze di Regolamentazione Prudenziale*, Temi di Discussione, no. 113

Benston, G.J. (1990), *The Separation of Commercial Banking and Investment Banking. The Glass Steagall Act Revised and Reconsidered* (London: Macmillan)

Cable, J. (1985), 'Capital market information and industrial performance: the role of West German banks', *Economic Journal*, **95** (March)

Capriglione, F. (1991), 'Note introduttive alla disciplina s.i.m. e dell 'organizzazione dei mercati', *Quaderni di Ricerca Giuridica*, Banca d'Italia, no. 25

Cavazzuti, F. (1989), 'Conflitti di interessi e informazioni asimmetriche nella intermediazione finanziaria', *Banca Impresa Società*, no. 3

Financial Services Act 1986 (London: HMSO)

Franks, J. and C. Mayer (1989), *Risk, Regulation and Investor Protection* (Oxford: Clarendon Press)

Gessler, E. (1979), *I Problemi Fondamentali dell'Ordinamento Creditizio della Germania Federale*, Relazione della commissione di studio del Ministero delle Finance della Repubblica Federale Tedesca diretta da Ernest Gessler (Bologna: Il Mulino)

Goode, R.M. (ed.) (1986), *Conflicts of Interest in the Changing Financial World*, The Institute of Bankers and Centre for Commercial Law Studies, Queen Mary College, University of London

Gower, L.C.B. (1984), *Review of Investor Protection* (London: HMSO)

Gualandri, E. (1991), 'Banche e mercati mobiliari Gran Bretagna' in G. Forestieri and M. Onado (eds), *Banche e Mercati Mobiliari*, (Milano, Egea)

Hall, M.J.B. (1987), 'Reform of the London Stock Exchange: the prudential issues', *Banca Nazionale del Lavoro Quarterly Review* (June)

Herring, R.J. and A.M. Santomero (1991), 'The corporate structure of financial conglomerates', *Journal of Financial Services Research*, no. 2

Jarc, F. (1991), 'Banche e mercati mobiliari Germania' in G. Forestieri and M. Onado (eds), *Banche e Mercati Mobiliari* (Milano, Egea)

Landi, A. (1991), 'Banche e mercati mobiliari: concorrenza o complementarità?' in G. Forestieri and M. Onado (eds), *Banche e Mercati Mobiliari* (Milano, Egea)

Lobuono, M. (1990), 'Deregulation dei mercati finanziari e processi di auto-regolamentazione' in *Banca Impresa Società*, no. 2

Marchetti, P. (1991), 'Gruppi bancaria, SIM, stabilità, regole di condotta', *Bancaria*

Nicoll, S. (1989), *The Securities Industry Handbook* (Cambridge, UK: Woodhead-Faulkner)

Pennington, R. (1986), 'How conflicts of interest may arise' in R.M. Goode (ed.), *Conflicts of Interest in the Changing Financial World*, The Institute of Bankers and Centre for Commercial Law Studies, Queen Mary College, University of London

Robertson, J. (1987), 'Conflicts and Chinese Walls' in S. MacLeachlan (ed.), *Life after Big Bang* (London: Graham & Trotman)

Sabani, L. and P. Sapienza (1990), *I Conflitti di Interesse in un'Istituzione Finanziaria Multiprodotto*, Centro di Economia Monetaria e Finanziaria 'Paolo Baffi', Università Bocconi, Quaderni di Ricerca, no. 44 (Luglio)

Saunders, A. (1985), 'Conflict of interest: an economic view' in I. Walter (ed.), *Deregulating Wall Street* (New York: John Wiley & Sons)

The Securities Association (1990a), *Revised Conduct of Business Rules. Consultative Document* (London)

The Securities Association (1990b), *Revised Conduct of Business Rules. Notes and Appendices* (London)

Stiglitz, J.E. (1985), 'Credit markets and the control of capital', *Journal of Money, Credit and Banking*, **17**, 2 (May)

Stiglitz, J.E. and A. Weiss (1988), *Banks as Social Accountants and Screening Devices for the Allocation of Credit*, NBER Working Paper, no. 2710

Wormell, J. (1985), *The Gilt-Edged Market* (London: George Allen & Unwin)

Wood, P.R. (1986), 'Financial conglomerates and conflicts of interest' in R.M. Goode (ed.), *Conflicts of Interest in the Changing Financial World*, The Institute of Bankers and Centre for Commercial Law Studies, Queen Mary College, University of London

CHAPTER 9
CREDIT LOSSES IN NORDIC BANKS

Ted Lindblom

INTRODUCTION

In the 1980s the central banks of the Nordic countries began to deregu-
late their financial markets. Within the space of a few years, several of
the existing regulations were abolished that had for long restricted
banks' lending volumes, interest rate setting and foreign exchange. For
the banks a door was opened to a new world; the changed environment
offered exciting business opportunities. The demand for new loans
seemed almost infinite, but simultaneously the competition between
banks, and between banks and other financial institutions, was strengthened. Therefore, many banks reorganised and decentralised their business. Competitiveness and market (customer) orientation became buzz
words and were considered by many banks to be strategical key factors
for success. Branches became profit centres and, within certain limits,
the authority to make credit decisions was often delegated to the local
branch manager. The new world, however, was also a world of which
most of the banks had no real experience and, apparently, very limited
understanding. Today it is obvious that the majority failed to realise the
magnitude of the underlying credit risk exposure when expanding the
loan portfolio.

In a three-year period banks in Norway more than doubled their
lending to the general public, from NOK 131 billion in 1983 to NOK
268 billion in 1986[1]. According to Reve (1990, 1992), the Norwegian
banks radically changed their image during this period. They stopped
being regarded as institutions that conducted themselves with dignity,
care and style. Instead they became aggressive and competitive organisations, often with a young dynamic marketing director, who saw new
lending possibilities everywhere. In short, the Norwegian banks were
now paying more attention to market shares than credit risks. Today we
are observing the consequences of this change of strategy. The Norwegian banks are suffering from severe credit losses and large banks have
merged, such as Bergen Bank and DnC (Den norske Creditbank). In
spite of such mergers, however, the Norwegian government has been
more or less forced to intervene and contribute with new (risk) capital
and guarantees. This has been found necessary for the survival of many
banks that were close to bankruptcy. Furthermore, only a few banks

174

would otherwise be able to manage the new capital adequacy rules by the end of 1992. As a direct consequence of these actions, more than 50 per cent of the Norwegian banks are now wholly or partly owned by the state.

The development in other Nordic countries is similar to that in Norway, but as Petterson (1992), the former vice president of Första Sparbanken in Sweden, points out when he studies the bank crises in Norway, the Norwegians are one or two years ahead. However, my intention is not to make another comparison between the banking crises in the Nordic countries. The purpose of this research project is to study and analyse the credit losses that individual banks within the Nordic countries have made. There are several interesting questions to be answered. For example, how have credit losses developed over time in the banks? How can these losses be explained? What impact have they had on the banks' profitability? What have the banks done to cover their credit losses - what measures have been taken?

This paper is focusing on the credit losses and financial performance of ten Nordic banks or, more correctly, banking groups[2]. Five are located in Norway and five in Sweden. In this initial phase the analyses are strictly empirical and almost entirely based on data from the banking groups' annual income statements and balance sheets. The presentation is limited to the development of credit losses and their impact on the banks' profitability. All presented figures/results are still preliminary.

THE BANKS' CREDIT LOSSES DURING THE PAST TEN YEARS

The title is perhaps a little misleading. The annual reports that I have available at the moment concerning the Norwegian banks do not cover the whole period of ten years. Furthermore, it should be noticed that the largest bank in Norway, Den norske Bank, was established only two years ago (1990) as a result of the merger between Bergen Bank and DnC. All figures concerning Den norske Bank before this year are based on the credit losses and financial performance of these two banking groups. The other banks examined in Norway are Kreditkassen, Fokus Bank, Landsbanken and Sparebanken Rogaland (SR-Bank). Except the latter, which is one of the larger savings banks in Norway, all the banks examined are commercial banks.

Also four of the Swedish banks examined are commercial banks. These are Gota Bank, Nordbanken (the former PKbanken), Svenska

Handelsbanken and Skandinaviska Enskilda Banken. Like Den norske Bank, Nordbanken was established in 1990. In this latter case, however, it was not a question of a merger between two more or less equally large banks, but an ordinary acquisition. When the former PKbanken acquired the provincial bank named Nordbanken, it changed its own name to Nordbanken. Besides the change of the name, this acquisition does not differ from other acquisitions that have taken place in both Norway and Sweden during the period studied. The fifth Swedish bank examined is Första Sparbanken (First Savings Bank).

Since all figures are based on annual reports, it is worth noting that most assets and liabilities are valued at cost rather than market value. Furthermore, the balances are end-year figures rather than the preferable average daily balances. The reason why the former figures are used in this study is that average balances are not shown by the annual report of every bank. This means that the presented evaluation of a bank's profitability, for instance, may differ from profitability measures based on average balances. Therefore, I have chosen to focus on the development over time. The actual trends are usually possible to discern by the end-year balances as well[3].

Regarding the credit losses, the problem is how they are measured and determined. The accounting principles may differ between different countries and, furthermore, the principles may change from one year to another. But it is even more crucial that a substantial part of a bank's credit losses for a certain year are estimates of expected future losses. Figure 9.1 shows how credit losses, in terms of provisions for loan losses, have developed for the five Norwegian banks since the beginning/middle of the 1980s.

A major part of the very high and increasing loan loss provisions between 1985 and 1989 for 'Den norske Bank' occurred in the former DnC. In 1984, for instance, about 90 per cent of Bergen Bank's and DnC's total provisions for loan losses occurred in DnC. Possibly, the merger into Den norske Bank in 1990 may have had a positive effect on loan losses, at least in comparison with Kreditkassen. As is shown in Figure 9.1, the rate of change for Kreditkassen has been much higher in 1990 and 1991. Regarding the three other banks, one should bear in mind that the loan loss provisions in Figure 9.1 are measured in absolute terms. The picture changes slightly when we compare the ratio between loan loss provisions and net loans to the general public (see Figure 9.2).

In Figure 9.2 it is even clearer that Kreditkassen has been very unsuccessful in avoiding credit risks in its loan portfolio, especially in 1991[4]. Furthermore, it is also shown that Den norske Bank has

Figure 9.1 **The development of provisions for loan losses for five Norwegian banks (NOK M)**

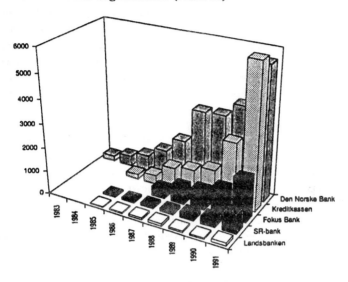

Figure 9.2 **Provisions for loan losses/net loans for five Norwegian banks**

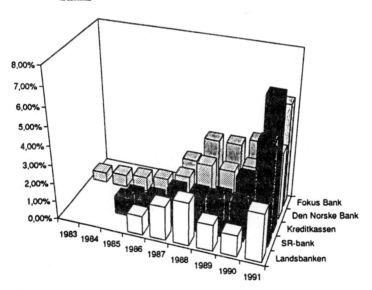

managed relatively well in comparison with three of the banks, i.e. Kreditkassen, Fokus Bank and SR-bank. On the other hand, a ratio of 3.7 per cent in 1991 between the provisions for loan losses and net loans is nothing of which to be proud. Quite the contrary. In reality the provisions for loan losses for Den norske Bank were higher than the bank's net interest income (the ratio was 1.2). Regarding Fokus bank and especially SR-bank, the situation looks much worse than in Figure 9.1. For SR-bank the ratio between loan provisions and net loans nearly tripled between 1990 to 1991.

The performances of the five Swedish banks do not differ too much from the Norwegian ones but, as was mentioned above, there is a time-lag. The examined banks' provisions for loan losses are shown in Figure 9.3.

Figure 9.3   The development of provisions for loan losses for five Swedish banks (SEK M)

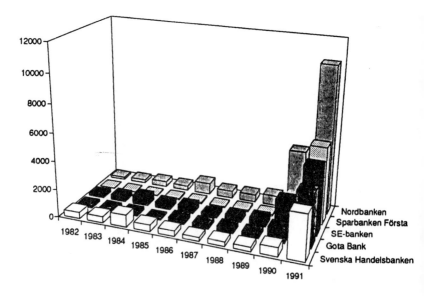

For the Swedish banks examined, the loan loss provisions began to increase remarkably in 1990. They were doubled for Svenska Handels-

banken, more than tripled for Gota Bank and SE-banken and increased
almost ten times for Nordbanken and Sparbanken Första. However, the
real increase took place in 1991. Nordbanken's loan loss provisions
especially were enormous, but none of the banks seems to have been
able to avoid extraordinarily huge credit losses. However, the situation
looks better for Svenska Handelsbanken and SE-banken when considering lending volumes (see Figure 9.4).

Figure 9.4 shows the ratio between loan loss provisions and lending
(including lending to financial institutions).

Figure 9.4   Provision for loan losses/lending for five Swedish banks

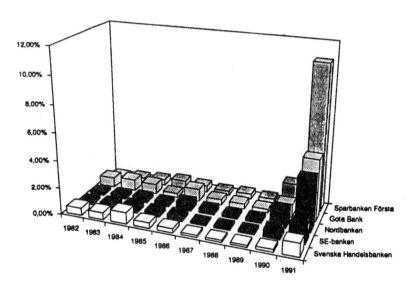

As can be seen from Figure 9.4, the situation for three of the banks
is most disturbing. One of them, Sparbanken Första, looks even worse
off than any of the Norwegian banks examined. Its ratio between loan
loss provisions and lending was nearly 11 per cent (10.7 per cent) in
1991[5]. The bank's provision for loan losses was then more than four
times as high as its net interest income. The corresponding figures for
the two other banks were 1.1 times (Gota Bank) and 1.5 times (Nord-

banken).   It has been necessary for the Swedish government and/or owners to give external support to each of these three banks.   The Swedish government has contributed with new risk capital and/or financial guarantees to Nordbanken and Sparbanken Första, and the insurance company, SPP/Trygg Hansa, has paid in capital to Gota Bank.

As was mentioned earlier, it should be noticed that actual credit losses do not necessarily coincide with the loan loss provisions made. Provision for loan loss covers both actual and expected (possible) credit losses.   In the beginning of the period the loan loss provisions were predominated by actual credit losses, but over the last two years this has changed.   In 1991 about 70-95 per cent of the banks' loan loss provisions were estimated possible credit losses.   Although there exist certain criteria from the Swedish Bank Inspection Board regarding the determination of actual and possible credit losses, it is inevitable that a bank's provision for loan loss is becoming a more and more vague and uncertain measure of the bank's real credit losses.   Thus, the comparisons between the banks are becoming more diffuse.

In Figure 9.5 the ratios between the Swedish banks' possible credit losses and provisions for loan losses are shown for the past five years. Is it only by pure chance that Gota Bank, Nordbanken and, especially, Sparbanken Första have had a relatively higher ratio of possible credit losses during the past five years?   Considering that every one of them has been rather eager to increase market share and expand its lending to commercial and industrial borrowers, I would suggest that the answer is no.   Both SE-banken and Svenska Handelsbanken have long been established as commercial banks.   Consequently, the 'breaking-in' banks have had to accept riskier customer categories and/or offer better lending conditions to the established banks' customers.   In both cases the credit risks are underpriced.

In earlier studies, like those of Reve (1990) and Petterson (1992), several plausible reasons have been suggested for the dramatically rising provisions for loan losses.   As was initially indicated in this paper, the changing strategies and behaviour of the banks are often considered to be very important reasons for this development; it seems almost as if the banks abandoned credit evaluations and rationing.   Probably, the banks' performance measures have stimulated branch managers to go for (risky) volume rather than (safe) long-term profitability.   This implies defective and underdeveloped management control systems.   Of course, there are also structural reasons, like the rather abrupt change from a regulated to an almost unregulated financial system and the rapid increase of real estate values and thereafter a complete collapse.   However, evidently

Figure 9.5 The share of possible credit losses of total provisions for loan losses for the five Swedish banks between 1987 and 1991

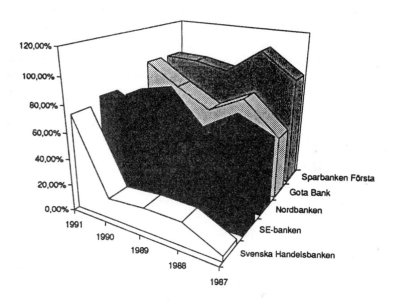

these as well as other environmental causes have an unnecessarily great impact on the banks' credit losses. With improved internal or management control systems it is very likely that most banks would have been better off. It cannot just be a coincidence that Svenska Handelsbanken has managed relatively better than the other banks; already in 1971 cost and revenue control systems were implemented in this bank.

CREDIT LOSSES AND THE BANKS' PROFITABILITY

In this section we are going to analyse the impact of credit losses on the return on equity (ROE). ROE could be expressed as the sum of two components, return on invested funds (ROIF) and return on financial leverage (ROFL)[6]. ROIF reflects the bank's operating risk and shows the bank's productivity and efficiency, that is how well it has been operating its business and investing its funds. It is defined as the ratio between operating income before taxes (revenues minus operating

expenses) and assets.   ROFL reflects the bank's financial risk and is
dependent upon both the bank's debt-equity ratio (D/E) and the difference between ROIF and the bank's (average) cost of debt funds (CDF).
With this approach of breaking down ROE it will be possible to distinguish and identify what impact the banks' operating efficiency and financial activities have had on the ROE. In Figure 9.6 the ROE (before tax)
is shown for the five Norwegian banks.

Not surprisingly, the banks' ROEs are heavily affected by the huge
credit losses in 1991. If there were not any loan loss provisions Den
norske Bank, for instance, would have obtained a ROE of +25 per cent
instead of -190 per cent. However, the large loan loss provisions are not
the only explanation for low or negative ROEs. Fokus Bank would have
had a negative ROE even if there had not been any provisions for loan
losses.

Figure 9.6 Return on equity before tax for five Norwegian banks[1]

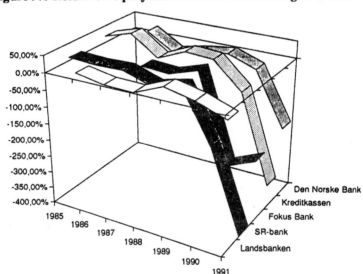

Note: 1.   ROE is defined as the net operating income before extraor-
dinary expenses (NOI) divided by equity capital (EC) and
justified untaxed reserves/capital (UR).   Expressed as an
equation:

$$ROE = NOI/(EC + UR*(1 - tax rate))$$

By definition, credit losses are included in a bank's operating costs and therefore affect its ROIF. Needless to say, the share of the credit losses has increased during the period studied. However, as is shown in Figure 9.7, credit losses or, more correctly, loan loss provisions are not the only reason for decreasing ROIFs. In each bank the ROIF would have diminished anyhow. In principle there may be two reasons for this. The ratio between revenues and assets (that is the yields) has either increased or decreased relatively less or more than the operating expense ratio (excluding credit losses). The first reason is shown to be the case in four of the banks, where both ratios have increased but the operating expense ratio has increased most; in the fifth bank, Den norske Bank, the yield has decreased. In fact, both the interest income ratio (interest income/assets) and the non-interest income ratio (non-interest income/ assets) have decreased. On the other hand, the bank's operating expense ratio has not increased as much as for the other banks. Regarding the dominant operating expenses (personnel expenses) only one of the banks (Landsbanken) has been able to reduce its ratio.

Figure 9.7 Return on invested funds (including loss effect) for five Norwegian banks

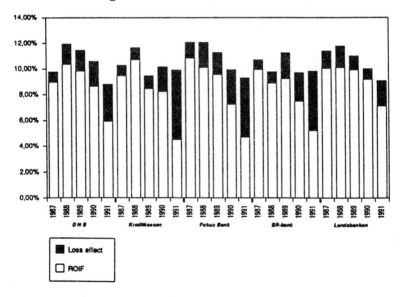

In Figure 9.8 the banks' ROFLs are shown for the past five years as well as the magnitude of loan losses (what we have called loan loss leverage or LLL). LLL expresses the impact provision for loan losses has had on the ROFL. Thus, ROFL minus LLL equals ROFL (excluding loan losses). Hence, without any loan loss provisions each of the banks would have obtained a positive ROFL for almost every year.

Figure 9.8   Return on financial and loan loss leverages for the five Norwegian banks

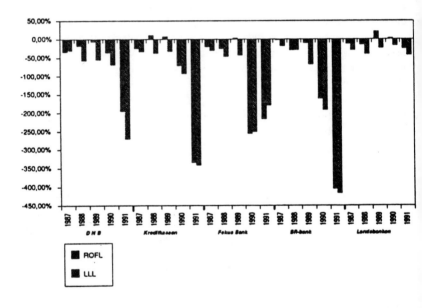

Regarding the banks' financial risk, ROFL, it is important to note that ROFL is the product of two components, the leverage spread, ROIF minus CDF, and the debt-equity ratio, D/E. Expressed as an equation:

ROFL = (ROIF - CDF)*D/E.

Thus, as long as the leverage spread is positive, ROFL will also be positive and thereby contribute to a higher ROE. The magnitude of the contribution depends on the magnitude of the debt-equity ratio. The higher the ratio, the higher the ROFL. However, in the case ROIF < CDF a high debt-equity ratio will seriously affect ROE negatively.

The analyses of the five Norwegian banks' ROFLs are clear-cut. Since credit losses reduce a bank's equity (*ceteris paribus*), the debt-equity ratio has increased for every bank between 1987 and 1991. Especially in 1991 the ratio dramatically increased in several of the banks. As is implicitly shown in Figure 9.8, the leverage spread has been negative in each year for two of the banks, Den norske Bank and SR-bank; the three other banks have had a positive spread only once or twice during the past five years. Since the CDF has decreased in each bank, the negative spreads are caused by the ever lower ROIFs, which are to a great extent explained by the huge credit losses, but also by declining efficiency (cf. Figure 9.7).

The situation seems not quite as dark for the five Swedish banks, at least not until 1990. As is shown in Figure 9.9, the banks' ROEs (before taxes) have been positive in every year between 1972 and 1989. Between 1986 and 1988/89 the ROE was, in fact, very good for three of the banks, when it was slightly above 30 per cent for Svenska Handelsbanken and between 25 and 30 per cent for SE-banken and Nordbanken. In 1990 the credit losses began to increase. This resulted in a negative ROE for Sparsbanken Första and, in 1991, the ROEs were negative for Gota Bank and Nordbanken too.

Is it then only because of the credit losses that ROEs are negative? Obviously, several of the Norwegian banks were also inefficient, and this led to low ROIFs. Certainly, the ROIF has declined for the majority of the Swedish banks too but, contrary to the Norwegian banks, the declining ROIFs are almost entirely explained by rising credit losses (see Figure 9.10).

If it were not for the credit losses, the ROIF would have increased for all the banks between 1987 and 1991. For some of the banks it has increased in spite of these losses. In this context it may seem strange that the ROIF (excluding credit losses) for Svenska Handelsbanken (SHB) decreases between 1990 and 1991. After all, this bank is known for its (superior) efficiency. One reason might have been the acquisition of the provincial bank, Skånska Banken, in 1990. This meant an additional network of 70 branches of which the major part (56 branches) was restructured and converted during 1991. As a consequence (?), the operating expense ratio increased slightly more than the bank's yield. However, when considering the whole five-year period, it seems as if the bank has been rather successful in cutting operating expenses. The

Figure 9.9   Return on equity before tax for five Swedish banks

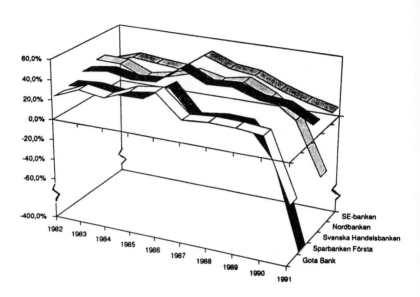

Figure 9.10   Return on invested funds (including loss effect) for five Swedish banks

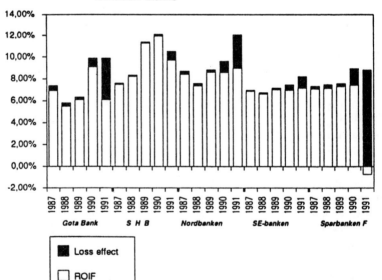

operating expense ratio (excluding personnel expenses and credit losses) has decreased almost five percentage points between 1987 and 1991.

Regarding the ROFL, only Svenska Handelsbanken and SE-banken have managed to obtain positive values during the whole period (see Figure 9.11). For Sparbanken Första the problems had already started in 1990 when the ROFL decreased thirty percentage points, from +8 per cent in 1989 to -22 per cent in 1990. The leverage spread changed from +0.4 per cent to -0.8 per cent, whilst the debt-equity ratio

Figure 9.11 Return on financial and loan loss leverages for the five Swedish banks

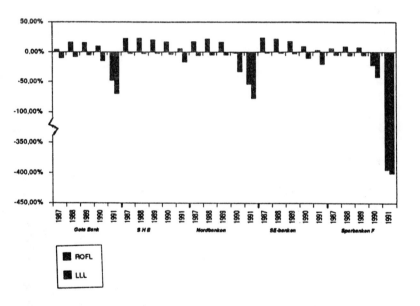

increased from 21.5 to 28.2. Doubtless the credit losses are the major causes of these changes, but it should also be noticed that the bank's CDF increased by 1.3 per cent (from 6.9 per cent to 8.2 per cent). In 1991 the situation became aggravated. Without substantial contributions (guaranteed by the Swedish government) from other savings banks, Sparbanken Första would not have existed any longer. However, in spite of an additional amount of SEK 3.8 milliards of so-called primary capital, the debt-equity ratio was almost doubled to 45.5. Since the leverage spread decreased to -8.7 per cent, the ROFL fell by more than 370 percentage points down to -395 per cent. Thus, in 1991, the ROFL was more than seventeen times as low as in 1990.

Nordbanken also had a negative ROFL in 1990, but only -1.7 per cent. As for Sparbanken Första and Gota Bank, the serious drop occurred in 1991. Although the bank managed to raise its ROIF, in spite of a loan loss provision ratio of 3.1 per cent, the leverage spread decreased to -2.1 per cent. The decrease was caused by an increase of the bank's CDF, which changed from 8.6 per cent to 11.1 per cent[7]. However, contrary to Sparbanken Första, the debt-equity ratio was strengthened (due to paid in capital from the Swedish government), so that the decrease of the bank's ROFL was restrained to -53.8 per cent. This is almost equal to Gota Bank's ROFL, which was -47.8 per cent. However, this very low ROFL is to a great extent explained by a decrease of the bank's ROIF (cf. Figure 9.9). Besides credit losses, this decrease was also caused by increased expenses for personnel and other operating expenses.

CONCLUSIONS

During the past one to five years, the credit losses have been substantial for the banks within the Nordic countries. For many other industries comparable losses and failures would have resulted in bankruptcies and radical structural changes. However, this is not valid for the banking industry; it is generally considered too important for the stability and efficiency of the financial system in a society. Both the Norwegian and Swedish governments have decided to rescue many of the suffering banks in order to prevent the financial systems from breaking down. In the short-term perspective these decisions are understandable and probably necessary, but are they desirable and efficient in the long run? They favour banks that have failed and, if not conserving the old established structures, so delay the natural processes of changes. In the worst scenario, inefficient banks survive at the expense of efficient ones; without any rescue operations, these banks might disappear anyway. Regardless of the true answer, it is obvious that the credit losses have shaken the countries to their very foundations.

In this study we have been focusing on individual banks. We can conclude that the credit losses for the examined banks have been severe.

None of the banks has managed to avoid huge losses; for many of them the provisions for loan losses have been enormous. However, the results must be interpreted cautiously: a bank's provision for loan loss is an estimation of its actual and expected possible credit losses. During the period studied, the banks' provisions for loan losses have shifted from being dominated by actual credit losses to being dominated by expected possible losses. This shift reflects an increasing uncertainty among banks about the magnitude of credit losses, but also it makes the analyses and evaluations of the performances of the individual banks imprecise. Hence, any comparisons between the different banks regarding credit losses and their impact on profitability are vague.

Bearing this in mind, we can also conclude that, for several of the banks, credit losses (loan loss provisions) do not seem to be the only reason for low profitability. The breaking down of the banks' returns on equity (ROEs) into the two components, return on invested funds (ROIF) and return on financial leverage (ROFL), reveals a certain amount of inefficiency in some of the banks. These inefficiencies were caused by a decreasing other income ratio and/or an increasing operating expense ratio. Furthermore, the approach of breaking down ROE shows that credit losses are not only serious because they affect the bank's ROIF: but their impact on the bank's financial strength is much more important and, in certain banks, burdensome. Since credit losses reduce the bank's equity capital (*ceteris paribus*), the debt-equity ratio increases proportionately to the losses. Hence, the bank's financial strength is weakened and thereby its financial risk rises. For all the Norwegian banks and three of the Swedish this has led to substantial losses. The high debt-equity ratios, in combination with the banks' negative leverage spread, have dramatically aggravated the economic consequences of the banks' credit losses, since the debt-equity ratio functions as a multiplier.

NOTES

1. Petterson (1992).
2. Cf. Vikkula (1991), who makes a few similar comparisons between some of the largest Nordic banks.
3. This statement is not general. It is based on comparisons between average and end-year balances in those annual reports where both figures are shown. In these reports greater differences only occurred when the trend changed to the opposite direction. In many

banks, for instance, this is the case regarding the lending portfolio, which has been increasing during the 1980s but is now decreasing.

4. In order to get a clearer picture, the order between the banks has been switched in Figure 9.2.
5. In this context is should be noticed that the denominator includes lending to financial institutions.
6. See, for example, Alberts (1989).
7. This increase is partly technical. In 1991 Nordbanken dissolved a major part of its untaxed reserves. Since 30 per cent of these reserves are regarded as a latent tax debt without any interest, the average interest expenses will naturally increase.

LIST OF REFERENCES

Alberts, W.W. (1989), 'Explaining a bank's ROE: an alternative approach', *The Bankers Magazine*, March-April

Petterson, K-H. (1992), *Den Norska Bankkrisen: Vad Kan Sverige Lära?*, Gothenburg

Reve, T. (1990), 'Hva gikk galt?', SAF, Bergen, Working paper no. 3

Reve, T. (1992), 'Learning to compete in a deregulated credit market: a lesson in banking failure', paper presented at the Fourth Annual Conference of the Society for Advancement of School Economics in California, Irvine, CA, 27-29 March and at the Bertil Danielsson Symposium in Gothenburg, 9-10 April

Vikkula, K. (1991), 'The competitiveness of Finnish and Scandinavian banks in the 1990s', *Kansallis Economic Review*, 4, and presented at the Bertil Danielsson Symposium in Gothenburg, 9-10 April 1992

Annual Reports

PART IV

SECURITIES MARKETS AND FINANCIAL CENTRES

CHAPTER 10

THE INTERNATIONALISATION OF BOND MARKETS

Richard Harrington

INTRODUCTION

One of the most striking features of the modern world is the rapid internationalisation of economic life as modern technology continues to
diminish the importance of distance. Of course this is not new in itself;
it is a trend which has been going on for centuries but, due to the revolution in microelectronics, the pace of change has increased markedly in
recent decades. This has affected all economic life and, indeed, political
life to the point where it has undermined traditional notions of sovereignty and of independent nation states. But nowhere have the changes been
more dramatic than in finance. It has become a common occurrence for
syndicates of banks from many countries to provide finance for a borrower in one country, denominated in the currency of another country,
with the whole deal arranged in yet another country. And it is perhaps
not surprising that banking should undergo such changes as a consequence of developments in microelectronics. Banking involves the
storage, accessing and updating of large amounts of data: the development of modern computers meant that all this could be done cheaply,
rapidly and across long distances.

The internationalisation of banking has been the subject of much
discussion and comment and of official concern, not least as far as the
maintenance of prudent behaviour by banks and of the supervision of
such behaviour is concerned. Much has been written on these topics[1].
Somewhat less attention has been paid to developments in securities
markets and security trading, although much the same trend of internationalisation has been taking place there. In recent years the process has
appeared to be acquiring greater momentum and it is now attracting
more attention from commentators and from official bodies[2]. This paper
seeks to provide an overview of what is happening and looks at some
potential implications.

SECURITY TRADING

Although modern security trading encompasses a wide range of different
assets, these can still be classified broadly into: 1) equity shares, invol-

ving claims of ownership on property and the income accruing thereto;
and 2) debt contracts or bonds, involving entitlements to prescribed
payments of interest. Dealing in equities remains predominantly national
although there have been a number of international issues including
certain sales of shares in companies being privatised. It is in the bond
market that the process of internationalisation has been proceeding rapidly and now appears inevitable.

It is convenient to distinguish four broad categories of bond.

Government bonds and public sector bonds with government guarantee

Such bonds are virtually free of default risk, are frequently issued in
large amounts and tend to be heavily traded. The larger issues provide
benchmark rates of interest in most national markets. Traditionally they
were almost invariably denominated in the local currency, were issued
mainly to domestic investors and were listed on the local stock exchange. This is still largely true today, although in recent years a
number of European governments have issued debt denominated in Ecu.

Government markets vary greatly in size depending on the size of
the country and on past and present financial policies. The three largest
are those trading bonds of the US federal government (nominal value in
excess of $1,650 billion at end of 1990); of the Japanese government
(nominal value in excess of US $1,160 billion equivalent); and of the
Italian government (nominal value in excess of US $590 billion equiva-
lent).

Private sector bonds and other public sector bonds issued in the domestic market

Traditionally, private sector bonds are issued by both financial and non-
financial corporations, although both the size of the total market and the
relative importance of these two types of issue vary greatly between
countries. The largest markets in corporate bonds are those of the
United States, Japan and Germany: in the United States issues are made
by a wide range of companies; in both Japan and Germany banks are the
predominant issuers. Other public sector issues include those of provincial and local authorities and of a variety of public agencies.

Bonds issued in one country by an issuer resident in another (foreign bonds)

These bonds which are normally denominated in the currency of the place of issue, constitute the traditional means of internationalisation of security trading. During the nineteenth century such bonds of foreign governments and public utilities were frequently issued in London and in Paris. Foreign issues remain substantial today only in a few markets notably Switzerland, the United States and Japan.

Bonds issued and traded by a number of international dealers in several countries (eurobonds)

These bonds, which were first issued in the early 1960s, are the clearest and best known example of the internationalisation of bond trading. They are issued and sold in a variety of countries; they are issued on behalf of a wide range of borrowers covering international organisations, national governments, public sector agencies and large corporations, both financial and non-financial; they may be denominated in any one of a number of currencies or in composite units such as the Ecu. Although the majority of eurobonds are straight fixed-rate bonds, a number of other forms of bond are issued, notably convertibles, bonds with warrants and bonds with variable interest rates.

THE INTERNATIONAL MARKET

Growth

The first and obvious manifestation of the internationalisation of security trading is the growth of issuing and trading in eurobonds and in foreign bonds. Table 10.1 gives figures of gross issues for selected years from 1975 to 1991. From this it can be seen that the volume of new issues has risen nearly tenfold in just over a decade. This rise is measured in terms of nominal US dollars, but after allowing for US inflation the rise in real terms would still be over sixfold[3]. At end-1991 the total stock of outstanding international bonds had a nominal value equivalent to US $1,651 billion. This figure is shown in Table 10.2 along with comparable figures for some of the larger domestic bond markets.

Table 10.1   Gross international bond issues

US$ billion

	Eurobonds	Foreign bonds	Total
1975	9.9	12.1	22.0
1980	25.6	11.3	36.9
1985	137.2	27.3	164.5
1988	183.7	43.1	226.8
1989	223.7	39.0	262.7
1990	212.4	50.8	263.2
1991			329.2

Source: Figures from the Bank of England ICMS database and published in Davis (1992) and Bank of England (1992)

Table 10.2   The stock of bonds outstanding: some comparisons

US$ billion

International bonds	1,651.4
US domestic market	6,088.3
Japanese domestic market	2,737.1
German domestic market	1,112.7
Estimated net international bank credit	**3,610.0**

Source: BIS, *Annual Report 1991-92*

Not only has the international bond market grown in volume, it has also grown in depth and in the range of instruments traded. Less than 40 per cent of outstanding bonds are denominated in US dollars and only just over 12 per cent in Japanese yen. The remainder are composed of bonds denominated in a wide range of other currencies, of which the Swiss franc, the Deutsche Mark, the pound sterling and the Ecu are the most important. Turnover in secondary market trading has also risen; this is discussed further below.

The growth in the size and diversity of the international bond market has occurred at a time when domestic bond markets have also been growing rapidly due, in a number of cases, to large and sustained government deficits and consequential large issues of government debt. But in a number of cases, there is evidence that private issues of debt are increasingly being made in the form of eurobonds and that traditional non-government domestic issues are declining. Before looking at this it should be stressed that the evidence concerns only most recent years and hence is necessarily limited and that therefore judgments must be tentative. This is inevitably the case as it is only in the past few years that many governments have permitted anything like free access for domestic investors to the international bond market. Hitherto exchange controls, taxation, listing requirements and other restrictions have all served to segment markets and to limit competition between domestic and international markets.

The United Kingdom abolished exchange controls during 1979 and 1980. France and Italy did so progressively over the 1980s, Sweden and Denmark reduced exchange controls during the 1980s, Spain, Portugal, Greece and Ireland are shortly to remove their remaining restrictions. Withholding taxes applied to non-residents in France and the United States were abolished in the 1980s, and it was made easier for non-residents to reclaim such tax in both the United Kingdom and Italy. A number of other controls on the timing or the types of bonds that may be issued in certain markets have also been removed or been modified in recent years. Some controls remain, notably the Swiss authorities continue to prevent the issue of eurobonds in Swiss francs, it remains necessary to comply with the detailed regulations of the Securities and Exchange Commission before issuing securities in the US market[4] and it is still necessary to have authorisation from the Ministry of Finance before issuing foreign bonds in Japan. Further, prudential regulations often limit the scope of financial institutions to hold certain types of asset or to issue certain types of debt.

The case of sterling

However, it is the case that there is more scope now for a convergence of domestic and international bond markets. Such a convergence appears to be taking place and nowhere is this trend more evident than in the United Kingdom. Table 10.3 shows gross sterling bond issues other than those of the UK public sector for the years 1980-91. This period of twelve years saw the re-opening of the London market to foreign issues after the ending of exchange controls and also saw a revival of issues by domestic companies after a number of years when high nominal rates of interest had reduced such issues to a trickle.

Two things stand out immediately. Firstly there is the substantial growth of the total market in sterling issues, and secondly there is the growing domination of eurosterling issues both for foreign borrowers and for domestic borrowers. During the four years 1980 to 1983 eurosterling issues (including FRNs) averaged 44 per cent of total issues; in the four years 1988 to 1991 the comparable figure was 84 per cent.

A number of reasons for this pronounced trend can be given:

- International investors are more familiar with issuing and trading procedures than they are with the procedures of the London Stock Exchange. They are also widely believed to have a strong preference for bonds issued in bearer form and for interest payments without deduction of withholding tax. All of these factors would make them prefer eurobonds.

- Many British investors are also likely to prefer to receive dividend payments gross rather than net of tax[5].

- This preference for eurobond issues has meant that they have tended to trade at a lower rate of interest than domestic sterling issues, even on occasions trading at rates of interest below those on government securities[6]. This means that issuers are likely to be able to offer slightly lower rates of interest on a euro-issue than on a domestic issue.

- Eurobond issues can be arranged more quickly than can domestic issues. This advantage may be decisive if the object of the issue is to take advantage of a temporarily favourable pattern of rates of interest.

- Eurobonds are normally issued unsecured but contain a negative pledge to the effect that future issues of bonds shall not be given any preferential security. Large companies able to borrow on the strength of their own reputation and/or explicit credit rating frequently prefer not to have to give any specific security. But, independently of any such preferences, once they have issued eurobonds with negative pledges they cannot then make an issue of secured bonds (debentures).

£ million

	Domestic issues			Eurosterling fixed rate			Total fixed rate	Eurosterling FRNs
	British	Foreign	Total	British	Foreign	Total		
1980	219	75	294	52	295	347	641	70
1981	7	440	447	0	249	249	696	0
1982	880	725	1,605	85	375	460	2,065	0
1983	300	595	895	145	688	833	1,728	505
1984	640	1,040	1,680	345	1,265	1,610	3,290	1,548
1985	597	710	1,307	522	1,450	1,972	3,279	2,275
1986	2,339	838	2,524	1,787	1,540	3,326	5,850	3,700
1987	2,030	0	2,030	3,544	4,413	7,957	9,987	1,247
1988	2,499	185	2,684	4,080	3,219	7,299	9,983	6,500
1989	5,280	645	5,925	3,292	3,303	6,595	12,520	5,150
1990	1,344	0	1,344	4,282	2,404	6,686	8,030	5,933
1991	996	0	996	6,520	5,051	11,571	12,657	4,285

Source: Bank of England
Note: 1. Including convertibles

These reasons suggest that the trend to eurosterling is unlikely to be reversed. But given that London-based security houses have a dominant share of eurobond trading, it is perhaps not surprising that in an era of financial liberalisation, sterling bonds issued in London should be issued in the form of eurobonds if this was deemed advantageous. But what about other financial centres and other currencies?

Other currencies

I have been unable to produce figures for bond issues in other currencies as detailed as those given for issues in sterling, but Table 10.4 gives information on nominal amounts of bonds outstanding at end-1990 denominated in a range of other currencies. The table compares totals of domestically issued bonds (excluding issues on behalf of the national government and public sector) and eurobonds. This table has two notable omissions. No figures are given for Swiss francs because there are

Table 10.4 Domestic issues and euro-issues: nominal amounts outstanding end-1990
US$ billion

	Domestic issues[1] (by residents and non-residents	Euro-issues	Euro-issues as a % of total
US dollar	1,796.1	525.9	22.6
Yen	766.9	115.9	13.1
Lira	128.3	14.0	9.8
French franc	89.3	27.5	23.5
£	37.5	106.6	74.0
Canadian $	50.0	47.9	48.9
Guilder	53.2	15.2	22.2
Australian $	11.5	25.8	69.7

Source: BIS (1991)
Note: 1. Excluding issues on behalf of the national government and public sector

no eurobonds outstanding in that currency: it is the policy of the Swiss authorities to have all Swiss franc bonds issues (by residents and by non-residents) made on the domestic market and to prevent such issues being made in the form of eurobonds. No figures are given for Deutsche Mark bonds because appropriate data were not available.

Table 10.4 shows a varied picture. On the basis of issues outstanding it is indeed in the sterling sector that euro-issues assume the greatest importance. But the position is not too dissimilar in the Australian dollar sector, and the total of euro-issues outstanding in Canadian dollars is only just less than that of domestic issues. The US dollar and the Japanese yen both have their own special features connected with very large domestic markets. Although euro-issues are large, it is likely that internationalisation will show up more in foreign holdings of domestic issues rather than in any decline in domestic issues as such. In the cases of the Dutch guilder and the French franc, euro-issues account for between one-fifth and one-quarter of all issues; in the case of the lira they account for less than 10 per cent. But all three of these currency sectors of the bond market have experienced measures of deregulation in recent years, with the ending of exchange controls in France and Italy of particular importance. In all three sectors there was a big increase in euro-issues in 1991[7].

The Ecu market

Another manifestation of the internationalisation of bond trading is the growth of the Ecu bond market. Although the first Ecu bond was issued only in 1981, by early 1992 the value of the Ecu bonds outstanding was almost Ecu 90 billion or around US $112 billion at then prevailing exchange rates. Issues of Ecu bonds in 1991 exceeded $33 billion equivalent, the average size of issue grew to Ecu 260 billion and turn-over in the secondary market increased greatly.

Interest rates

Insofar as a genuine international market in securities is emerging, the interest rate differentials on different types of bond within the same currency sector ought to be increasingly predictable. Differences in actual rates will, of course, remain due to differences in creditworthiness, marketability, costs of transactions, tax and so on, but the differences would be expected to be increasingly stable in that different types of bonds were increasingly substitutable.

The most detailed recent study of this is by Benzie (1992) using data from Salomon Brothers. He compared the returns on five-year government bonds with those on euro-issues and/or foreign issues of similar maturity in eight different currency sectors. Benzie derived correlations of returns in each case for the two periods, January 1978 to December 1984 and January 1985 to October 1990. The results were quite striking; in most cases measured correlations between returns were high, often greater than 0.9, and in most cases the correlations were noticeably higher in the second period than in the first. Benzie summed up his results in the following words:

The principal conclusion to emerge from this work is the increasing substitutability of domestic and international bond portfolios denominated in the same currency. In particular, as far as the sterling, Canadian dollar, French franc, Swiss franc and Japanese yen sectors are concerned, yields on international and domestic bond portfolios were much more closely correlated in the late 1980s than they were in the late 1970s and early 1980s.

GOVERNMENT BONDS

Government bond markets have traditionally been distinct national markets, each having its own customs and practices. The issuers were national governments and their agencies, and they tended to have close relationships with bond dealers in their own domestic markets. This remains true but nonetheless these markets are also becoming more open and more international. On the issuing side, a number of governments of small and medium-sized countries have issued bonds denominated in US dollars and other foreign currencies, while the governments of France, Italy and the United Kingdom have issued bonds denominated in Ecu. A number of markets have been reformed in ways that have made it easier for non-residents to purchase bonds, and there is evidence that among large investors there is growing willingness to hold the bonds of a number of different governments, and especially of those that make large liquid issues.

Detailed information is limited and there is also the problem that there are inevitably cycles in foreign investment in particular government bond markets as investors move in and out of currencies due to expectations about movements in exchange rates and interest rates. But notwithstanding this, some trends are appearing.

In the American government bond market, although foreign holdings rose sharply during the 1980s, they do not seem to have grown much faster than the market as a whole. At the end of the decade, the share of foreign ownership (including official holdings) of federal government bonds was around 20 per cent, much as it had been ten years earlier[8]. There does appear to have been a rapid growth of foreign holdings of German government bonds. Again the total market grew rapidly during the 1980s as the federal government sought to finance large budget deficits. At end-1991 foreign holding of all German public sector debt was estimated to be over DM 271 billion or around 45 per cent of total marketable debt[9]. In Britain foreign ownership of government bonds tends to be a fairly small proportion of total marketable debt. At end-March 1991 some 13 per cent of the total was foreign-owned, but of this nearly half was accounted for by official holdings[10]. In Italy, where foreign holding of government debt was traditionally very low, various government measures have resulted in a growing foreign interest; in the two years 1990 and 1991 some L 30,000 billion (US \$25.5 billion) debt was sold to non-residents amounting to about one-eighth of total sales of debt[11].

Another indication of the growing international holding of domestically issued bonds is the recent rapid increase in the amount of trading of such bonds that is settled on the international clearing systems Euroclear and CEDEL. The turnover of domestic fixed-rate securities settled through the two systems rose from around \$700 billion in 1987 to nearly \$3,000 billion in 1991, not far short of the value of eurobond settlements[12].

CONCLUSION

National financial markets are becoming more and more interlinked. This paper represents a preliminary look at one segment of the financial market, albeit a very important one, the bond market. The picture is one of rapid change. It is becoming less meaningful to talk about national bond markets and more realistic to talk about different currency segments of a world bond market. The size and domestic regulation of both the American and Japanese markets may ensure they do remain individual markets for some time yet, but within Europe the trend towards the international holding and trading of bonds is likely to continue.

At the microeconomic level this means that the different financial centres are more and more in direct competition with each other for the trading of both domestic issues and euro-issues: indeed the distinction between the two is likely to become of less and less significance. At the macro-level, it is likely to mean a greater willingness to shift funds into or out of currencies in the light of expected movements in exchange rates. This will mean it will be harder for central banks to defend exchange rates which lack credibility. It adds to the arguments in favour of opting for completely fixed exchange rates along the lines of the proposed economic and monetary union (EMU).

NOTES

1. See for instance the major study by Pecchioli (1983).
2. See for instance Benzie (1992) and Davis (1992).
3. Between 1980 and 1991, the US GDP deflator showed a rise in US prices of 64 per cent, or an average annual rate of 4.6 per cent. See Federal Reserve Bank of St Louis (1992).
4. Some modifications have occurred in the SEC requirements. Shelf registration, introduced in 1982, allows issuers more scope to time public issues, and more recently the regulations on private placements have been liberalised allowing unregistered securities to be sold to qualified (or large) investors.
5. It is usually assumed that such a preference indicates a desire to avoid paying tax. In many cases this may be so, but it may just indicate a desire to delay paying tax.
6. See Bank of England (1988) and Benzie (1992).
7. See Bank for International Settlements (1992, pp. 173-79).
8. See the *Economic Report of the President 1990*, Appendix Table C 86.
9. See the *Monthly Report* of the Deutsche Bundesbank, Appendix Table 10.9.
10. See Bank of England (1991).
11. See Banca d'Italia (1992).
12. See Bank of England (1992).

LIST OF REFERENCES

Banca d'Italia (1992), *Abridged Report for the Year 1991*

Bank for International Settlements (1991), 'The international and domestic bond markets', in *International Banking and Financial Market Developments*

Bank for International Settlements (1992), *62nd Annual Report* (June)

Bank of England (1988), 'Recent developments in the corporate and bulldog sectors of the sterling bond market', *Quarterly Bulletin* (February)

Bank of England (1991), 'The net debt of the public sector: end-March 1991', *Quarterly Bulletin* (November)

Bank of England (1992), 'Developments in international banking and capital markets in 1991', *Quarterly Bulletin* (May)

Benzie, Richard (1992), *The Development of the International Bond Market*, BIS Economic Papers, no. 32

Davis, E.P. (1992), 'The eurobond market' in D. Cobham (ed.), *The Economics of the London Financial Markets* (London: Longman)

Deutsche Bundesbank, *Monthly Report*

Economic Report of the President 1990 (Washington DC: US Government Printing Office)

Federal Reserve Bank of St Louis, *International Economic Conditions* (quarterly)

Pecchioli, R.M. (1983), *The Internationalisation of Banking: the Policy Issues* (Paris: OECD)

CHAPTER 11
THE DEVELOPMENT OF EUROPEAN CAPITAL MARKETS: THE MAIN TRENDS AND THEIR IMPLICATIONS

Tad Rybczynski

SUMMARY AND CONCLUSIONS

The main findings of this exercise, whose aim is to provide an overview of the key features of the present evolution of the European capital markets, their likely consequences and implications, can be summarised as follows.

The European capital markets are expanding in size and scope and are changing in character. The increase now under way covers the activities of the domestic markets of the twelve members of the European Community (EC), as well as of the markets in the countries of the European Free Trade Association (EFTA) now being integrated into the European Economic Area, which will be subject to EC rules and regulations. It is reflected in the increase in the number of listed companies' and public bodies' securities listed in stock exchanges (indicative of a continuing rise in the reliance of private sector companies on external funds raised through capital markets rather than from banks and other savings collecting institutions), a steadily growing use of capital markets by European and foreign public bodies and overseas companies, as well as a growing advance in the activities of the secondary markets. The main factors propelling this increase in size and geographical scope and a growing variety of financial instruments, now extending to derivatives and synthetic products, are the strong trend towards securitisation of the financial system, the privatisation policies being pursued by governments in Europe and overseas, and a rising recourse to capital markets by European and other public sector bodies.

The increase in size is accompanied by important changes in the character of the markets involving, above all, internationalisation and segmentation into two sectors. Internationalisation covers a rising volume of cross-border transactions in primary and secondary markets, associated with freedom of movement of capital and diversification by investors and companies seeking lowest-cost finance. Segmentation covers the division into wholesale and retail markets, each with different characteristics. This is due to the spread of institutional investors to the countries on the continent of Europe and overseas.

Increase in the size and scope, and changes in the character of the capital markets, together with rapid advances in technology, are having a profound impact on the structure of the industry. All stock exchanges are now in the process of modernisation and streamlining involving, first, the adoption of technologically advanced methods of price dissemination, information, trading, and clearing and settlement; secondly, the restructuring in the number of agency broking, broking/dealing and market-making firms; thirdly, linking of regional exchanges with central national and foreign exchanges.

Modernisation is undertaken with the view of retaining and improving relative position and becoming an important regional, national or international financial centre. This modernisation of exchanges is accompanied by a trend towards disintermediation among participants in the capital markets consisting in investors trying, with the help of new technology, to develop methods of dealing directly with other investors as regards their secondary market business.

On the European level, the proposal to create an EC-regulated price and company news information service, 'Euro-quote', has been abandoned. In its place it is planned to have 'Euro-list', a new service covering 150 large European companies. The inclusion on 'Euro-list' will automatically list companies in all EC and EFTA exchanges. This new approach is a reflection of an intense competition, especially among London, Frankfurt and Paris, to become the leading European financial centre. An important part in this competition, linked to the changes in the character of the market, is London's plan to create a new wholesale market.

Partly in response to rapid technological advance, partly as a means of helping their capital markets to gain a leading position or to prevent too much business drifting away, and partly as a move to create a Single European Financial Market, the regulatory framework continues to be changed, both on national and European (now Pan-European) levels. As regards the Pan-European level, the EFTA countries will now be adopting all EC directives relating to financial matters, above all the Second Banking Co-ordination Directive, and the yet-to-be-agreed Investment Services Directive. On the EC level, a number of directives complementary to the banking co-ordination and investment services directives, but bearing on capital markets, such as insider trading, are still in the pipeline.   On the domestic level, the regulatory framework is being modernised in the United Kingdom, France, Italy, Germany and other member countries - a process likely to continue for some time.

The prospects ahead are that the basic trends mentioned can be expected to continue.   The size of European markets (including their liquidity) and their scope are likely to continue to increase for various reasons: growing internationalisation; further growth in the size of companies, and lower cost and flexibility of capital market funds; a more rapid pace of privatisation, partly due to the endeavours of governments to contain the growing burden of welfare provision, mainly pensions and health; and, above all, a continuing rise in the relative importance of the institutional investor, trading wholesale and linked to the advance in funded pension and also health schemes, as well as the spread of collective savings institutions, often with special tax privileges.

This development, already leading to a two-tiered structure of the industry and dividing it into large multinational investment/securities houses and small and medium-size specialised firms, can be expected to gain momentum.

The regulatory framework is likely to advance further.   On the new European level, the Investment Services Directive, intended to introduce a 'level playing field', can be expected to be agreed upon within the next twelve to eighteen months, and there is likely to be progress on complementary matters such as insider trading directives and other items.

What the result of competition will be among three main stock exchanges, London, Frankfurt and Paris, and among them and other exchanges, will depend on the regulatory framework in each country and on the European level, the cost, flexibility and attraction of each centre and also on the location of the new European Central Bank when, and if, it is created.

PURPOSE AND SCOPE

This note, which examines the nature of the changes in the capital markets in Europe, has as its main purpose to provide a sharp but short overview of the key factors behind the changes now in train, and to assess their repercussions on the size, structure and character of the European financial industry in the years to come.

The European capital (and credit) markets are passing through an important and profound transitional phase.   This change can be said to have started in the mid-1980s when the United Kingdom introduced the so-called 'Big Bang', when important changes were introduced altering the regulatory framework and the basic institutional structure of the markets, and spread later to other European and overseas countries, changing the scope and nature of their securities and allied business. The wave then set in motion has been gathering strength and momentum ever since and is likely to be with us for some time.

Three basic features characterise the changes now under way. They are an increase in the size and scope and changes in the character of the European capital markets; the continuing adjustment of stock exchanges and firms to the new and continually altering external environment; and changes in the regulatory framework governing the working of the markets, both on the European Community and domestic levels.

The section which follows discusses macroeconomic developments determining the size and character of the markets by reference to the behaviour of the basic underlying trends and factors responsible for them. This is followed by a section which examines the response of the members of stock exchanges and the industry to the new and changing conditions, reflecting the impact of new technology, the new institutional framework and the different economic climate. The changes in the regulatory framework are the subject of the next section, in response to the Single Financial Market Programme, but against the background of the world developments in this area. The final section tries to see what are the implications of the basic trends for the future developments of the European capital market, its main structural elements and its role in the European and world financial system. This section also tries to see what would be the longer-term implications on capital markets of the European Central Bank (Euro-Fed) should such an institution be created, even in a strictly limited form in the closing years of the present decade. A few concluding observations are contained in the final section.

CHANGES IN THE SIZE, SCOPE AND CHARACTER OF THE EUROPEAN CAPITAL MARKETS

The size and scope of the market

The European capital markets have continued to increase in absolute size and also relative size, that is as measured by reference to their role as financial intermediaries. Estimates available show that the total number of domestic companies with listings in major EC exchanges amounted in 1990 to some 5800 and of overseas companies to some 1420. The number of domestic securities, excluding fixed-interest and public sector securities, amounted in 1990 to well over 6000, and of overseas securities to over 2100; of non-public sector fixed-interest securities to some 37,000 and of public sector debt securities to over 3500. Alongside the EC market there were nearly 1200 domestic companies listed in major EFTA countries' stock exchanges, where there were also some 830 listed foreign companies and nearly 9000 fixed-interest securities. These figures compare quite favourably with similar figures calculated for the United States and Japan (see Table 11.1). Such guesstimates as can be made indicate that the amount of new money (gross and net) raised using capital markets has also been increasing in absolute terms and, more importantly, as compared with flows through the banking system.

The increase in size of the EC capital markets is now accompanied by their geographical expansion and a rise in the number of types of securities. The geographical expansion involves the integration of the EFTA capital markets following the agreement between the EC and EFTA on the removal of all obstacles to the movement of capital, labour and services between the two groups and the EFTA countries' undertaking in principle to accept all the EC rules and regulations relating to the financial area.

A rise in the geographical coverage of European capital markets, which also include euromarkets centred in London, and whose size, measured by number of securities and their value as well as new issues, has been increasing, has been accompanied by a continuing increase in the variety and number of products, which include a number of synthetic products denominated in baskets of various currencies including the Ecu, as well as derivatives.

The increase in absolute and relative size of EC capital markets - as well as other European markets now linked into the EC markets - has been due to the securitisation of the financial systems in Europe, the rapid spread of privatisation, a steady increase in their use by non-EC countries as well as a growing reliance on them by public bodies in Europe and other countries.

The trend towards securitisation has involved a greater reliance of non-financial corporations on external funds raised through capital markets and a greater use of them by the public sector, as compared with funds raised through banks by way of bills and similar instruments and by direct appeal for direct savings to the household sector using various government savings instruments and publicly-owned savings banks.

Table 11.1 Companies and securities listed in the EC, EFTA, United States and Japan in 1990

Exchanges	Companies (numbers)			Securities (numbers)					Turnover equity 1991 (£ billion)
	Domestic	Overseas	Total	Domestic	Overseas	Fixed	Public	Total	
EC									
London	2,006	553	2,559	2,081	742	3,893	450	7,166	244.7
Frankfurt (Fed. of Exch)	649	555	1,204	776	616	15,838	...	17,230	181.2
Paris	443	226	669	...	...	...	...	...	48.1
Amsterdam	260	236	498	303	307	1,007	159	1,776	17.1
Madrid	427	2	429	...	...	...	...	...	17.5
Barcelona	419	7	426	405	2	431	247	1,085	...
Brussels	182	159	341	298	179	31	103	611	3.1
Copenhagen	258	10	268	336	14	2,274	90	2,714	4.5
Milan	220	-	220	...	...	106	1,197	...	12.3
Lisbon	152	-	152	174	-	374	...	548	0.5
Oporto	245	-	245	...	...	...	...	...	...
Luxembourg	550	183	733	1,400	229	7,424	1,078	10,131	0.08

continued

Table 11.1   (continued)

Exchanges	Companies (numbers)			Securities (numbers)					Turnover equity 1991 (£ billion)
	Domestic	Overseas	Total	Domestic	Overseas	Fixed	Public	Total	
EFTA									
Basle	151	236	387	411	284	2,259	...	2,954	...
Zurich	182	240	422	335	247	2,448	...	3,030	207.4[1]
Geneva	354	718	1,072	292	261	1,608	311	2,472	...
Stockholm	121	11	132	...	...	...	...	...	...
Helsinki	73	4	77	132	5	552	76	765	...
Vienna	99	52	151	128	59	1,982	-	2,169	9.7[1]
Other									
New York	1,678	96	1,774	2,174	110	2,912	-	5,196	871.7[1]
NASDAQ	3,875	256	4,131	271	101	-	4,706	706	-
United States	789	70	859	986	77	259	-	1,332	...
Tokyo	1,627	125	1,752	1,634	125	1,368	97	3,224	470.1[1]
Osaka	1,138	-	1,138	1,144	-	1,069	96	2,309	-

Source: World Stock Exchange
Note: 1. 1990

Some indication of the long-term trend towards securitisation of corporate non-financial sector finance is shown by an examination of the sources of funds of non-financial corporations in relation to gross (and also net) investment outlays (Table 11.2). The percentage of funds raised by share and bond issues in four major European countries, the United Kingdom, Germany, France and Italy, has shown a steady increase for some time now. This has also been true of the United States, Canada and Japan.

The trend towards securitisation, as defined previously, can be explained first by reference to the lower cost and flexibility of funds raised using capital markets rather than banks, and indeed directly from other financial intermediaries such as insurance companies and so on. That sizeable corporations can now raise additional funds more easily and cheaply, relying on domestic, foreign and international capital markets, there is little doubt. One of the important factors working in favour of the lower cost of capital market finance is the new capital requirements on banks required by the regulators in accordance with the Basle Accord, which imposes high risk coefficients on loans or holdings of equity in business enterprises. Not only is the cost of capital funds lower, but also capital markets instruments can be combined flexibly, with a rich variety of instruments offering opportunities to reduce interest rate and exchange risk by way of swaps, futures and options.

Accompanying the attraction of capital markets for sizeable companies has been a change in preferences of households to hold a larger share of their financial wealth in the form of stock exchange securities. Such information as is available indicates that holding of debt securities, long-term loans, shares, and other financial assets, excluding cash and deposits, as a percentage of GDP, has been growing very fast in three main European countries, Germany, France and Italy as well as in the US and Canada.

Some indication of this trend is shown in Table 11.3 which provides estimates of major types of financial assets held by households in four European countries, France, Italy, Germany and the United Kingdom, as well as, for comparative purposes, the United States, Canada and Japan. The table shows that cash and deposits held by households as a percentage of GNP/GDP have been declining and that in Germany, Canada and the United States they have, for all practical purposes, remained stable since 1980 and only increased in Japan. In contrast, their holdings of debt securities, shares and other assets, among which holdings of equity in pension and insurance funds are most important, have been increasing steadily.

Table 11.2 Sources of finance of non-financial corporations (gross)

Percentages of investment outlays

Country	Period	Retentions	Share issues	Loans	Bonds	Others
Germany	1970/79	75	...	...	40	8
	1980/84	79	...	...	38	8
	1985/89	86	2	...	30	10
France	1970/79	62	10	45	5	45
	1980/84	68	13	52	10	32
	1985/89	80	29	5	8	22
UK	1970/79	85	3	...	28	10
	1980/84	110	7	...	20	4
	1985/89	112	16	...	15	2
Italy	1970/79	49	8	...	56	9
	1980/84	52	15	...	44	9
	1985/89	65	6	...	28	6
US	1970/79	75	2	24	10	12
	1980/84	86	-1	36	8	8
	1985/89	108	-24	25	12	9
Japan	1970/79	50	5	...	68	48
	1980/84	59	7	...	55	15
	1985/89	58	8	...	59	18

Source: OECD

Table 11.3   Composition of household financial assets

Percentage of GNP/GDP

Country	Period	Cash & deposits	Debt securities & long-term loans	Shares	Other, incl. insurances & pension funds
France	1976/79	76	5	9	12
	1980/84	68	9	12	13
	1985/90	60	5	48	20
Italy	1979	62	13	4	20
	1980/84	52	18	20	12
	1985/88	50	40	10	25
Germany	1970/79	55	8	3	18
	1980/84	62	14	2	24
	1985/88	63	18	3	32
UK	1986	60	8	30	96
Canada	1971/79	51	22	30	40
	1980/84	54	20	32	48
	1985/89	54	20	33	55
Japan	1973/79	92	10	2	20
	1980/84	110	20	8	30
	1985/90	125	21	20	45
US	1979/80	62	22	49	100
	1980/84	65	33	38	112
	1985/89	67	29	45	110

Source: OECD

The implications of securitisation for the character of the markets and for the financial industry are discussed later.

The second main factor responsible for the increase in the size of the European capital market has been the now rapidly developing trend towards privatisation. One lasting legacy of the new economic philosophy and policies developed in the 1980s has been the acceptance of the need to privatise as large a proportion of publicly-owned and controlled assets as possible, as well as to shift a great proportion of 'welfare' spending undertaken by government, particularly as regards pensions, health and education, to privately-funded schemes. Privatisation of state-owned assets has now become a part of economic policy in Europe as well as other developed and developing countries. In addition to helping public sector finances, this policy, which can be said to be in its initial phase, except for the United Kingdom, has still a long way to go, and is raising the size and the role of capital markets in Europe and other countries.

Alongside the policy of privatising publicly-owned or controlled assets, economic policy in European countries has started shifting towards the privatising of some or part of welfare services such as pensions, health and education which, at present, are paid for on a 'pay-as-you-go' basis. Privatisation of welfare services has two effects on capital markets. First, by shifting the financing of such activities, it will increase the business of existing companies, above all insurance companies in the private sector, private or listed on the stock exchange. This will raise the value of companies already listed and may cause previously unlisted companies to obtain listing. Second, it will probably lead to the creation of new companies involved directly or indirectly in this activity, some of which will probably wish sooner or later to obtain listing. In the former case the value of existing companies with listing, such as insurance companies, will increase; in the latter case the probability is that some of the companies will, in due course, obtain stock exchange listing. At the same time, new funding activities will increase funds available for investment, including investment in listed securities.

Two other factors responsible for the growth of European capital markets comprise a growing use made of them by the EC public bodies and non-EC enterprises and public bodies. This development reflects relative ease, now that capital movements are no longer controlled, to seek lowest-cost sources of capital as far as users of funds are concerned on the one hand, and on the other, highest risk-related return combined with diversification as far as world investors are concerned.

Changes in the character of the market

Two basic features characterise the development of capital markets and their structure. They are first, the continuing trend toward steadily increasing internationalisation and second, the segmentation of the markets into two sections, the wholesale and retail markets. Internationalisation of European capital markets has involved a rise in the relative share of new issues made in European domestic markets and euro-markets by non-EC and non-European entities; second, growth in the number of EC and other European and non-European securities listed in the EC (and EFTA) capital markets; third, a rise in the number (and value) of EC (and EFTA) securities held by non-residents; and, finally, an increase in the relative importance of cross-border business in the EC secondary markets involving intra-EC, intra-European and non-European business.

Some indication of a rise in issues by non-EC residents is given by a value of non-domestic bond issue in the EC countries in the last five years and an increase in the gross issues of bonds in the euromarkets in the same period shown in Table 11.4.

Table 11.4   New bonds issues by non-residents in the EC markets and Switzerland, and new issues in the euromarkets

$ billion

	1987	1988	1989	1990	1991
EC countries	2.6	3.6	5.1	7.0	8.3
Switzerland	24.3	26.3	18.6	23.2	20.2
Euro-markets	159.9	199.7	232.0	199.7	269.1

Source: OECD

Such estimates as are available show that the number of new listings in EC and other European exchanges continues to grow (Table 11.5).

Among the EC countries the four main centres attracting overseas
companies are London, Frankfurt, Paris and Luxembourg, the last of
these offering the advantages of especially tax favourable treatment for
unit trusts.

Table 11.5   New listings of foreign companies

	1988	1989	1990
London	34	49	-54
Frankfurt	74	91	...
(Association of Federations)			
Luxembourg	9	15	...
Paris	16	16	-21
Other EC	22	19	...
Zurich	17	...	...

Source: London Stock Exchange

The third element of internationalisation of capital markets has been
a rapid rise in cross-border (and cross-exchange transactions carried out
in off-shore centres) equity and bond business. Estimates available show
that cross-border equity transactions in the secondary markets have been
rising steadily, reflecting mainly higher turnover (Table 11.6). Of the
world total of $2.1 trillion turnover in equity, about 20 per cent repre-
sents intra-EC transactions, about 10 per cent transactions between the
EC and EFTA, about 35 per cent transactions between the EC and the
rest of the world, and nearly 5 per cent transactions between EFTA and
the rest of the world excluding the EC.

Such guesstimates as can be made tend to suggest that cross-border
bond activity (in secondary markets) has been substantially greater than
in equities and amounted in 1991 to between $5-6 trillion. This figure
reflects rapid growth of the bond market (Table 11.7) and a rise in
turnover. Propelling the growing cross-border transactions in secondary

markets has been the policy of geographical diversification of assets by investors and, above all, the rapid growth of institutional investors discussed later.

Table 11.6   Gross cross-border equity transactions and ownership of foreign shares

	1988	1989	1990	1991
Cross-border and cross-exchange transactions ($ trillion)	1.6	2.2	2.3	2.1
Foreign investors' holdings of world market capitalisation (per cent)	5.5	7.7	7.4	8.1

Source: Baring Securities

Table 11.7   World and EC bond market

$ billion, nominal value

	1975	1980	1985	1990
International	...	132	410	1,419
Domestic	...	3,168	5,450	11,367
Total	...	**3,300**	**5,860**	**12,786**

Source: BIS

The second outstanding change as regards the nature of the EC, other European, and other capital markets has been their segmentation into the wholesale and retail markets. This division reflects the growth of institutional investors comprising pension and insurance funds as well as savings collecting bodies other than banks, such as unit and investment trusts. Institutional investors now have around three-quarters of UK equities, about 60 per cent of equities in the United States, and account for a growing proportion of equities and other securities in other industrial countries (see Table 11.8). Institutional investors are diversifying their holdings to include foreign securities and tend to trade in large blocks quite frequently, indeed continually, to take advantage of changes in their perception of markets, currencies and different securities.

Table 11.8 Institutional assets as a percentage of GNP

	1975	1985	1995[1]
Switzerland	40	60	90-95
US	40	52	60
Japan	10	20	40
Germany	8	19	45
UK	40	75	80

Source: BIS
Note: 1. Estimates

The emphasis on continual trading in large quantities, normally exceeding $250,000 for equities and $500,000 for bonds, has led to the rapid growth of the wholesale market, which is playing a rapidly increasing role as compared with the retail markets whose importance is decreasing. The emphasis of institutional investors is on cost and speed of execution as compared with emphasis on protection required by individual investors.

The main factors behind the rapid growth of institutional investors are demographic trends and governmental policies to transfer part of the burden of welfare provision and, above all, pensions to the private sector by encouraging funded pension and health schemes. At present private funded pension schemes on the Continent are rare since most of such business is undertaken by governments on a 'pay-as-your-go' basis, as in France, Italy, Belgium, and by individual companies using cash flow for internal investment, as in Germany, but on a government underwritten basis. In addition, institutional investors, which also comprise collective savings institutions such as unit and investment trusts, are gaining in importance because of special tax privileges accorded to them to spread the habit of holding shares by individuals.

CHANGES IN THE STRUCTURE OF THE INDUSTRY

The structure of the capital market industry which, apart from non-financial companies and their business in the primary markets, comprises fund management companies and financial intermediaries linked to the industry (that is market-makers, broker/dealers and agency brokers, and financial exchanges), has been experiencing important and profound changes.

The fund management industry is now assuming a structure based on four divisions. The four sections comprise: first, very large, often vertically integrated, investment units, engaged in the search for disintermediation; secondly, medium-size units, which do not have a sufficiently large base to develop full independence, including integration of various activities which the newly emerging technology-based infrastructure allows; thirdly, small and medium-size boutiques specialising in activities in various segments, covering either geographical areas or industries or markets or certain segments of the derivatives and/or synthetic instruments; and, finally, a new breed of managers engaged in managing funds by using products produced by boutique or niche managers.

The emergence of large, often vertically integrated, units reflects the growth of institutional investors and, above all, pension funds. Their thrust has been towards integration, that is the elimination of intermediaries covering different activities in the chain of investment from research to custody with the aim of reducing costs. This trend now extends to the use of electronic trading networks which eliminate dealer, agency broking, broking/dealing and also market-makers, taking advantage of new technology. The new systems now being introduced, which comprise Instinet, Posit and Select, are fully automated systems providing dealing, confirmation and reporting facilities. The trend towards disintermediation propelled by big users, together with the expansion in the geographical scope and product variety, including derivatives, has been exerting strong pressure on exchanges and is raising a number of important issues, especially as regards liquidity.

The medium-sized fund management companies, which include insurance companies, unit trusts, and so on, are gradually coming under pressure but are being constrained by the highly imperfect and growing market where information is far from full. Consequently, neither their performance nor their costs are easily, if at all, ascertainable. Nevertheless, in this sector one can notice a trend towards mergers and amalgamation with other financial institutions, domestically and internationally. The boutique or niche segment is still expanding especially in the area of derivatives and quantitative management, although some signs of a trend towards larger units are beginning to appear.

A new segment is that of fund managers managing funds indirectly by selecting and changing boutique and niche managers in accordance with their performance. Unlike the trend towards disintermediation characterising large units, this group in fact appears to a certain extent to 'unbundle' at least some of the activities constituting the chain of fund management business. What is in fact happening is that some of the managers in the second segment mentioned, the medium-sized and small units, are increasingly transforming themselves into members of this group.

To a large extent the changes in the structure of the European capital market industry affecting market-makers, broking/dealing, agency brokers and exchanges are a reflection of the pressures put on them by companies using them for the purpose of raising funds, by investing institutions, and by competition among themselves to gain a proper place in the newly emerging Single European Financial Market and especially competition among London, Paris and Frankfurt to become a leading European financial centre.

As far as the creation of an EC-regulated price and news information service is concerned, the ambitious plan to create a 'Euro-quote' has now been abandoned because of the unwillingness to support this essentially French-backed project by London and Frankfurt. This has now been replaced by three different approaches, the first of which is the creation of a Euro-list. Such a list would comprise some 150 companies, which would have to have a minimum market capitalisation of 1.5 billion Ecus or turnover in their shares of at least 250 million Ecus. They would be listed on all European exchanges which are members of the Federation of European Stock Exchanges, which includes all EFTA countries.

Inclusion on the Euro-list will remove the need for separate listing on the exchanges which are members of the Federation of European Stock Exchanges and will now also embrace those of the three non-EC Scandinavian countries, Norway, Sweden and Finland, as well as Switzerland and Austria. The inclusion in the Euro-list will be cost-saving to the companies concerned, in that there will be no need for multiple listing applications, and will facilitate the distributions of various announcements in various markets with different mixes of the wholesale and retail business with their different requirements. The users of the wholesale markets engaged in block trading emphasise cost and liquidity. Intermediaries operating in it require considerably longer time-lags between dealing and their disclosure, and a considerably more flexible and lighter regulatory framework than that required in domestic markets. Of course, the London SEAQI International competes direct with Euro-list in that it aims at the same universe of European countries. However, it also aims to attract large non-European companies and is not restricted to price and company news dissemination but also provides full dealing facilities.

Alongside these two approaches to wholesale business, individual stock exchanges are now engaged in the process of modernisation designed to improve their competitiveness. This is the third approach. This development must be looked at as complementary to the competitive struggle to catch as large a share of the trading in secondary markets as possible. It is now increasingly realised that the euromarket, with its special rules agreed by the International Securities Market Association (ISMA), formerly the Association of International Bond Dealers (AIBD) is supported by the integration of the two clearing systems, Euroclear and CEDEL, and its new reporting system (Trax) is also a competitor. Also, primary markets are bound to be anchored in various domestic markets and will continue to cater for retail business (transacted in the secondary markets). Consequently, future developments will be concerned above all with the linking of markets within Europe and between European and non-European markets, including also the integration of the settlement systems. This development, involving separation of wholesale equity markets, wholesale government and allied securities markets, euromarkets and retail markets is driven, not only by economic or cost, but also by political considerations. This is so because it is now clear that, in the absence of political unification, individual countries would insist on having their own capital markets (whatever their size and character) because this is considered an integral part of their sovereignty and a necessary link in the chain to complement their fiscal policy.

Closely linked to the modernisation and automation of the national stock exchanges has been restructuring of the intermediaries. The main feature of the development now under way is first, the acceptance of the system of dual capacity in the countries where the functions of market making and acting as agent had been separated; second, concentration of market-making and broking/dealing in the hands of (universal) banks, either directly or indirectly through special subsidiaries, accompanied by rationalisation; and, third, interpenetration of various domestic market intermediaries and markets by other European and non-European firms through purchasing previously independent firms and setting up subsidiaries and branches.

By now all EC and other European countries have removed legal and other barriers separating market-making, agency and banking and investment banking activities. As a result, universal banks are now undertaking these activities, directly or indirectly. As a consequence, capital market intermediary activities, as deposit banking activities, tend to be dominated by a relatively small number of institutions surrounded by a relatively small and decreasing number of independent agency brokers whose business tends to be limited to special areas.

The concentration and rationalisation of the intermediaries and the emergence of an oligopolistic structure dominated by banks has been accompanied by a trend towards interpenetration involving large banks, European and non-European, and investment banking houses establishing presence in other European (and non-European) countries.

The overall result of these developments among intermediaries is the emergence of a two-tier oligopolistic structure of market-makers, broker -dealers and agency brokers dominated by a relatively small number of large universal and investment banks surrounded by medium-size and small units operating essentially on a regional basis.

CHANGES IN THE EUROPEAN REGULATORY FRAMEWORK

Changes in the European regulatory framework have two dimensions. The first has to do with the rules emanating from Brussels and applicable to all EC members, and now also to EFTA members; the second concerns new measures introduced by individual countries and is concerned with the operations of their capital market intermediaries.

The EC dimension of the regulatory framework includes the Investment Services Directive, which involves a single passport for investment banking activities (issues in primary markets, trading in secondary markets by firms offering such services), and allied directives concerned with the functioning of the markets, as for example 'insider trading'.

The EC regulation of investment firms is essentially concerned with their capital adequacy. This matter is also being dealt with by the Bank for International Settlements (BIS), G-10 Committee on Banking Supervision and the International Organisation of Securities Commissions (IOSCO), a body bringing together national securities regulators.

The Capital Adequacy Directive, and the Investment Services Directive now being discussed in Brussels, try to reach a compromise between the approach to and the demands of the universal banks which are involved in securities business, pure investment banking houses and, above all, the UK and US firms, which do not engage in deposit banking.

What is at issue, and has not so far been resolved, is capital requirements against various risks and the way risk is measured. The former covers various types of risk, long equity positions, short positions, debt positions and risk on derivatives. The measurement problem is concerned with the problem of whether risk should be measured on a gross basis or a net basis.

What ultimately emerges will have a profound impact on the development of the markets and their location. Against the background of increasing division of investors into large institutional investors concerned with efficiency, cost and liquidity and retail investors concerned with transparency, the emphasis of UK regulations is primarily on cost and liquidity, supportive of wholesale markets. The Continentals and the BIS, G-10 group and the Securities and Exchange Commission (SEC) of the United States (which plays an important role in IOSCO) put the main emphasis on transparency and protection of retail investors. This attitude is explicable in terms of importance of retail business on the Continent and a powerful lobby favouring retail business in the United States.

A compromise favouring European (and the SEC) approach would favour Continental universal banks; that favouring the British approach would favour British investment firms. However, there is reason to think that a high capital adequacy requirement would lead to the emergence of off-shore markets depriving Europe of the benefits of truly integrated capital markets. The emergence of new off-shore centres, or an increase in the business of the existing centres, would favour London to a certain extent in that London has large expertise in managing funds through off-shore centres.

The second element in the regulatory framework of the European dimension comprises various directives already approved, implemented, about to be implemented, in the pipeline, or only under debate in general terms, such as harmonisation of various aspects of corporate finance and capital markets, such as insider trading, tax, and so on. This aspect of the Euro-dimension has still a long way to go.

On the domestic level, the regulatory framework is being restructured in virtually all EC and other European countries in response to market developments. Broadly speaking, the thrust at present is to ensure transparency while preserving adequate strength of capital market intermediaries. In the United Kingdom it is proposed to streamline the structure of self-regulatory bodies, reducing their number and simplifying reporting and monitoring requirements but treating wholesale markets in a different manner from the retail market. At the same time the London Stock Exchange, as mentioned previously, is preparing new rules to govern the operations of SEAQ International.

France is also streamlining the new regulatory structure installed initially in 1988 and in the light of pressures and the recent collapse of an important stockbroking firm. At the same time discussion has started about the way of setting up rules for conducting takeovers and insider trading. New legislation introduced in Italy also contains rules covering the behaviour of investment activity to be undertaken only by newly created special companies. Outside the European Community, Switzerland has been introducing new rules as regards the type of shares and voting rights attached to them.

PROSPECTS AHEAD

There is little doubt that the EC and European capital markets can be expected to continue to grow. The fundamental forces responsible for this development comprise continuing securitisation of the financial system; privatisation; the demographic trends leading to the setting up of funded pension schemes, as is already happening in France, and encouragement, including tax relief, to fund health schemes; and growing use of capital markets by governments to finance their deficits as well as by other public bodies. Such guesstimates as can be made suggest that the impact of the forces will be stronger in Europe than in North America and also to a certain, though rather limited, extent in Japan.

Likewise, the prospects are that the EC and European capital markets will continue to assume a two-tier character and become increasingly internationalised. The division into wholesale markets engaged in block trading and retail markets will become stronger as international investors, pension funds, insurance companies, mutual funds and similar organisations increase in absolute size and relative importance as depositories and users of new savings. Again this trend is likely to be much stronger in Europe than in North America and also, to a small degree, than in Japan, where the division is already quite marked.

Also the trend toward internationalisation involving cross-border trading in secondary markets and greater use of the European primary market can be expected to gain momentum. This is because of further reductions in constraints imposed on insurance and pension funds on foreign investment in Europe and non-European developed countries, the spread of awareness of the benefits of diversification, and the availability of derivatives facilitating hedging. In as much as further progress will be made towards irrevocably fixed foreign exchange rates and European economic and monetary union (EMU), the European capital markets can be expected to be among the main beneficiaries.

The structure of the industry can be expected to continue to change. Such indications as are available suggest that, linked to the emergence of two different segments of the markets, wholesale and retail, there will also come into being - it is already appearing - a three-tier structure of capital market intermediaries. The first tier will comprise large international market-makers and broker/dealers with a presence in all major world financial centres and membership of major stock exchanges. They will be providing their services predominantly to large institutional investors with a worldwide interest in diversifying portfolios and using derivative instruments. Because of the economies of scale and coverage of all exchanges, including those dealing in derivatives, they will compete on cost and efficiency, placing business where the combination of them is best. They will be capable of shifting their business from order-driven to quote-driven exchanges as required.

The second tier would comprise regional broker/dealers, and market-makers specialising in certain areas and possible products, such as bond and equities with or without derivatives.

Finally, there will be small to medium-size agency brokers offering their service to private individuals and, possibly, smaller institutional investors such as small charities.

In the longer run the question for large and medium firms will be not so much competing among themselves as competing with commercially run systems such as Instinet, Posit, and others.

These changes can be expected to be associated with the linking of national exchanges, where they still have independent existence, and also of national exchanges once the last stage of EMU comes into effect. This development, however, is unlikely before the first decade of the next century at the earliest.

Closely linked with this aspect of future changes is the impact of the location of the future European Central Bank on the location of the dominant capital market in Europe. Since the new central bank will operate in money markets, exchange rate markets and, probably, also in securities markets - depending on the functions entrusted to it - there is reason to believe that such activities will attract money, credit, capital and foreign exchange and possibly capital markets. This impact is still inadequately explored but the possibility that this may occur must not be dismissed out of hand.

CONCLUDING REMARKS

This exercise has tried to bring out the main features of the present developments in European capital markets in order to provide a compact but sharp overview of the key elements and the implication they carry. The basic factors influencing the size and character of the markets are fairly clear. However, the way the industry will be changing will be influenced not only by technology but also by new institutional arrangements now in train; by search for lowest cost on the part of stock exchanges and capital market intermediaries; by the evolution of the regulatory framework on the European, national and international level; and also by the decisions about the location of the proposed European Central Bank and its method of operation. This will not become clear for some time yet.

CHAPTER 12
THE COMPETITIVENESS OF EUROPEAN INTERNATIONAL FINANCIAL CENTRES

Jean-Paul Abraham
Nadia Bervaes
and
Anne Guinotte

COMPETITION BETWEEN FINANCIAL CENTRES: A SPECIFIC ASPECT OF FINANCIAL COMPETITION

In the last decades, progress in transport technology, telecommunications and data processing has heavily stimulated the worldwide dispersion of financial operations. Given the necessary equipment and decision-making power, the dealer in a remote office can trade with his colleagues all over the world through the SWIFT system and other systems of telecommunication. In spite of these worldwide professional 'home banking' opportunities, financial activities tend to remain geographically concentrated in some areas and places, old and new. When transactions with overseas - with and among non-residents - are important in these places, we call them international financial centres (IFCs). Their activity adds an international, geographical and institutional dimension to financial activity, which we will try to discuss in this paper.

Economic analysis of geographically localised *financial* activity has lagged behind the development of regional studies of *economic* activity. Most studies have a historical and/or descriptive and/or promotional character. The latest full-scale book on international financial centres (Park and Essayad 1989) was the offshoot of a conference organised to assess the competitive edge of ... Anchorage, Alaska, as an IFC! In the last 25 years, the sparse economic literature has been dominated by a few big names. In chronological order they are: Kindleberger (1974), Reed (1981), Dematte (1981), Choi, Tschoegl and Yu (1986), Helsley and Levi (1988), Park and Essayad (1989), Goldberg, Gardener and Molyneux (1990).

Meanwhile, the concept and the activity of IFCs have developed and changed in at least four respects:
- The *number* of IFCs has increased in a significant way. Worldwide dispersion of financial *activity* has also meant worldwide dispersion of IFCs.

- The *variety* of IFCs has become much larger. Obviously, Luxembourg, the Bahamas, Singapore, Hong Kong and Bahrain differ in many respects from London, New York, Paris and Frankfurt.
- *Business* in the IFCs has increased in an explosive way. The 'financial bubbles' of the 1980s have been mainly bubbles in the major IFCs.
- As a cause and also as a consequence of the three previous factors, *competition* among financial centres has strengthened significantly. Each centre tries to attract customers and business and to augment its part of the global financial pie. Competition in financial services no longer stems only from individual financial institutions, banks or non-banks, or from individual nations, but also from IFCs. These act, of course, in interdependence with financial institutions and governments, but do not identify themselves completely with them. The policy of Wall Street, the City of London and the Damrak does not necessarily identify itself with that of the respective authorities and financial participants.

The financial markets and public opinion in general have been flooded with publications, audio- and video-shows promoting the strengths of a particular IFC and minimising its weaknesses. In Belgium, the authorities have even invited the financial community, in a very persuasive way, to join them, all over the world, in a series of 'roadshows' aimed at promoting Brussels as an IFC.

In this general context, our study concentrates on three questions:

- Given the variety of IFCs, how can we *classify* them according to various criteria? No reasonable comparison and evaluation of IFCs can be made, if they are not classified in advance into various types and categories.
- How can we *compare* IFCs, assess their strengths and weaknesses, and isolate their specific competitive edge?
- How can we *apply* the previous analysis to the case of *Brussels* and analyse, in this respect, the material and documents prepared for the international roadshows which were held in 1991?

Our analysis concerns mainly, but not exclusively, the comparison between financial centres in Europe. This limitation has not only been introduced for practical reasons, but also because the development of a single financial market in the European Economic Community, and more generally the Europe 1992 plan, is due to increase the competitive pressure on IFCs located in the EEC area.

CLASSIFYING IFCs: MAJOR CRITERIA AND SOME APPLICATIONS FROM THE LITERATURE

It would be tedious and futile to provide a full encyclopaedia of classification criteria in this article. In the literature, most classifications were established for specific purposes and have no general significance. More important for us is to reduce those various classifications to a few archetypes, each of them based on a simple clear-cut approach. In this respect, we may distinguish two main approaches to the classification of IFCs. The first distinguishes and classifies the IFCs according to the main function they are supposed to perform. The second aims at setting up a hierarchy of IFCs, to rank them according to the importance of the international financial links and the intensity of their activity. Some examples of the functional and the hierarchical ranking approach are given below. It may be argued that the two approaches are not mutually exclusive, but complementary. This is indeed true. Nevertheless, in some classifications the dominating note is functional, while in others ranking considerations come to the fore.

The functional approach to classification: combining two applications

Although partially outdated by the developments of the 1980s, the classification of Dufey and Giddy (1978) remains the standard starting point for a functional approach to IFCs. These authors distinguish three possible basic functions of an IFC:

- *traditional capital export*: the transfer abroad of a domestic savings surplus, as performed by London during the Golden Age of the Gold-Sterling Standard and by New York after World War II and before the Interest Equalisation Tax of 1963
- *an entrepôt function*: where the IFC intermediates between the investors from abroad, who want to invest their savings, and the borrowers at home or abroad
- *offshore banking*: where financial services and intermediation are provided exclusively for non-residents and are not subject to domestic regulations concerning monetary and prudential control and taxation

Park and Essayad (1989) devote more attention to the sources and destination of funds and suggest some ranking between IFCs. They distinguish:

- *primary centres*, in highly industrialised countries which operate

heavily both on the demand and the supply side of funds
- *funding centres*, which concentrate on *inward* financial intermediation
- *collection centres*, specialising in *outward* financial intermediation
- *booking centres*: offshore centres without much financial infrastructure, which function as a financial entrepôt for non-residents

The most interesting feature of this approach is to link the classification of IFCs with the *nature* and not only with the *volume* of activity in those centres. Unfortunately, this is also the major weakness of the approach. The nature of activity is rapidly *changing* in the major centres, more specifically towards services and in general towards fee business. This business is not always linked to the traditional financial intermediation on which the classification of Dufey and Giddy, and to a certain degree that of Park (1982) is based. In the entrepôt centres, like London, the services provided in the entrepôt are often more important than the in- and outflow of funds.

Another problem arises from the very fact that the activity in major IFCs is nearly always a *mix* of different functions. This mix is also subject to rapid change. Internal equilibrium and balance of payments problems have spectacularly reduced the traditional capital export function of Wall Street, the City of London and now, after German reunification, of Frankfurt, to the benefit of entrepôt functions and even some elements of offshore banking like the IBF (International Banking Facilities) in New York. At the other extreme, Luxembourg has been rapidly enriching its offshore banking by services linked to the entrepôt function: portfolio management, SICAVs, etc. Altogether, our experience is that the practical use of the functional approach for classifying IFCs is limited to splitting up the very diversified set of IFCs into broad categories. Inside these categories, some centres can be considered as *prototypes* of a specific kind of geographical distribution of international financial activity.

In Table 12.1A, we have tried to combine and to update the classification of Dufey and Giddy, and Park in order to distinguish a dozen functionally different *categories* of IFCs. In Table 12.1B, we have roughly classified, according to these categories, the 37 centres which we are considering in our ranking exercise below. As this functional approach concentrates on financial intermediation, we have used the importance of foreign financial assets (FFA) and liabilities (FFL) as statistical criteria. The data are given in Appendix 12A. The outcome does not mean very much as long as no ranking is introduced between major and less important centres. The classification shows that the

Table 12.1A Categories of IFC according to a functional approach

	Entrepôt	Traditional capital export	Offshore
Primary	Highly industrialised home country Worldwide collection and distribution of funds Large array of financial services Professional expertise Efficient financial infrastructure and telecommunications Flexible regulatory framework (no exchange control, no monetary control for non-residents)	Highly industrialised home country Important domestic savings surplus Excellent financial infrastructure No control of international capital movements	Highly industrialised home country Efficient telecommunications Favourable taxation system for non-residents Flexible regulatory framework

continued

Table 12.1A (continued)

	Entrepôt	Traditional capital export	Offshore
Funding	Inward financial intermediation International network of suppliers of funds	Not relevant	Inward financial intermediation Favourable taxation system for non-residents Flexible regulatory framework
Collection	Outward financial intermediation Efficient management and placement of funds	Outward financial intermediation Domestic savings surplus	Outward financial intermediation Favourable taxation system for non-residents Flexible regulatory framework

continued

Table 12.1A (continued)

	Entrepôt	Traditional capital export	Offshore
Booking	Collection and distribution of funds of non-residents without much financial value added No extensive financial infrastructure	Not relevant	Collection and distribution of funds of non-residents without much financial value added No extensive financial infrastructure Favourable taxation system for non-residents Flexible regulatory framework

Table 12.1B   Functional classification of 37 IFCs

	Entrepôt	Capital exports	Offshore
Primary (FFA and/or FFL >250)	London Tokyo Paris	Zurich Frankfurt	Hong Kong Singapore Luxembourg
Funding (FFL > FFA)	**Major** (FFA/L > 100) Brussels Milan		
	Average (30 < FFA/L < 100) Toronto Vienna Stockholm Madrid Helsinki Mexico City		
	Minor (FFA/L < 30) Oslo Manila Rio de Janeiro Santiago Melbourne Bangkok Seoul Johannesburg Athens Montevideo Buenos Aires		
Collection (FFA > FFL)	**Major** (FFA/L > 100) Amsterdam		
	Average (30 < FFA/L < 100) Bahrain	United Arab Emirates	

continued

Table 12.1B (continued)

	Entrepôt	Capital exports	Offshore
	Minor (FFA/L < 30) Copenhagen Cairo Jakarta Lisbon Kuala Lumpur		
Booking	The Bahamas	Panama City	

Source: Data from Appendix 12A
Note: FFA: Foreign financial assets of commercial banks in a given IFC (US$ billion)
FFL: Foreign financial liabilities of commercial banks in a given IFC (US$ billion)

entrepôt function has been developed in a large number of IFCs. Outside the primary centres, the category of funding centres predominates. Many major and minor centres are used to attract funds.

Ranking approach to classification: examples from the literature

Many studies on the history of financial centres focus on the development from local into regional, from regional into national, and from national into international centres of financial activity. They often end up with an implicit or explicit hierarchical system, putting at the top of the list those centres which develop a worldwide activity.

A typical example of this approach can be found in Kindleberger's well-known study on the *Formation of Financial Centers* (1974):

> The borrowing and lending pattern starts locally and extends to a national center, with perhaps intermediate regional stops, finally becoming international. Specialization grows in instruments and by hierarchical market. (p.9)

For money payments there can be no doubt of the efficiency of a central financial market at the apex of a national system, and of a single international market as the apex of national financial centers.

(pp. 6-7)

This approach explains the development of the large traditional centres. But it is no longer sustainable as the basis of a hierarchical classification, in view of the emergence of offshore centres of various kinds, which start from nothing and nowhere and rapidly become significant members of the club.

In the last decade, more systematic studies have been published, which try to classify and rank the IFCs on the basis of empirical quantitative analysis. Three excellent examples of this approach are the studies by Reed (1981), Choi, Tschoegl and Yu (1986) and Goldberg, Helsley and Levi (1988). Using cluster and discriminant analysis, Reed concentrates on the organisational structure of IFCs and ranks them on this basis. Relevant variables are:

- banking concentration: localisation of local bank headquarters
- international financial activity: foreign financial assets (FFA) and foreign financial liabilities (FFL)
- international telecommunications (number of international cables)
- international investment: net foreign direct investment
- industrial concentration: corporate asset multiple[1]

Choi, Tschoegl and Yu focus on the attraction exerted by the IFCs on foreign banks and find as relevant variables:

- the volume of economic activity in a given IFC (GNP per capita, multiplied by the population of the IFC)
- the number of foreign banks already established as this suggests a bandwagon effect or significant economies of scale

Goldberg, Helsley and Levi examine the size of the financial sector as an indicator of the importance of an IFC and end up with two main relevant variables:

- the stage of economic development in a given IFC (as represented by GNP per capita)
- the importance of foreign trade, which has a positive impact on the size of the financial sector for imports and (rather surprisingly!) a negative one for exports

These studies highlight the determinants of international financial activity and contribute in this way to explaining not only *that* a given IFC is important, but also *why* it is important. Furthermore, it proves easy to derive a hierarchy from such an analysis, as well as a ranking of the various IFCs. Reed has not only made this ranking for the recent past, but also in a historical perspective, which goes back to the beginning of the century. Table 12.2 shows the constant competition between London and New York at the top of the table and the importance of a large 'subtop' group in the beginning of the 1930s and 1980s.

The ranking approach: an exercise in classification for 1990, using factor analysis[2]

Our own attempt to classify IFCs on the basis of 1990 data is derived from the Reed analysis. It tries to rank IFCs according to their importance, measured, on the one side, by the international links of the financial institutions active in a given IFC and, on the other side, by the volume of their outstanding foreign assets and liabilities.

More specifically, our nine explanatory variables can be listed as follows:

$X1 = $ LBHDQ: the number of domestic banks with their headquarters in a given IFC: this variable measures the concentration in a given IFC of the decision-making unit in the domestic banking system

$X2 = $ LBDIL: the number of IFCs having a link with a given IFC via the domestic banks with their headquarters in that IFC: this measures the importance of the international network of the domestic banks of the category LBHDQ

$X3 = $ LBRDIL: the number of IFCs having a link with a given IFC via a *domestic* bank having only a *representative office* in this IFC

$X4 = $ FBDIL: the number of IFCs having a link with a given IFC via a *foreign* bank established in this IFC

$X5 = $ FBRDIL: the same, but for *foreign* banks which have only a representative office in the IFC

$X6 = $ FBO: the number of foreign banks established in a given centre

$X7 = $ FBRO: the same, for foreign banks with only a representative office in the IFC

$X8 = $ FFA: foreign financial assets of commercial banks in a given IFC

$X9 = $ FFL: foreign financial liabilities of commercial banks in a given IFC

The study concerns 37 IFCs for which data or proxies for all the variables could be gathered for (mainly) the year 1990: Amsterdam, Athens,

Table 12.2 Historical ranking of IFCs according to their organisational structure

Group	1900	1915	1930	1940	1960	1975	1980
1	London New York	New York London	London New York	London	London New York	London	London New York
2	Paris Hong Kong	Hong Kong Paris Berlin	Paris Yokohama Berlin Hong Kong Amsterdam Montreal Tokyo Osaka	New York Paris Berlin	Paris Tokyo Hong Kong Hamburg San Fran- cisco	New York Tokyo Paris	Paris Frankfurt Tokyo Hamburg Hong Kong Zurich San Fran- cisco Chicago
3	72 centres	30 centres	14 centres	32 centres	14 centres	15 centres	33 centres
4	-	41 centres	50 centres	40 centres	55 centres	43 centres	36 centres

Source: Reed (1981, Table 2.1)

the Bahamas, Bahrain, Bangkok, Brussels, Buenos Aires, Cairo, Copenhagen, Frankfurt, Helsinki, Hong Kong, Jakarta, Johannesburg, Kuala Lumpur, Lisbon, London, Luxembourg, Madrid, Manila, Melbourne, Mexico City, Milan, Montevideo, Oslo, Panama City, Paris, Rio de Janeiro, Santiago, Seoul, Singapore, Stockholm, Tokyo, Toronto, the United Arab Emirates (UAE), Vienna and Zurich. Furthermore, eighteen additional IFCs, for which no data for FFA and FFL could be found, have been included in our estimation procedure: Algeria, Baghdad, Bogota, Bombay, Caracas, the Cayman Islands, the Channel Islands, Chicago, Dublin, Los Angeles, Moscow, New York, Riyadh, San Francisco, Shanghai, Taipei, Tehran and Tel Aviv.

Our analysis has been restricted to 208 banks out of the top 1000 commercial banks listed in the July 1990 issue of *The Banker*. We found out in which of the 55 IFCs under study, these 208 banks were present, at least with a representative office. So, we had to examine 55 x 208 = 11,440 relations. The big absentees in our study are the IFCs in the United States, because we had to restrict our main analysis to countries where there is only one dominant IFC and where *national* data for foreign assets and liabilities can be used as proxies for the assets and liabilities of this dominant IFC. This procedure could obviously not be used for the United States, where New York, Chicago, San Francisco and Los Angeles are to be taken into account. Consequently, these IFCs could only be included in the additional list and are, unfortunately, not considered in the final ranking. The basic data for the 37 IFCs which have been included in the ranking are given in Appendix 12A.

If our economic approach is similar to the Reed study, we differ from this study by the statistical tool used for classification. Instead of clustering, we have applied factor analysis, according to the principal components method. Technical details are given in Appendix 12B. Factor analysis aims at describing the covariances between many variables in terms of a few underlying, unobservable dimensions, which are called factors. By this analysis, we can single out how many factors contribute, independently of one another, to a description of the status of an IFC and a ranking of the IFC according to these factors.

The loading of a variable i on a given factor f is a measure of the importance of this factor in explaining variable i. In our case, where the variables are standardised and the factors orthogonal (i.e. non-correlated), the loadings represent the correlation between the variable i and the factor f. Consequently, the squared loading of a variable on a factor indicates what proportion of the variance of this variable is explained by this factor. Using some stopping criteria, we finally restricted our analysis to three factors which, as seen in Table 12.3, explain cumulatively 88 per cent of the global variance of our nine variables.

Table 12.3   Rotated factor scheme of the factor loadings

Variable	Factor 1	Factor 2	Factor 3
LBHDQ	0.43945	*0.76537*	0.16374
LBDIL	0.57232	*0.66119*	0.15520
LBRDIL	-0.01941	*0.93840*	0.15491
FBDIL	*0.93769*	0.05419	-0.07617
FBRDIL	-0.18214	0.12557	*0.93393*
FBO	*0.95627*	0.06750	-0.01898
FBRO	0.24455	0.19069	*0.89192*
FFA	*0.88560*	0.32843	0.10992
FFL	*0.88550*	0.32236	0.09271
(a)	3.97612	2.17496	1.76949
(b)	0.44179	0.68345	0.88006

Notes: (a)   Sum of the squared factor loadings
          (b)   Cumulative proportion of the total variance explained by the factors considered
          (c)   Italic type indicates high correlation

Examining the other data of Table 12.3, we find a very high correlation between Factor 1 and the variables FBO (the number of foreign banks in the IFC) and FBDIL (the number of IFCs having links with the IFC considered via these foreign banks). On this basis, we may interpret Factor 1 as the *openness to abroad* of the IFC considered, which is expressed by the penetration and the activity of the foreign banks. The high correlation between F1 and FFA (Foreign Assets) and FFL (Foreign Liabilities) fits completely into this interpretation of F1.

Factor 2 can be described as *the internationalisation via the domestic banks*, on the basis of the high correlation between F2 and LBHDQ, LBDIL, LBRDIL, all variables in which the domestic banks are involved.

Factor 3 is highly correlated with FBRDIL and FBRO, which both reflect the *representative presence of foreign banks* in the considered IFC. This represents a weaker openness to abroad than under F1.

Finally, Table 12.3 shows that 44 per cent of the global variance is explained by F1, 24 per cent by F2 and 20 per cent by F3. This illustrates and underlines the predominant significance of the penetration of foreign banks for the status of an IFC and for the development of its international activity. The presence of 155 top foreign banks - 75 per cent of our sample - of which 127 have a branch and are without a representative office, is certainly a key factor in the present status of London as the number one IFC in the world. This foreign presence is also important in Brussels where, in 1990, 53 top foreign banks were located, of which 37 were established in the form of a local branch. Corresponding figures for other IFCs are given in Appendix 12A.

Ranking of IFCs on the basis of factor analysis can be made via *factor ratings*, which are linear combinations of our nine original standardised variables. In these combinations, the weights are represented by scoring coefficients, which are presented in Appendix 12B. In this way, we can rank our 37 financial centres on the basis of their ratings for each of our three factors F1, F2, F3. This gives us the three rankings of Table 12.4A. Consequently, each IFC has a rank in each of the three rankings. As shown in this table, London, for example, has rank 1 on the basis of F1, rank 17 on the basis of F2 and rank 22 on the basis of F3. The corresponding rankings for Brussels are 10, 12 and 24.

On the basis of these rankings, we can classify the IFCs, in Table 12.4B, into three groups, according to whether they score their highest ranking on F1, F2 or F3. In our interpretation this means that we split up our population of IFCs into: F1, a group which scores best on openness to abroad; F2, a group which specialises in internationalisation of domestic banks; F3, a group where the IFCs concentrate relatively more on the representative activity of foreign banks.

The majority of the IFCs of Group 1 are offshore centres or centres such as Luxembourg, Singapore and Hong Kong, which initiated their take-off by attracting foreign banks through favourable monetary and/or tax regimes. London and Brussels are also members of this club. This is explained by their traditional financial openness and their longstanding open-door policy toward foreign banks. The conclusion to be drawn

from this first group is that offshore banking obviously supposes openness to abroad and penetration of foreign banks. Conversely, the case of
London and Brussels indicates that openness to abroad does not necessarily require a high degree of offshore banking.

The IFCs of Group 2 are all centres with a very strong domestic
banking system. It is no coincidence that the big three at the top of the
list are Tokyo, Frankfurt and Paris. Their international dimension is
more closely linked to the internationalisation of their local banks, than
to an open-door policy towards foreign banks, which in some cases
started rather late. Finally, Group 3 comprises a certain number of less
important IFCs, mainly in developing countries. In these centres, the
activity of foreign banks is often limited to representative offices, which
concentrate on commercial and financial relations, without involving
themselves directly in operations.

Table 12.4A   Ranking of IFCs according to principal components

Group 1 (Ranking for F1)		Group 2 (Ranking for F2)		Group 3 (Ranking for F3)	
IFC	Rank	IFC	Rank	IFC	Rank
London	1	Tokyo	1	Mexico City	1
Hong Kong	2	Frankfurt	2	Tokyo	2
Tokyo	3	Paris	3	Frankfurt	3
Singapore	4	Milan	4	Rio de Janeiro	4
Luxembourg	5	Seoul	5	Hong Kong	5
Paris	6	Amsterdam	6	Buenos Aires	6
Bahrain	7	Zurich	7	Jakarta	7
The Bahamas	8	Madrid	8	Bangkok	8
Frankfurt	9	Stockholm	9	Zurich	9

continued

Table 12.4A (continued)

Group 1 (Ranking for F1)		Group 2 (Ranking for F2)		Group 3 (Ranking for F3)	
IFC	Rank	IFC	Rank	IFC	Rank
Brussels	10	Helsinki	10	Paris	10
Panama City	11	Melbourne	11	Melbourne	11
Zurich	12	Brussels	12	Stockholm	12
Toronto	13	Toronto	13	Santiago	13
Manila	14	Vienna	14	Kuala Lumpur	14
Kuala Lumpur	15	Rio de Janeiro	15	Johannesburg	15
Amsterdam	16	Copenhagen	16	Bahrain	16
Seoul	17	London	17	Copenhagen	17
Madrid	18	Athens	18	UAE	18
Cairo	19	Oslo	19	Madrid	19
Milan	20	Johannesburg	20	Lisbon	20
Buenos Aires	21	Buenos Aires	21	Cairo	21
Jakarta	22	Montevideo	22	London	22
Santiago	23	Lisbon	23	Toronto	23
Montevideo	24	Bahrain	24	Brussels	24
Bangkok	25	Jakarta	25	Seoul	25
UAE	26	Cairo	26	Singapore	26
Lisbon	27	UAE	27	Montevideo	27
Athens	28	Manila	28	Panama City	28
Oslo	29	The Bahamas	29	Athens	29
Vienna	30	Kuala Lumpur	30	Milan	30
Mexico City	31	Santiago	31	Oslo	31
Copenhagen	32	Luxembourg	32	Amsterdam	32
Rio de Janeiro	33	Bangkok	33	Manila	33
Helsinki	34	PanamaCity	34	Vienna	34
Melbourne	35	Mexico City	35	Helsinki	35
Johannesburg	36	Singapore	36	Luxembourg	36
Stockholm	37	Hong Kong	37	The Bahamas	37

Table 12.4B   Grouping of IFCs according to their highest ranking

Group 1 (IFCs having highest ranking for F1)		Group 2 (IFCs having highest ranking for F2)		Group 3 (IFCs having highest ranking for F3)	
IFC	Rank	IFC	Rank	IFC	Rank
London	1	Tokyo	1	Mexico City	1
Hong Kong	2	Frankfurt	2	Rio de Janeiro	4
Singapore	4	Paris	3	Buenos Aires	6
Luxembourg	5	Milan	4	Jakarta	7
Bahrain	7	Seoul	5	Bangkok	8
The Bahamas	8	Amsterdam	6	Santiago	13
Brussels	10	Zurich	7	Kuala Lumpur	14
Panama City	11	Madrid	8	Johannesburg	15
Manila	14	Stockholm	9	UAE	18
Cairo	19	Helsinki	10	Lisbon	20
		Melbourne	11		
		Toronto	13		
		Vienna	14		
		Copenhagen	16		
		Athens	18		
		Oslo	19		
		Montevideo	22		

This ranking exercise clearly builds a hierarchy among IFCs, according to their respective importance, but at the same time highlights some characteristic features of the development of IFCs; openness to abroad, presence of foreign banks on an operational or representative basis, internationalisation of local banks. This leads directly to the question: how to use these indicators and classifications in order to *compare* IFCs and to assess their respective comparative advantage? On what basis did London, Hong Kong, Singapore, Tokyo develop into IFCs with a worldwide impact? What is their competitive edge at present?

COMPARING IFCs AND THEIR COMPETITIVE EDGE[3]

Comparative advantage and IFCs

> *Most of the theoretical underpinnings of international trade find application in the financial services sector.*
>
> (I. Walter 1988, p.105)

For an international economist, the most obvious way to approach international division of activity and competition between financial centres is to consider these centres as producers, exporters and/or importers of financial services. Just as Ricardo considered England and Portugal - both nations - as producers and traders of respectively cloth and wine, we can approach London as an exporter of syndicated eurocredits or of electronic trading of securities through SEAQ, and Luxembourg as a producer of private banking and favourable tax facilities.

The Heckscher-Ohlin theorem suggests the comparison of the factor endowments of the various IFCs. Each sector is expected to specialise in the services which embody relatively more of its abundant factor, such as professional expertise (skilled labour) in London and capital from a saving surplus in Frankfurt and Zurich. In order to make such an approach operational for explaining the present relations between IFCs, numerous qualifications and additional factors have to be taken into account:

- *international factor movements* are very often more important for services than for goods. Hence, free entry for foreign capital, for example in the form of an open-door policy for foreign banks and for foreign skilled labour, as in Luxembourg, is a key factor in the competition between IFCs.

- factor endowments and comparative advantage, especially in the service sector, are not primarily given by nature, but are *man-made*. They are changed by human effort and innovations. What Porter (1990, p.73) recently emphasised for the competitive advantage of nations, applies even more to IFCs:

  National prosperity is created, not herited. It does not grow out of a country's natural endowment, its labour pool, its interest rate, or its currency's value, as classical economics insists. A nation's competitiveness depends on the capacity of its industries to innovate and upgrade.

- success in banking and in financial business in general depends very much on the *political, economic and technological environment* in which financial institutions have to operate.

Again we may apply *a fortiori* one of Porter's statements on the competitiveness of nations to that of IFCs:

> When a national environment permits and supports the most rapid accumulation of specialized assets and skills, companies gain a competitive advantage. When a national environment affords better ongoing information and insight into product and process needs, companies gain a competitive advantage. When the national environment pressures companies to innovate and invest, companies both gain a competitive advantage and upgrade those advantages over time.

- The financial industry tends to be a very *regulated* one. Differences in *monetary, exchange* and *banking regulations* play an important part in the rise and fall of IFCs.
- The *tax sensitivity* of financial operations is very high, especially in Europe, where taxation is heavy in many countries. Identification of IFCs with tax havens is not infrequent.

With these qualifications in mind, we have tried to make a compilation of the factors which are commonly quoted in the literature as sources of competitive strength or weakness of an IFC. In Table 12.5 we list 47 criteria, which we have classified into three categories according to the qualifications made above.

Table 12.5 List of criteria for competitiveness of IFCs

Category	Criterion
A. Factors of production	
1. Availability of capital	
- size of domestic saving	1
- attraction of foreign capital	2
2. Quality of human resources	
- skilled domestic labour	3
- professional expertise	4

continued

Table 12.5 (continued)

Category	Criterion
3. Infrastructure	
- geographical location	5
- transport and telecommunications facilities	6
- operation costs of a financial institution (rent, services ...)	7
- time zone (cf. Tokyo, New York)	8
- location of	
· important international institutions	9
. multinationals	10
B. Man-made environment	
1. Environment	
- economic growth of the country	11
- inflation	12
- strength of the currency	13
- importance of banking activity	14
- bank secrecy	15
2. Technology	
- automatic continuous system for transactions	16
- circulation of information	17
- settlement of transactions	18
3. Characteristics of financial market	
- diversity and size of markets	
. money market	19
. foreign exchange market	20
. capital market	21
- volume of transactions	
. on the stock exchange	22
. outside the stock exchange	23
- dominant influence of a few superstar shares	24
- openness to abroad	
. presence of foreign banks	25
. international assets and liabilities	26

continued

Table 12.5   (continued)

Category	Criterion
4. Innovation	
- availability of sophisticated financial instruments	27
- functioning of markets for derivatives	
. futures	28
. options	29
- attitude towards innovation	30
5. Financial tradition	
- stock exchange capitalisation	31
- turnover	32
- importance of bond market	33
6. Political tradition	
- (absence of) state intervention	34
- political stability	35
C. Regulatory framework	
1. Regulation	
- market regulation	
. money market: degree of deregulation	36
. capital market: degree of deregulation	37
- takeover bid and money-laundering control	38
- organisation of stock exchange	
(e.g. Switzerland: federation)	39
- absence of exchange control	40
2. Fiscal regulation	
- withholding tax	41
- stamp tax	42
- stock exchange tax	43
- corporate tax	
. resident financial institutions	44
. non-resident financial institutions	45
3. Commissions	
- transaction costs	46
- type of commissions	47

Source: Guinotte (1991), schéma 2-5, pp.64-65

Group A covers primarily *factor endowments*: financial capital, human resources, infrastructure. Group B concentrates on the man-made *environment*: economic growth, inflation, monetary stability, technology, financial markets, innovative climate, political and financial tradition. Finally, group C covers the *regulatory* framework at large: regulation of financial markets, tax regulations and regulation of costs and fees. This list of criteria is the basis for the questionnaire used in the survey, which will be discussed in the next section.

Specification, quantification and weighting problems

Most of the current literature on strengths and weaknesses of IFCs is promotional. It highlights the effective or potential strengths of a particular IFC and conceals its weaknesses as much as possible. When we try to examine these aspects in a more balanced way, on the basis of the criteria listed in Table 12.5, the usual problems of specification, quantification and weighting have to be tackled. It may be possible to compare the volume of banking and stock exchange transactions quite easily, by gathering turnover statistics in various IFCs. However, it is much more difficult to find a representative indicator of political stability and of the degree of deregulation, let alone to obtain a reliable quantitative expression for this indicator.

Our experience is that the current literature provides, on the one hand, global statements on the comparative edge of a particular IFC and, on the other hand, piecemeal indications of peculiar aspects, for which the IFC concerned has a comparative advantage. The former are very difficult to verify without having a global scheme and the latter are often too fragmentary to be assembled easily in a global scheme. Such a procedure would have required supplementary work of an extensive team and is therefore far beyond our means.

Instead, we have asked a certain number of financial experts to evaluate our six European IFCs in a detailed way, by giving each of them a rating for the 47 criteria in Table 12.5. The centres concerned were London, Paris, Frankfurt, Zurich, Luxembourg and Brussels. The survey was held during Spring 1991, at a moment when modernisation and reform in places like Frankfurt and Brussels had not reached full momentum. Ten persons from the banking and/or academic world were willing to join us in this exercise[4]. We supplied them with some fragmentary data from the literature and, afterwards, we tried to compare their evaluation with other sources. Having a ranking approach in mind, we asked the experts to give each of the six IFCs a rating from 1 to 5, with 1 being the best. We also associated them in the process of weighting the 47 criteria, in order to allow a *global* evaluation of the six IFCs. More specifically, we asked them whether they considered a criterion as 'dominant' (rating 1), very important (rating 2), important (rating 3), less important (rating 4), or not important (rating 5).

As shown in Table 12.6, we analysed the answers on the basis of the arithmetic average and the variance of the individual ratings. We globalised the weighting system by computing the average ratings of four 'blocks' of criteria: factor endowments, environment, regulatory framework, taxation and other costs (see end of Table 12.6).

For the comparison between the six IFCs, we have analysed the answers mainly on the basis of the average of ratings for each criterion (Table 12.7).

Finally, we have globalised the results for each IFC by first re-grouping the ratings according to our four blocks and weighting them by the global weights indicated at the end of Table 12.6[5]. According to our ranking idea, the IFC with the *lowest* rating is the number 1, the outstanding centre in the group of six. It is obvious that the limited number of participants denies any statistical representativeness to our inquiry. Rather, the exercise should be interpreted as the consultation of experts, on the basis of a standardised questionnaire and a scoring system that aims at ranking criteria and financial centres.

Results of the survey: weighting the criteria

As shown by Table 12.6, the criteria considered as 'dominant' by our club of experts can be summarised as follows:

(i) *factor endowments*
- availability of foreign capital
- professional expertise

It is striking that these factors are considered as much more important than geographical location, quality of transport and telecommunications, and operating costs of financial institutions. This somewhat contradicts the historical view and the Kindleberger approach, which explains the growth of IFCs by their location in harbour cities and other privileged areas of international trade.

(ii) *Environment*
- diversity and size of financial markets
- openness to abroad

Table 12.6 Weighting the importance of factors of competitiveness for IFCs

		Average	Variance	IFCs
Factor endowments				
Dominant	Attraction of foreign capital	1.50	0.25	LON LUX
X< 2	Professional expertise	1.40	0.24	LON
Important	Size of domestic saving	2.40	0.64	FRAN ZÜR
2 ≤ X< 2.5	Skilled domestic labour	2.30	1.21	LON
	Transport & telecommunication facilities	2.20	0.96	LON
	Location of multinationals	2.30	0.81	LON
Less important	Operating costs	2.80	0.76	BRUX
2.5 ≤ X< 3	Time zone	3.00	1.0	LON LUX
Not Important	Geographical location	3.30	0.41	BRUX
X> 3	Presence of important international institutions	3.10	1.89	LUX BRUX

continued

Table 12.6 (continued)

Environment		Average	Variance	IFCs
Dominant				
X< 2	Diversity and size of the markets[1]	1.60	0.64	LON
	Openness to abroad[1]	1.50	0.65	LON
	Innovation[1]	1.80	0.49	LON PAR
	Political stability	1.60	0.44	LUX ZUR
Important	Importance of banking activity	2.00	0.40	LUX LON
2 ≤ X< 2.5	Bank secrecy	2.00	1.00	LUX ZUR
	Technology	2.10	0.89	LON
	Volume of transactions on and outside stock exchange	2.00	1.40	LON
	Stock exchange capitalistion	2.10	0.69	LON
	Turnover	2.10	0.89	LON
	Importance of bond market	2.00	0.60	LON
Less important	Absence of state intervention	2.70	1.21	LON LUX
2.5 ≤ X≤ 3	Economic growth	2.80	0.96	FRAN
	Strength of the currency	2.50	0.85	FRAN
Not important	Inflation	3.10	1.29	FRAN
X> 3	Dominant influence of a few superstar shares	3.70	0.81	LON

continued

Table 12.6 (continued)

		Average	Variance	IFCs
Regulatory framework				
Dominant	Deregulation of the money market	1.80	0.76	LON PAR
X< 2	Of the capital market	1.40	0.44	LON LUX
	Exchange control	1.50	0.45	ALL
Less important	Take-over bid and money-laundering control	2.80	0.56	ZUR LUX
2.5 ≤ X≤ 3	Organisation of stock exchange	2.80	0.56	LON
Taxation and costs				
Dominant	Transaction costs	1.80	0.56	LON
X< 2	Fee charges	1.80	0.76	LON PAR
Important	Withholding tax	2.20	0.96	LUX
2 ≤ X< 2.5	Stamp tax	2.10	0.89	LUX LON
	Stock exchange tax	2.10	0.89	LON LUX
	Corporate tax on foreign financial institutions	2.40	0.61	LUX
Less important	Corporate tax on domestic			
2.5 ≤ X≤ 3	financial institutions	2.70	0.44	ZUR
continued				

Table 12.6 (continued)

Globalisation by averaging ratings of criteria in each group

	Average	Weight
Factor endowments	2.46	0.280
Environment	2.20	0.250
Regulatory framework	1.98	0.225
Taxation and other costs	2.16	0.245
Total	8.80	1.000

Source: Guinotte (1991, pp. 73-80)

Note: 1. Aggregation of criteria of the same categories, the averages of which are quite similar. The average presented in column 3 is the lowest of the various criteria. The variance is the highest of the criteria that have been aggregated

- innovation
- political stability

The importance given to openness to abroad seems to be linked with the 'availability of foreign capital', quoted above. It confirms the importance of F1 in our factor analysis. Rather surprising is the lack of importance of the inflation rate in the IFCs.

(iii) *Regulatory framework*
- deregulation of monetary and capital markets
- (absence of) exchange controls

For the efficiency/stability dilemma which dominates the discussion on regulation, the experts clearly favour the efficiency factor.

(iv) *Taxation and costs*
- transaction costs
- fee charges

Taxes are also considered as important, but less than the 'private' costs of financial transactions. It should be stressed that the importance given to these costs is not at all incompatible with the 'benign neglect' of operating costs of a financial institution (see (i) above). Low fees are supposed to attract business, which makes rather high operating costs acceptable.

As far as globalisation is concerned, the end of Table 12.6 indicates that the weights implicitly given to the four blocks of criteria are not very different. The block *Factor endowments* carries a somewhat higher weight (28 per cent).

Results of the survey: London as absolute number one

Table 12.7 globalises the results of the rating of our six European IFCs for the 47 criteria. Some comments can be made per block of criteria:

(i) *Factor endowments*
The London rating is excellent, precisely for the criteria which are considered as essential: attraction of foreign capital and professional expertise. Luxembourg is also considered excellent for the first of these criteria.

(ii) *Environment*
Again, London has the most favourable ratings for most of the dominant criteria: diversity and dimension of financial markets, openness to

abroad, innovation. But London is also outstanding for other criteria: importance of banking activity and technology. Zurich and Luxembourg enjoy much consideration for political stability, banking activity and bank secrecy.

(iii) *Regulatory framework*
All the IFCs considered enjoy absence of exchange control, which is no longer a comparative advantage, at least among each other. Again, London has the most favourable rating for the dominant factors: deregulation of monetary and capital markets. This also applies to Luxembourg, at least for capital markets.

(iv) *Taxation and costs*
Again and again, London scores most favourably for the dominant factor: costs and fees and financial transactions. The absence of withholding tax is a well-known comparative advantage of Luxembourg.

The global ratings and the final ranking in Table 12.7 reflect the features discussed above. With a rating of 'only' 1.69, London outscores by far all other IFCs, including the number 2, which is Luxembourg (rating 2.28). Paris and Frankfurt have analogous ratings and can be ranked *ex-aequo* as number 3. Zurich (2.64) and Brussels (2.91) close the list. It has been noticed that London ranks first in each of the blocks of criteria considered in the inquiry. Finally, in Table 12.8, we have compared the results of this rather limited inquiry with those of a survey held in 1986 by the French Centre d'Observation et de Prospection Sociale. This survey covers the answers of 1000 participants, institutional investors and business executives in the United Kingdom, Germany, Switzerland, France and the Benelux countries. The final outcome of both inquiries is strikingly convergent, except for the competitive edge of Luxembourg, which is rated higher than Frankfurt and Zurich in our study. This is probably linked to the fact that in our inquiry the proportion of Belgian participants, who are sensitive neighbours of the Luxembourg IFC, is substantial.

But, for the remainder, the similarity is striking: London tops the list and is followed at quite a distance by the group. The situation does not seem to have changed very much in the last five years. The key question is then whether the interpenetration of IFCs of the European Economic Community in the framework of the Europe 1992 project is likely to increase or to reduce the important differences which have been noticed in both inquiries. In other words, will IFCs that have historically a very large domestic basis, like Paris, Frankfurt and

Zurich, catch up with the leader London? And will IFCs in small
countries, whether onshore, like Brussels, or offshore, like
Luxembourg, be able to stay in the race with the Big Brothers?

Table 12.7   Global ratings for six European IFCs

IFC	Criteria	Average	Rating
London	Factor endowments	1.95	0.546
	Environment	1.59	0.398
	Regulatory framework	1.44	0.324
	Taxation and costs	1.73	0.424
	Total	**1.69**	**1.692**
Paris	Factor endowments	2.74	0.767
	Environment	2.44	0.610
	Regulatory framework	2.26	0.509
	Taxation and costs	2.57	0.630
	Total	**2.52**	**2.516**
Frankfurt	Factor endowments	2.63	0.736
	Environment	2.66	0.665
	Regulatory framework	2.28	0.513
	Taxation and costs	2.29	0.561
	Total	**2.48**	**2.475**
Luxembourg	Factor endowments	2.67	0.748
	Environment	2.65	0.663
	Regulatory framework	1.94	0.437
	Taxation and costs	1.77	0.434
	Total	**2.28**	**2.282**
Zurich	Factor endowments	2.73	0.764
	Environment	2.54	0.635
	Regulatory framework	2.42	0.545
	Taxation and costs	2.83	0.693
	Total	**2.64**	**2.637**

continued

Table 12.7   (continued)

IFC	Criteria	Average	Rating
Brussels	Factor endowments	2.63	0.736
	Environment	3.30	0.825
	Regulatory framework	2.60	0.585
	Taxation and costs	3.11	0.762
	Total	**2.91**	**2.908**

Comparison

	London		Paris		Frank-furt		Luxem-bourg		Zurich		Brussels	
	Rating	R	Rating	R	Rating	R	Rating	R	Rating	R	Rating	R
Block 1	0.546	1	0.767	6	0.736	2	0.748	4	0.764	5	0.736	2
Block 2	0.398	1	0.610	2	0.665	5	0.663	4	0.635	3	0.825	6
Block 3	0.324	1	0.509	3	0.513	4	0.437	2	0.545	5	0.585	6
Block 4	0.424	1	0.630	4	0.561	3	0.434	2	0.693	5	0.762	6
Total	1.692	1	2.516	4	2.475	3	2.282	2	2.637	5	2.908	6

Source: Guinotte (1991, pp.96-8 and 100-3)
Key: R = rank
        Block 1 = Factor endowments
        Block 2 = Environment
        Block 3 = Regulatory framework
        Block 4 = Taxation and costs

Table 12.8   Comparative ratings for six European IFCs

	Our survey	COPS survey
London	8.35	7.89
Paris	6.29	6.67
Frankfurt	6.38	7.25
Luxembourg	6.92	5.89
Zurich	5.96	6.97
Brussels	5.24	5.62

Notes: 1. COPS = Centre d'Observation et de Prospection Sociale
2. Ratings: 0 = minimum; 10 = maximum

HOW TO BECOME A SIGNIFICANT IFC: THE CASE OF BRUSSELS

I predict, very tentatively, that Brussels will emerge as the financial center of the European Economic Community, for the following reasons: It serves as headquarters for the Commission; it attracts foreign corporations and will ultimately attract foreign and European banks; it tolerates the world intellectual medium of exchange, the English language. ... While the advantages of centralisation are less compelling than they were in the middle of the nineteenth century, they still exist. Thus I predict that, despite cultural resistance and only with difficulty, centralisation will take place, but not before the late 1980s.

(C.P. Kindleberger 1974, p.71)

This 1974 prophecy by a prestigious writer clearly did not materialise, certainly 'not before the late 1980s'. As a matter of fact, our survey puts Brussels at the bottom of the list of the six IFCs under scrutiny (cf. the last section of Table 12.7). The failure of this brave promotional attempt is easy to explain. First, it derives from the inadequacy of a historical approach, which analyses the growth of IFCs as a process of cross-border centralisation of financial activities. As mentioned earlier, an IFC no longer necessarily stands at the 'apex of national financial centres'.   Secondly, in the process of European integration, the emergence of a *financial* capital can occur quite independently from the development of an *administrative* and *political* capital.   Financial activity has its own specific determinants, which may be quite independent of other socio-political factors.   Moreoever, the experience of Germany and the Community itself shows that integration in a federative way does not lead to centralisation in one single place.   Finally, the *performance of Brussels as a financial centre* in the late 1970s and most of the 1980s was rather average, with a remarkable commercial banking activity, but striking weaknesses for capital markets and markets of derivative financial products.

According to Tables 12.9 and 12.10, which summarise the results of our survey for Brussels, most ratings on specific fields tend to cluster around the average number of 3.   The strengths of Brussels are mainly related to its geographical and time zone location, its low operating costs for financial institutions, its openness to foreign banks, the presence of important international institutions, its favourable corporate taxation for foreign firms (through ' co-ordination centres') and, most of all, the absence of exchange control.   However, this last advantage is shared by most other IFCs under review.   Well-known weaknesses are the absence of a significant options market, before the start of Belfox, and the very modest size of the stock exchange.   In the last few years, significant efforts have been made to enhance the international financial status of Brussels by fostering the competitiveness of the Belgian economy, by linking the Belgian franc to the Deutsche Mark and by modernising the domestic money and capital markets.

These efforts have been publicised in a series of roadshows which, in 1991, led the leaders of the financial community successively to Zurich, London, Amsterdam, Tokyo and Taipei.   A definite plus point of this initiative was the very fact that the Belgian delegation comprised high-ranking representatives of the public sector (the Ministry of Finance, the central bank, public credit institutions), of private banks and the stock exchange.   The governor of Banque Nationale and in some cases the Minister of Finance headed the delegation in the places visited. All this was highly appreciated by the local audiences.

It seems interesting to analyse the materials prepared for these roadshows according to the 47 criteria of competitiveness in our survey and to evaluate in this way the case of Brussels as a significant IFC (Table 12.10).

When one looks through the various items of Table 12.10, three main tendencies emerge.

Table 12.9 Evaluation of Brussels according to 47 criteria

Class	Range	Number	Remarks
Excellent to good	X < 2	1	Absence of exchange control (rating 1.60)
Good to average	2 < X < 3	19	Most favourable ratings: - operating costs of banks (2.10) - geographical location (2.30) - important international institutions (2.30) - time zone (2.40) - strong currency (2.40) - favourable corporate taxation for non-residents (2.40) - number of foreign banks (2.40)
Average to bad	3 < X < 4	24	
Bad to very bad	X > 4	3	- options market (4.00) - stock exchange capitalisation (4.10) - stock exchange turnover (4.20)

Firstly, Brussels is being promoted as a *medium-sized onshore IFC*. For obvious reasons, the emphasis has been put neither on size, nor on regulatory or fiscal facilities. The delegation has been careful enough to avoid over self-estimation and aggressiveness against other IFCs. 'Brussels has no ambition to challenge the City as the most important

Table 12.10 The case of Brussels: the argumentation of the roadshows in the conceptual framework of our survey

	Criteria	Our survey		Road show materials	
		Average weight given to the factor (1 = of first importance)	Average rating for Brussels (1 = excellent)	Variance	Argument	Weight given to argument (our assessment)
A	B	C	D	E	F	G
1	Size of domestic saving	2.40	2.60	1.24	High and stable rate of financial savings	+ +
2	Attraction of foreign capital	1.50	3.10	0.49		
3	Skilled domestic labour	2.30	2.80	0.56	Quality and skill of multi-lingual workforce	+
4	Professional expertise	1.40	2.90	0.89		
5	Geographical location	3.30	2.30	0.61	At the crossroads of Western Europe	+

continued

Table 12.10 (continued)

A	Criteria B	Our survey C	D	E	Road show materials F	G
6	Transport and telecom-munications facilities	2.20	2.80	0.76	'Best infrastructure on the continent and arguably the world' (sic). Highways, rail network, waterways and ports, international airport. No mention of telecommunications	+
7	Operation costs of a financial institution	2.80	2.10	1.49	Human dimension and scale of Brussels	+
					Readily available and less costly office space	+
					Good housing, international schools	+
					Gastronomical capital of Europe (sic)	+

continued

Table 12.10 (continued)

A	B (Criteria)	C	D	E (Our survey)	F (Road show materials)	G
8	Time zone	3.00	2.40	0.64		
9	Important international institutions	3.10	2.30	0.81	'Burgeoning home of EEC and NATO'	+
10	Multinationals	2.30	3.00	0.80	Attraction of dynamic companies and services at cutting edge of technology and communications.	++
11	Economic growth of the country	2.80	2.60	0.64	GNP growth rates above EEC and OECD averages	+
					Surpluses on current account	
					Price stability	+
					Sustained high competitiveness as imperative precondition for balanced economic growth	++
						+++

continued

Table 12.10 (continued)

A	B	C	D	E	F	G
	Criteria	Our survey			Road show materials	
12	Inflation	3.10	2.50	0.65	Towards budget deficit down to 3% of GNP	+
					Strong and stable rate of exchange	+++
					Pegging of the BEF to the strong EMS currencies	+++
13	Strength of the currency	2.50	2.40	0.84		
14	Importance of banking activity	2.00	2.90	0.49		
15	Bank secrecy	2.00	3.40	0.44		
16	Automatic continuous system for transactions	2.10	3.40	0.24	Quote-driven market for OLOs and treasury bills through system of primary dealers	+++
					CATS and OBLICATS system on the stock exchange	+

continued

Table 12.10 (continued)

| | Criteria | Our survey | | | Road show materials | |
A	B	C	D	E	F	G
17	Circulation of information	2.10	3.10	0.69	New central clearing system for OLOs and treasury bills, managed by the central bank	+ +
18	Settlement of transactions	2.40	3.60	0.84		
19	Diversity and size of money market	1.60	3.40	0.64		
20	Diversity and size of foreign exchange market	1.60	3.10	0.89	Modernisation of management and market of Belgian short public debt by reform of treasury bills	+ + +
					Promotion of a market for private commercial paper and CDs	+

continued

Table 12.10 (continued)

A	B	Our survey			Road show materials	
		C	D	E	F	G
21	Diversity and size of capital market	1.60	3.50	0.89	Modernisation of management and market of Belgian long-term public debt by OLOs	+++
22	Volume of transactions on the stock exchange	2.10	3.70	1.21		
23	Volume of transactions outside the stock exchange	2.00	3.50	0.65		
24	Dominant influence of a few superstar shares	3.70	3.70	0.41		
25	Presence of foreign banks	1.50	2.40	1.64		
26	International assets and liabilities	1.90	2.90	1.29		
27	Availability of sophisticated financial instruments	1.80	3.30	0.21	OLOs and treasury bills (cf. 20 and 21)	+++
					Undertakings for collective investments (SICAV, SICAF,...)	++

continued

Table 12.10 (continued)

A	B	Our survey			Road show materials	G
	Criteria	C	D	E	F	
28	Functioning of markets for derivatives: futures	1.80	3.90	0.29	BELFOX announced as becoming operational in early autumn 1991: futures as national government bonds	++
29	Functioning of markets for derivatives: options	1.80	4.00	0.40	BELFOX: put and call options on most actively traded shares and on the BEL 20 Index	++
30	Attitude towards innovation	1.90	3.50	0.65		
31	Stock exchange capitalisation	2.10	4.10	0.69	Medium size of stock exchange capitalisation Diversified stock exchange with Belgian and foreign securities	+ +

continued

Table 12.10 (continued)

A	B Criteria	Our survey			Road show materials	
		C	D	E	F	G
32	Turnover	2.10	4.20	0.56	See 31	
33	Importance of bond market	2.00	3.70	1.41		
34	(Absence of) state intervention	2.70	2.90	0.09		
35	Political stability	1.60	2.70	0.41		
36	Degree of deregulation of money market	1.80	2.70	0.61	Fine tuning of monetary policy by interventions of central bank on the market itself	+ +
37	Degree of deregulation of capital market	1.40	2.60	0.64		
38	Take-over bid & money-laundering control	2.80	3.00	0.20		

continued

Table 12.10 (continued)

| A | B | Our survey | | | Road show materials | |
	Criteria	C	D	E	F	G
39	Organisation of stock exchange (eg. Switzerland: federation)	2.80	3.10	0.29	Modernised stock exchange: stronger intermediation, more market transparency, lower taxation and costs	++
40	Exchange control	1.50	1.60	0.64		
41	Withholding tax	2.20	3.10	0.49	No withholding tax on OLOs and treasury bills for non-resident investors	++
					Full exemption on capitalisation SICAVs	+
42	Stamp tax	2.10	3.50	0.85	No tax on transactions on OLOs and treasury bills	+
43	Stock exchange tax	2.10	3.60	0.44		

continued

Table 12.10 (continued)

A	B	C	D	E	F	G
	Criteria		Our survey			Road show materials
44	Corporate tax resident, financial institutions	2.70	3.00	0.40		
45	Corporate tax non-resident, financial institutions	2.40	2.40	0.84		
46	Transaction costs	1.80	3.10	0.49	Reduction of transaction costs on stock exchange operations	+
47	Type of commissions (free/fixed)	1.80	3.10	0.29		

Sources:
1. Criteria and survey: Guinotte (1991: A, B Annex IIa; C, D, E Annex IIc)
2. Road shows (1991): column F mainly on the basis of the general report; column G subjective weighting by the authors on the basis of the written documents and oral reports from the road-shows

financial center of Europe' (sic)[6].   As to taxation, the only strong
emphasis is put on the absence of withholding tax for non-residents.

Secondly, the recent *macro-economic performance of Belgium* and
the strong position of the Belgian franc are being stressed, over and over
again, as determining factors of the attractiveness of Brussels as an IFC.
The specific points mentioned in this context are:

- the linking of the Belgian franc to the Deutsche Mark
- the growth rate of the Belgian economy in recent years
- the price stability and the competitiveness of the Belgian economy[6]
- the favourable balance of payments position with a substantial
  current account surplus and a reversal of the capital outflow
- the reduction of the budget deficit from 13 to about 6 per cent of
  GNP. It appeared from the discussions that this last point raised
  several questions from the audiences. Progress towards the final
  goal of reducing the deficit to 3 per cent of GNP, in order to quality
  for the third stage of EMU, becomes the main challenge for
  Brussels as an IFC.

Thirdly, short- and long-term government paper, that is treasury
bills and OLOs[7], have been presented as the most attractive new financial instruments for non-residents. It has been suggested that this is the
typical way in which clever Belgians convert the liability of their high
public debt into a valuable international financial asset. Government
paper is being considered as the showpiece of the modernised money and
capital markets in Belgium.

In contrast to the arguments about government paper, those relating
to the stock exchange and associated markets appear to be much less
convincing, especially when considering the long delay in starting Belfox, the new futures and options market. Quite incomprehensible in the
context of the present paper is the lack of emphasis on the international
activity of commercial banks and the openness of Belgium to foreign
business and foreign financial institutions. This benign neglect can be
explained, but not justified, by the fact that this openness to abroad is a
permanent, but not a *new* feature of the Belgian financial system. As in
many travels, the suitcases for the roadshows have been filled with the
new gadgets, but the basics have been left at home.

This leads into a more fundamental reflection on the future of smaller onshore IFCs and on the way in which this future can be fostered.
Taken out of this context, the assertion that Brussels 'has no ambition to
challenge the City' sounds rather ridiculous when the pertinent question
is whether smaller centres can survive as *international* financial centres
in conditions of worldwide globalisation of markets and delocalisation of

transactions. The answer to this question refers to the traditional *specialisation-diversification* dilemma.

Both classical international trade theory and the recent industrial theories, stress the importance of specialisation, niche strategies, unbalanced growth, etc. According to this view, a smaller IFC should not try to do everything but, as suggested in previous sections of this paper, concentrate on products and markets in which it has a competitive edge. It can reduce its weaknesses in other fields by *co-operating* with other IFCs. In this respect, the (important) question may be raised whether Brussels does not have the excessive ambition of trying to do too many things without having the means and the critical size to implement them in an efficient way. We can imagine that, for options on equities, it would have been easier for Brussels to become a subsidiary for Belgian shares of the European Options Exchange, which has been successfully built in Amsterdam.

On the other hand, the choice of government paper in Belgian francs as a basis for the development of an IFC seems quite justified: this instrument has distinctive national features; it is not an anonymous product; it enjoys a high rating; it is diversified and covers a very large segment of the yield curve (autumn 1991: 3 months up to 12 years); the market is large (4000 billion Belgian francs of quoted paper, of which more than 1200 billion is dematerialised OLOs); and liquidity is enhanced through the intervention of active primary dealers. This is really the specific, significant financial product 'made in Belgium', even more so than Belgian chocolates.

But even this instrument has its limitations as *the* engine of the development of Brussels as an IFC. Firstly, it is an instrument in *Belgian francs*, which has become a strong franc, but remains the small and relatively unknown currency of a small country. At this moment, there is still ample scope for enlarging the share of instruments in Belgian francs in international portfolios, but limits might be reached in the medium term. Secondly, the status of this instrument is closely dependent on the credibility of economic, budgetary and financial policies in Belgium. There is no scope at all for substantially and rapidly enlarging the supply of government paper without reducing the quality and the international rating of this paper. On the contrary, at even weak indications of economic and financial mismanagement, the market may be flooded by Belgian paper out of international portfolios. Foreign ownership of debt instruments is usually less stable than domestic ownership.

The conclusion to be drawn from this analysis is that, as a basis for an IFC, government paper in Belgian francs should (i) be supplemented by other financial instruments and (ii) that this *additional* diversification should be directed towards *international* financial instruments instead of *domestic* instruments made international. In our opinion, this could be done by giving a new impetus to the *Ecu market* in Brussels[8]. Belgian banks have strongly participated in the early start of the Ecu. Recently, this expansion has slowed down, both for policy reasons and because of market developments. Monetary authorities have preferred to 'Germanise the Belgian franc', instead of 'domesticating the Ecu' by assimilating it to the Belgian franc as a quasi-domestic currency.

In the marketplace, placement possibilities of Ecu-denominated paper in Belgium have dwindled because the interest differential between the Ecu and the national currency is not significant enough to induce Belgian investors - the well-known Belgian dentist - to invest in Ecu paper. Ecu transactions tend to be limited to interbank professional activity. This position seems impossible to sustain in the long run. The Ecu is slowly, irregularly, but nevertheless definitely evolving toward the single EEC currency. International transactions in Belgium, as in other EEC countries, will increasingly be made and financed in Ecu. More slowly, the Ecu will also penetrate domestic markets. All important financial institutions are now preparing for this fundamental change. It would be a pity if Brussels should 'miss the bus' at the very moment it is striving to assert itself as a significant IFC. Quite recently, the Belgian Treasury has taken the lead in a renewed interest for Ecu transactions by announcing issues of OLOs and commercial paper denominated in Ecu. Commercial banks should follow suit in substituting credits in Ecu for placements in Ecu and in promoting the commercial uses of the Ecu by assimilating Ecu payments to payments in domestic money. Summarising, we feel that a dynamic Ecu market in Brussels should be a significant complement and a useful instrument of diversification in fostering the international status of Brussels.

CONCLUSIONS

International financial competition can no longer be analysed only at the micro level of *banks* and at the macro level of *nations*. It has to be extended to the *meso* level represented by international markets and international financial centres. Progress in technology and telecommunications has favoured the worldwide dispersion of IFCs. These IFCs have to be classified and compared on the basis of the *functions* they perform and the *competitive* edge they enjoy. The comparative advantage of IFCs depends only to a minor extent on physical factor endowments and geographical location. It has increasingly become *man-made*, determined by such factors as professional expertise, size and variety of financial markets and other environmental factors, but also very strongly by the regulatory framework and the taxation system for non-residents.

Our inquiry has shown that London still tops by far the list of the six European IFCs which we studied. It scores best in all factors considered as crucial for the competitive edge of an IFC. The key question for the competition among IFCs in the 1990s is, therefore, whether European financial integration will widen or narrow the gap between London and its competitors. Our analysis suggests that, as the regulatory framework and the taxation systems become more uniform in the EEC countries, as a result either of institutional competition or European harmonisation, the factors of professional expertise, size and variety of markets and technological advance will favour the City of London even more, in spite of higher costs and some explosive financial scandals.

Smaller centres will have to react by specialisation and co-operation. The promotional actions favoured by Brussels have rightly put the emphasis on the opportunities provided by the new markets of short- and long-term government paper in Belgian francs. The attractiveness of this financial instrument, typically 'made in Belgium', is enhanced by the favourable macroeconomic performance of the country in recent years and by the linking of the Belgian franc to the Deutsche Mark. We contend, however, that this instrument should be supplemented by other, more international ones. In this framework, a new impetus should be given to the Ecu market in Brussels.

Appendix 12A Basic data for factor analysis

Centres	LBHDQ	LBDIL	LBRDIL	FBDIL	FBRDIL	FBO	FBRO	FFA	FFL
1 Amsterdam	3	33	8	8	3	21	6	146.27	122.33
2 Athens	1	4	4	6	3	12	6	2.59	12.30
3 Bahamas	0	0	0	8	0	28	0	175.42	176.51
4 Bahrain	1	6	2	15	2	26	26	70.47	67.48
5 Bangkok	1	0	0	7	4	9	29	1.79	3.31
6 Brussels	4	15	8	9	3	37	16	164.52	205.53
7 Buenos Aires	1	9	5	10	7	20	32	1.27	9.37
8 Cairo	1	2	0	9	2	11	18	8.52	4.26
9 Jakarta	1	3	2	8	5	11	38	6.03	1.79
10 Frankfurt	8	26	14	12	7	36	46	295.29	159.90
11 Helsinki	4	5	8	4	1	4	4	22.24	42.58
12 Hong Kong	1	18	2	22	7	103	32	355.64	310.13
13 Johannesburg	1	1	3	0	5	0	12	0.68	2.37
14 Copenhagen	3	6	5	4	6	5	8	23.92	23.44
15 Kuala Lumpur	1	4	0	10	3	12	22	2.54	1.90
16 Lisbon	1	1	0	6	4	8	9	4.16	1.66

continued

Centres	LBHDQ	LBDIL	LBRDIL	FBDIL	FBRDIL	FBO	FBRO	FFA	FFL
17 London	8	40	4	34	1	127	28	923.63	1,028.05
18 Luxembourg	1	4	0	13	0	57	1	279.57	245.25
19 Madrid	5	13	13	14	4	36	24	29.03	45.96
20 Manila	1	0	0	11	1	19	7	3.51	5.78
21 Melbourne	3	9	9	4	6	4	20	7.18	18.12
22 Mexico City	1	4	3	1	17	2	64	3.02	36.05
23 Milan	4	13	14	12	2	33	18	62.68	117.11
24 Montevideo	1	2	0	9	3	11	5	1.45	1.71
25 Oslo	1	5	2	3	2	5	7	6.68	21.07
26 Panama City	0	0	0	12	2	24	8	9.92	10.65
27 Paris	6	31	14	19	5	47	32	275.89	292.20
28 Rio de Janeiro	1	20	7	3	9	6	27	3.55	19.44
29 Santiago	1	1	0	9	5	11	13	0.38	3.33
30 Seoul	8	15	10	12	2	36	24	8.78	13.40
31 Singapore	2	8	1	23	1	91	18	306.06	308.37
32 Stockholm	4	6	11	4	7	5	14	20.01	53.33

continued

Appendix 12A (continued)

Centres	LBHDQ	LBDIL	LBRDIL	FBDIL	FBRDIL	FBO	FBRO	FFA	FFL
33 Tokyo	17	27	13	18	9	64	46	842.06	879.72
34 Toronto	3	20	6	12	2	24	22	48.82	70.81
35 UAE	1	1	0	8	5	12	8	16.81	5.79
36 Vienna	2	4	7	5	2	7	5	58.91	65.95
37 Zurich	2	16	15	9	7	32	25	355.60	280.48

Sources: LBHDQ, LBDIL, LBRDIL, FBDIL, FBRDIL, FBO, FBRO: Personal computation on the basis of *The Bankers' Almanac and Yearbook*, 1990

FFA, FFL: *IMF International Financial Statistics Yearbook*, 1990: US$ billion. Country data used as proxies for corresponding data of IFC.

Appendix 12B Factor scores

For our purpose of classification of financial centres, we have used the scores of individual centres on each factor. Although the common factor scores cannot be computed directly, they can be estimated in a variety of ways. The estimated factors can be considered as approximations to the common factors and are defined as linear combinations of the original variables. Consequently, each estimated factor score is computed as a linear combination of the standardised values of the variables that were factored:

$$F_j = a_{1j}z_1 + a_{2j}z_2 + .. + a_{9j}z_9$$
$$f_{jk} = a_{1j}z_{1k} + a_{1j}z_{1k} + .. + a_{9j}z_{9k} \quad (j = 1..m)$$

Or, in matrix form:

[factor scores] = [scoring coefficient]^T [standardised variables]

$$\mathbf{F} \quad = \quad \mathbf{A}^T \quad\quad\quad \mathbf{Z}$$

The coefficients a_{ij} are called scoring coefficients and $\mathbf{A} = [a_{ij}]$.

Standardised scoring coefficients

	Factor 1	*Factor 2*	*Factor 3*
LBHDQ	-0.02223	0.38668	-0.06136
LBDIL	0.04469	0.28720	-0.03682
LBRDIL	-0.21258	0.61127	-0.12609
FBDIL	0.29338	-0.15612	-0.02843
FBRDIL	-0.05363	-0.09880	0.57703
FBO	0.29861	-0.16502	0.00664
FBRO	0.07046	-0.14028	0.54946
FFA	0.22122	-0.00110	0.02561
FFL	0.22192	-0.00108	0.01575

The weights for the first linear combination are chosen so that the set of unstandardised factor scores on the first factor has maximum

variance. Then, subject to the second set of factor scores being uncorre-
lated with the first, we choose the weights for the second linear combination so that the set of scores on the second factor has maximum variance. This same principle will be applied as we find additional linear
combinations. The standardised scoring coeffecents resulting from our
analysis are shown above. The resulting factor ratings have mean zero
and variance one. The contribution of each original variable to the
variance of the scores on each factor is given by the square of that variable's loading (correlation) with the factor.

NOTES

Ackowledgements

The authors are very much indebted and grateful to the following: P.
Baufays (Brussels), E.P.M. Gardener and P. Molyneux (Bangor), B.
Jadoul (New York), O. Lefebvre (Brussels), F. Lierman (Brussels), P.
Praet (Brussels), P. Reding (Brussels), Ph. Romagnoli (Brussels) and E.
Willeaume (Brussels) for participating in an inquiry about the competi-
tive edge of six European financial centres; P. Stockman (Leuven) for
technical advice and assistance in applying and interpreting factor analy-
sis; H. Boon and L. Leenaert for formatting and typing text and tables.

1. The number of industrial firms, among the 200 most important in
   the world, which have their headquarters in a given IFC, multiplied
   by the assets of these firms.
2. This section and Appendix 12A summarise the empirical study of N.
   Bervaes (1991, part II, chapter II).
3. This section is primarily based on chapter 2 of Guinotte (1991).
4. The present authors use this opportunity to thank the experts very
   sincerely for their kind, competent and benevolent co-operation in
   an exercise which has proved to be more complicated than was initially expected by the authors.
5. For example, the global rating of London in Table 12.7 is computed
   as follows:

	1 Average rating in the group (Table 12.7)	2 Weight (Table 12.6)	3 Contribution to global rating 3 = (1 x 2)
Factor endowments	1.95	0.280	0.546
etc.	....	.....	.....

Global rating   1.69   1.0   1.692

6. Address in London by P. Maystadt, Minster of Finance, read by G. Brouhns, Director General of the Treasury
7. OLO = obligations linéaires/lineaire obligaties
8. For a more detailed analysis, see Wauters (1990, 4, pp. 143-55)

LIST OF REFERENCES

Association Belge des Banques (1988), *La Belgique: un Avenir de Place Financière Internationale*, Aspects et Documents, no. 67, 18 pp.; *Huit Défis pour la Place Financière Belge*, Aspects et Documents, no. 83, 19 pp.

Bervaes, N. (1991), *Financiële Centra in de Wereld: Literatuuroverzicht en Empirische Momentopname Volgens Factoranalyse* (K.U. Hortholieke Universiteit Leuven), mimeo, 155 pp.

Choi, S.; A.E. Tschoegl and C. Yu (1986), 'Banks and the world's major financial centres, 1970-1980', *Weltwirtschaftliches Archiv*, **122**, 1, 48-64

Dematte, Claudio (1981), *International Financial Intermediation: Implications for Bankers and Regulators*, Banca Nazionale del Lavoro

Dufey, G. and I. Giddy (1978), *The International Money Market* (Englewood Cliffs, New Jersey: Prentice-Hall Inc.), 283 pp.

Gardener, E.P.M. and P. Molyneux (1990), *Changes in Western European Banking* (London, Unwin Hyman), 300 pp.

Goldberg, M.A.; R.W. Helsley and D. Levi (1988), 'On the development of international financial centres', *Annals of Regional Science* (February), pp. 81-94

Guinotte, A. (1991), *La concurrence entre les Centres Financiers Européens dans la Perspective de l'Europe 1992* (Namur, FNDP), mimeo, 213 pp.

Kindleberger, C.P. (1974), *The Formation of Financial Centers: a Study in Comparative Economic History*, Princeton Studies in International Finance, no. 36 (Princeton, New Jersey: Princeton University Press), 82 pp.

Park, Y.S. (1982), 'The economics of offshore financial centres', *Columbia Journal of World Business* (Winter), pp. 31-35

Park, Y.S. and M. Essayad (1989), *International Banking and Financial Centres* (Boston: Kluwer Academic Publishers), 271 pp.

Porter, M.E. (1990), 'The competitive advantage of nations', *Harvard Business Review* (March/April), pp. 73-93

Reed, H.C. (1981), *The Pre-eminence of International Financial Centres* (New York: Praeger Publishers), 148 pp.

Road shows (1991), *Brussels at the Leading Edge of Finance*, collective map for the 1991 roadshows (Brussels), mimeo

Walter, I. (1988), *Global Competition in Financial Services*, p. 105

Wauters, E. (1990), 'De Ecu en de ontwikkeling van Brussel als internationaal financieel centrum', *Revue de la Banque - Bank- en Financiewezen*, no. 4, 143-55

Index